George T. S. (Taylor Shillito) Farquhar

The Episcopal History of Perth

1689-1894

George T. S. (Taylor Shillito) Farquhar

The Episcopal History of Perth
1689-1894

ISBN/EAN: 9783744661126

Printed in Europe, USA, Canada, Australia, Japan

Cover: Foto ©ninafisch / pixelio.de

More available books at **www.hansebooks.com**

The Episcopal History of Perth

1689-1894.

BY

REV. GEO. T. S. FARQUHAR, M.A., OXON.

CANON AND PRECENTOR OF PERTH CATHEDRAL AND
SUPERNUMERARY OF THE DIOCESE.

"*Through many griefs her upward path has lain.*"

PERTH: JAMES H. JACKSON, 20 HIGH STREET

MDCCCXCIV.

Printed at Jackson's Printing Works, Perth.

Behold how Israel, driven from the shore,
  Moves down into th' embraces of the sea!
  Though striving from affliction thus to flee,
You weltering flood must whelm them evermore!
But look! despite the billows' threatening roar,
  Its curse is silenced by Divine decree:
  'Tween lapsing walls the tribesmen still go free,
Trusting to Heaven for that which lies before.
O Church of the Fair City, it is thou!
  Thee would the waves have buried until now!
Yet, since our God so far has cleft a way
  Through thy long woes, faith tells me thou wilt stand,
  Ere all be done, upon the further strand,
And chant with Miriam thine exulting lay!

                                    G. T. S. F.

Preface.

In 1887, when there was no longer any doubt that the nave of Perth Cathedral would be erected, it occurred to me that a leaflet containing some account of the past of the institution might be useful in the interests of the building fund. The frequent discovery, however, of new material, combined with the incessant calls of pastoral work, constantly delayed me and changed the character of my undertaking. Had it not been that my position, as member of a Cathedral staff, sets me free from the overwhelmingly arduous duty of preaching two sermons every Sunday to the same congregation, my attempt would probably have come to nothing. As it is, the reader has the result now before him in the present volume.

My object has simply been to do what has never been attempted before, viz. :—to bring to light the full Truth concerning the History of the Church in Perth during the last two centuries, or somewhat longer.

It may indeed be argued by some that, as the Truth in this case proves to be of so troubled a character, it would have been better to leave it in its former obscurity; but my idea is this: that on all occasions (and, therefore, in the present instance), the Truth is the best foundation on which to build. It has its own sure way, sooner or later, of rewarding its followers. We cannot altogether say how, in the matter here dealt with, it will do so; but that such will ultimately be the case, we are confident. This much at least is clear, that, if there is something in the record to humble us (and that itself may not be a bad thing), there is also something to enlighten us. We now see that, if we have failed, since the Revolution, to carry a great proportion of the population with us in this place, the reason has not been that our principles have been unimpededly before the public, and nevertheless rejected by them, but that (if we may use a somewhat heathenish phrase) they have never been allowed a fair chance. For more than 100 years (1689-1792) penal laws—subtly designed at once to depress Scottish Episcopacy and to encourage the so-called "English" schism—were in force against us. Then, after all excuse was taken away from that division by our acceptance of the "powers that were" in 1788, hidden foes of the Church continued it here till 1846; and when at last our flock was revived in the City, in the latter year, it happened to be at the most distracting crisis of the Oxford movement—*i.e.*, the year after Newman's secession. Thus (if we may risk an Irish bull) there have *always* been *exceptional* difficulties, not arising from our essential principles, in the Church's way in Perth; and, therefore, the very manifestation of these causes of depression is a ground of hope for the future. It is reasonable to expect that a time will come—(it has come)—when there are no exceptional difficulties, either of external persecution or of internal dissension, to hinder us. And other benefits, such as the force of the noble examples of faithfulness here recorded, must arise from the relation of the Truth concerning our past.

However, it may be thought that, excellent as my aim is, I have developed it at too great length. Since my subject only concerns a handful of people in a

Scottish town of secondary importance, it is here treated with excessive fulness. But is there no force in the following consideration? Undoubtedly the biography of a single individual is an interesting form of literature. So also is the history of a nation. But it does not seem to me to follow that therefore everything that lies between an individual biography and a national history must be uninteresting. On the contrary, it appears that an account of the fortunes of a society, such as a congregation, will have its own attraction too. It will be surely all the more so, if it be given not merely in skeleton outline, but enriched with local, personal, and contemporary touches, which inevitably demand a certain amount of space. I hope that thus the student of our common nature, as well as the Scottish Churchman, may find some points of interest here. This would justify the writing of the history of any congregation at some length, and it ought certainly to do so in the case of a narrative, which, like the following, deals with events exhibiting anything but a monotonous character.

Once more. Some of those, who agree with me so far and allow that the Truth on this subject was worth telling and telling at some length, may still object that I have not unfolded it on strictly undenominational lines. I plead guilty to this charge. I have to confess that undenominationalism utterly fails both to win my affections and to satisfy my mind. I believe, on the contrary, that those beliefs, which, in this country, are in popular phraseology known as *Episcopalianism*, are Orthodox, and therefore Catholic. And so, while admitting that the following narrative is not written from an undenominational stand-point, but from that of the system, which I believe to be true, I avow that I consider this to be not a fault but a merit.

A last objection, which may be brought against me, is this: that, because I am a Churchman, therefore I have written uncharitably of those, who adhere to different systems. Now, as Churchmanship consists of the acceptance, not only of the Apostolical Ministry founded by Christ in the days of His Flesh, but also of the things committed to the charge of that Ministry, such as the Commandment of Love, it follows that, so far as I have departed from Charity, in that degree have I departed from Churchmanship. It is I, not the Church, that must thus bear the blame of any unkindness, which may appear in these pages. But I earnestly hope there is none. Certainly I have striven hard so to write as to do justice to every one's motives. Where the facts, indeed, appear to me to establish an unfavourable case, I have not scrupled to state my opinion. But then, I hope, these conclusions have been reached not through way of prejudice, but through processes of reason; and I am open to correction. But wherever there is something to be said on both sides, I trust that I have allowed it, and, if virtue has appeared anywhere, I shall be disappointed indeed, if I can be shewn not to have been magnanimous enough to do it justice.

After all, I cannot hope to have avoided every mistake either as to facts or the spirit, in which I have written, or the judgment which I have exercised, and I therefore hope the result of my labours will be received in a kindly and tolerant spirit.

It now only remains for me to express my thanks in varying degrees for help generously given (through the loan of MSS., etc.) to the following:—The Most

Rev. the Primus ; the Right Revs. the Bishops of Edinburgh and (late) of S. Andrews ; the Very Rev. the Dean of S. Andrews ; the Revs. Canon Skinner Wilson ; Canon Cole, late of Doune ; Canon Keating ; J. G. Simpson, Vice-Principal of our Theological College ; Dr. Gordon, late of S. Andrew's, Glasgow ; Dr Walker, Monymusk ; Chr. Bowstead of Pitlochry ; and last, but *by no means least*, J. Ferguson, Parish Minister of Aberdalgie and Presbytery Clerk. Also to the following laymen :—Ex-Lord Provost Wilson of Perth ; the Keeper of the Advocate's Library ; John Thomas, Esq., Sheriff Clerk of Perth ; Erskine Beveridge, Esq., Dunfermline ; J. Miller, Esq., Perth ; W. L. Watson, Esq. of Ayton ; J. Whyte, Esq., M.D., Perth ; W. Wordsworth, Esq. ; R. S. Fittis, Esq., Perth ; and J. R. Anderson, Esq., Convener of our Foreign Mission Board. Also to Miss Christian Bruce of Dunimarle for the sight of the Robert Lyon relics.

I shall be happy indeed if my "History" is found worthy of a place beside the works of the Rev. W. Walker, L.L.D. ; the Rev. J. D. Craven ; the Rev. Canon Archibald, and others of a like nature. *Benedictus benedicat!*

GEORGE T. S. FARQUHAR.

20 BALHOUSIE STREET, PERTH,
S. James' Day, 1894.

Contents.

Book I.—Disestablishment and Disendowment.

CHAPTER	PAGE
I.—How the First Storm Gathered Round Perth, 1688-9,	3
II.—How the Episcopal Clergy were Ousted from Perth, 1689-90,	8
III.—How the Neighbouring Parishes were Purged and Planted, 1689-99,	15
IV.—How the Neighbouring Parishes were Purged and Planted, 1699-1709,	26
V.—How the Church Battled for Existence in Perth, 1691-1707,	39
VI.—How a New Bishop was Appointed and the Prayer Book Introduced to Perth, 1704-9,	53
VII.—How the Revs. Messrs. Smith, Rhynd, and Walker were Sentenced by the Presbytery, 1709-10,	59
VIII.—How the Revs. Messrs. H. and T. Murray and W. Stewart were Sentenced by the Presbytery, 1711-12,	71
IX.—How the Presbytery "brought the Whole Matter to a Period," 1712-15,	81

Book II.—Penal Laws and Divisions.

X.—How the Church in Perth was Involved in a Second Disaster, 1715-19,	93
XI.—How Perth was Implicated in the College and Usage Controversies, 1720-26,	105
XII.—How the Last Years of the Rev. Henry Murray's Incumbency were Passed, 1727-35,	122
XIII.—How the Rev. Robert Lyon was Settled in Perth, 1735-39,	131
XIV.—How there was a Schism in the Perth Congregation, 1740,	137

CHAPTER	PAGE
XV.—How Bishop Rattray became Primus, Died, and was Succeeded, 1738-44,	143
XVI.—How Matters went in Perth, 1740-45.,	153
XVII.—How Robert Lyon followed Prince Charlie, 1745,	161
XVIII.—How the Church in Perth was Overwhelmed by a Fourth Great Disaster, 1746,	168
XIX.—How the Rev. Robert Lyon suffered Death at Penrith, 1746,	178
XX.—How the Persecution Raged from 1746 to 1756,	187
XXI.—How the Two Congregations Fared, 1750-76,	199
XXII.—How the Ecclesiastical Succession was Continued in Perth, 1776-91,	215

Book III.—Repeal and Exhaustion.

XXIII.—How Perth Churchmen Contributed to the Repeal of the Penal Laws, 1788-92,	225
XXIV.—How the Repeal of the Penal Laws was followed by the Extinction of the Church in Perth, 1792-1809,	233
XXV.—How the Land Lay Desolate, 1810-46,	246

Book IV.—Revival.

XXVI.—How the Scottish Congregation was Revived in Perth, 1846,	265
XXVII.—How the Schism of 1740 was Healed, 1842-48,	273
XXVIII.—How the Idea of a Cathedral began to take Root, 1847-49,	280
XXIX.—How the Church of S. John, Princes Street, was Built, 1849-51 (to 1873),	286
XXX.—How the Cathedral was Partly Built, Constituted, and Consecrated, 1849-50,	292
XXXI.—How the Cathedral Fared till Bishop Torry's Death, 1850-52,	307
XXXII.—How Bishop Torry Authorized a Scottish Prayer Book, 1847-52,	316
XXXIII.—How Bishop Torry Died and was Buried, and how Bishop Wordsworth was Elected, 1852-53,	324

CHAPTER	PAGE
XXXIV.—How the Cathedral was Accepted by the Diocesan Synod, 1853,	333
XXXV.—How Matters went in Perth during Bishop Wordsworth's first Three Years, 1853-56,	343
XXXVI.—How the Thirty Years' War Raged, 1856-86,	351
XXXVII.—How Peace enabled a New Start to be made, 1885-89,	368
XXXVIII.—How the Nave of the Cathedral was Built, 1886-90,	377
XXXIX.—How the Nave was Consecrated, 1890,	392
XL.—How the Cathedral Fared during Bishop Wordsworth's last Three Years, 1890-92,	403
XLI.—How Bishop Wordsworth Died, and Bishop Wilkinson Succeeded, 1892-93,	410
Epilogue, 1894,	418

BOOK I.

Disestablishment and Disendowment.

CHAPTER I.

HOW THE FIRST STORM GATHERED ROUND PERTH, 1688-9.

WHEN our narrative begins, we find ourselves upon the following scene. As regards place, it is the City of

ERRATA.

Preface page xi., line 14, for J. Whyte, Esq., M.D., read F. J. Whyte, Esq., M.D.
Page 371, line 19, for £300 read £200.
Page 387, line 8, for T. T. Oliphant, Esq., read K. T. Oliphant, Esq.

but the works of man are different. And this indicates that the time is not the present. It is, in fact, October, 1688. Regarding the scene, as we do, from an ecclesiastical standpoint, two chief differences strike our attention. The first of these is that instead of the many sacred edifices, which at present find a place in the Fair City, only one is to be found in the whole Burgh. The venerable spire of old S. John's emerges above the surrounding roofs, but it has no companions. And, if we advance and enter, we find that, instead of the Choir, Transepts and Nave being divided by partitions as now (1894) into the separate Churches,

CHAPTER I.

HOW THE FIRST STORM GATHERED ROUND PERTH, 1688-9.

WHEN our narrative begins, we find ourselves upon the following scene. As regards place, it is the City of Perth, lying between its two "Inches," on the banks of that noble, rushing river, the Tay. But the town is not to fill the whole of our view. It occupies the centre, indeed, and is the most conspicuous object, but round it in a circle are gathered, about equally in every direction, a group of parishes to the number of nearly thirty. We need not pause at present to identify each of these by name, since the ensuing story will erelong make us familiar with all of them. But there is one circumstance, which we must here notice in connection with the whole view. Nature, indeed, is seen to be the same as it is in the nineteenth century, but the works of man are different. And this indicates that the time is not the present. It is, in fact, October, 1688. Regarding the scene, as we do, from an ecclesiastical standpoint, two chief differences strike our attention. The first of these is that instead of the many sacred edifices, which at present find a place in the Fair City, only one is to be found in the whole Burgh. The venerable spire of old S. John's emerges above the surrounding roofs, but it has no companions. And, if we advance and enter, we find that, instead of the Choir, Transepts and Nave being divided by partitions as now (1894) into the separate Churches, called respectively the East, Middle, and West, only the West is partitioned off from the Middle. Although the latter is alone fitted up for public worship, yet it and the East or Choir open into each other.

But there is also a second and more important difference in the ecclesiastical situation. We make enquiries and find that although there are Kirk-Sessions, Presbyteries, black gowns and, within certain limits, *ex tempore* forms of prayer, the Established Church is Episcopal. We are in the Diocese of S. Andrews, and under the rule of Archbishop Ross (or Rose). Of this Prelate, indeed, his enemies (being bitter) say :—" He is a poor, ignorant, worthless man, in whom obedience and fury (two very opposite qualities!) are so eminent that they supply all other defects." His friends, however, who know him better, say : - " This Archbishop is a man of sound judgment and great integrity." As touching his income, he is far better off than any of his brethren on the bench. For, while the Bishop of Edinburgh enjoys a revenue of £93 per annum; the Bishop of Brechin, £76; the Bishop of Dunblane, £43; and the others not much more, our Primate receives £1500. The Parish Ministers of Perth are Adam Barclay, M.A., Incumbent of the first charge, who has only succeeded to the living a month or two ago. His predecessor, Mr. William Hay, resigned it last February on being consecrated Bishop of Moray. The minister of the second charge is David Anderson, M.A., who has been in his place since *October 20th, 1680*. And, if we travel round all the parishes in the neighbourhood, as we shall have occasion before long to do, we shall find that each of the clergy holds the Episcopal licence. And, what is more, in the south-west of Scotland, indeed, there is a bitter animus on the part

Threatening Prospects. 5

of a turbulent faction against the Established Church, but in the vicinity of Perth it is strong in the affections of the people.

Thus, things are in a very satisfactory state, and the public in a very contented frame of mind. But ominous news reaches the City from outside. By his infatuated attempt to force Romanism upon an unwilling nation, King James VII. has alienated all sympathies from himself. In fact, in England, where the enterprise has been more open and persistent, seven of the Bishops, the most loyal supporters of the dynasty, have had to suffer imprisonment, and are casting about in their minds whether some sort of Regency to restrain the King cannot be devised. Two also of the Scottish Prelates, Glasgow and Dunkeld, are in disgrace at Court for opposing the Royal designs. And since this is the state of mind of the most loyal section of the community, we are distressed, but not surprised, to hear that on *November 5th*, William, Prince of Orange, and husband of one of the King's daughters, has landed in the south at the head of an army, and that the ill-advised monarch, finding his troops untrustworthy, has fled to France and left the way open, not merely to a constitutional Regency such as the Bishops desired, but to a revolution, and the recognition of the Dutch adventurer as King.

It is soon known, indeed, that the revolutionary Prince is in favour of what is called "Moderate Episcopacy." But, whatever comfort may be drawn from that, is completely dissipated by the news that follows. From the south-west of Scotland comes intelligence that large numbers of the Clergy are being "rabbled" out of their livings by a furious and fanatical mob. In *January, 1689*, Bishop Rose alienates William's sympathies by hinting that not merely expediency, but also "reason and justice," would influence the conduct of the Scottish Bishops. A convention also assembles in Edinburgh on *March 14th*, the elections to which (if a modern political phrase may be allowed), have been so "jerrymandered" that Churchmen cannot but dread the very worst from its proceedings. Quickly following upon this comes the formal proclamation of William and Mary as King and Queen, together with a decree that the Clergy are to read the proclamation from their pulpits, abjure King James, whom they were bound by oath to support, and pray publicly for the newcomer and his Consort. The Scottish Council also invite information to be laid against all Episcopal Clergy, who fail to obey. And lastly, in July a Bill is passed by the Convention (which has now transformed itself into a Parliament) to the effect that "Prelacy and all superiority of any office in the Church of this kingdom above Presbyters is hereby abolished." It is, of course, absolutely preposterous to suppose that a secular Convention has the slightest power really to *abolish* a spiritual office which they did not and could not create, but our friends in Perth recognise that, though, of course, the Episcopate is not abrogated but lives on by Christ's authority, yet it is now a stern reality that the holders of that sacred office are to be forthwith reduced to the state which their predecessors occupied before the days of Constantine. They are to be stripped of all the Church's worldly possessions and status.

The prospect is truly alarming. Can nothing be done? Cannot a single blow be struck on behalf of the old *régime?* Yes! there is a brilliant gleam of hope. The gallant Viscount Dundee, disgusted at the disloyalty

Killiecrankie. 7

and injustice of the Convention Parliament in Edinburgh, has withdrawn from the capital : collected what forces he has been able and retired to Blair-Athole. From this in May he suddenly swoops down on Perth and causes infinite consternation to the party of the Revolution there by making some Whig Lairds prisoners. On his departure he is entertained by Lord Stormont, who thereby gets himself into trouble with those now endeavouring to secure authority for their side. On *July 27th*, within a week after the passing of the Disestablishment Act, a battle is fought in the Pass of Killiecrankie between Dundee and General Mackay, who commanded the Dutch Prince's forces. The result is that, though the latter are defeated, yet the gallant Viscount is killed and in his grave are buried all immediate hopes of retrieving the day in favour of the exiled Monarch. The Earl of Dunfermline, indeed, rashly ventures another action near Perth, but is defeated with the loss of 400 men; and William is now *de facto* King.

Although, therefore, the Clergy still hold possession of their livings in this neighbourhood, it is evident that the storm, which has already burst so furiously upon their brethren in the south-west, is drawing with alarming rapidity close to the Fair City.

CHAPTER II.

HOW THE EPISCOPAL CLERGY WERE OUSTED FROM PERTH, 1689-90.

In the last Chapter we saw the doom of the Episcopal Church in this part of the country, in common with the same in the rest of Scotland, resolved upon. We have now to observe how the process of putting the abstract decree into practice began to be carried out in this region. Those, who do not reflect, are very apt, when they have ascertained that the Disestablishment Bill was passed on *July 22nd, 1689*, to imagine that there and then the Episcopal *régime* was no more. But that to decree the expulsion of the Clergy, whatever it might be elsewhere, was in the Perth district a very different thing from expelling them will speedily become evident, as we trace the course of events. That the Clergy here were popular is evident from the following testimonies. The Presbyterian Dr. Carlyle, of course, states in a general way that "more than two-thirds of the people of the country and most part of the gentry were Episcopals." And another Presbyterian, Dr. Scott of Perth, the well-known compiler of the *Fasti*, after transcribing the narrative of affairs at this crisis, honestly states it as his opinion that "in the north of Scotland . . not only the nobility and gentry but also the bulk of the people were fondly attached to the Episcopal Incumbents." This he gives under the year 1689 and then he adds :—"*In the Presbytery of Perth the Episcopal Ministers were deprived not with the minds of the people but contrary thereto."* And, if it is objected that these are later opinions the same cannot be said of the following. It was written, not by a Scottish Churchman, but by the Rev. Mr. Morer, an English Chaplain who accompanied King William's forces into Scotland. "The Church of Scotland," he says, "is at this time under the claw of an enraged lion : Episcopacy abolished : its revenues alienated : the Clergy routed, some by form of sentence and others by violence and popular fury : their persons and families abused: their houses ransacked, with many other injuries and indignities." This, he goes on to say, was due to an extreme faction : for everywhere the gentry, and northward the people too were favourable to Episcopacy. He knows it from his own personal experience, because, for example, *"at Perth I was readily admitted into the Church and Pulpit, though the Magistrates refused the same favour to Lord Cardross, a Privy Councillor, and the Lord Argyle, on behalf of two Cameronian preachers."*

Our Incumbents, then, being in possession of their parishes not only by legal right, but also "with the minds of the people," how was their expulsion carried out ?

Our method of replying to this question will be simply to give the narrative of proceedings in each parish mainly as taken, not from any Episcopal source (for none such is forthcoming), but from the Perth *Presbytery Records* and to let them speak for themselves. By thus giving the story substantially from our adversaries' chronicle, it is hoped that at least no overwhelming prejudice will be allowed to colour the narrative in favour of the disestablished Church. And the order, in which each parish will be brought forward, will be merely that of time. Those parishes, from which the

Episcopal Incumbents were first driven and in which Presbyterian successors were first "planted," will be first dealt with and the rest will follow in due order.

The first Church to become vacant was that of Perth itself. The story of this will fully occupy the remainder of this Chapter. It seems that the parish Clergy here were full of hope during Viscount Dundee's enterprise. At least Mr. John Blair, Minister of Scone, when he heard that King William's troops had been defeated at Killiecrankie exclaimed, " It is the best news in the world ! " And Mr. *David* Anderson, Minister of the second charge in Perth was evidently of the same mind, for we read that in the street " he met with one, Mr. James Robertson, residenter in Balhousie, who was a Conventicler." Confident no doubt that he was still strong in his position as Parish Minister, he took the opportunity of expostulating with his Dissenting friend. The latter, however, "laid hold on his gown, when he was going to pass from him and told him what had happened (*i.e.*, that Dundee was killed) and that King William's troops were on the way to Perth ! " Naturally Mr. Anderson was "greatly troubled" at the news. " His countenance changed," and he did not think it safe to await the arrival of the revolutionary forces. Before their coming, therefore, he withdrew himself some distance from the town. It was evidently a case where discretion was the better part of valour. What could one or even two unarmed Clergy do against an army flushed by recent success ?

When the forces arrived in the City, a preacher, Mr. *John* Anderson by name, who had been Minister of Auchtergaven under Cromwell and after that a holder of Conventicles, was taken under their formidable

Perth Clergy Ousted.

patronage and protection. Until *May, 1691,* he was escorted to and from the Pulpit of S. John's by a guard of soldiers.

Our two Ministers were also confronted by civil, as well as military, force. It must be remembered that so far, although the Episcopal Church had been disestablished by law, Presbyterianism had not yet been put in its place. There were at this time ten months, which the " Voluntaries " of the nineteenth century must hail as exhibiting the ideal of ecclesiastical arrangement. There was no established Church in Scotland. There could, therefore, be no pretence of depriving our Perth Clergy of their cure of souls by any professing spiritual authority. This, however, did not trouble the minds of the new rulers. The Privy Council continuing its own wrong traditions, felt itself quite equal to the task, and on *September 3rd, 1689,* ratified the violence of the soldiery and dissolved the spiritual bond, which a successor of the Apostles had established between the Revs. Adam Barclay and David Anderson on the one side and their Parish on the other. They were deprived for not reading the Proclamation of Estates and not praying for King William and Queen Mary. No formal settlement of Mr. John Anderson in their place was attempted but he was allowed to go on preaching under the patronage of the soldiers.

But how was old S. John's permanently settled with Presbyterian Ministers? Not by any means speedily or with the goodwill of the citizens, as the following narrative will show.

In *May, 1690,* a motion for the establishment of Presbyterianism passed the Scottish Parliament and received the Royal assent. The legislators were afraid for an abnormal time to face the people at a general election but they took upon themselves to declare that the Genevan polity satisfied the wishes of the people. The government of the Church was now conferred by the secular power, not upon the existing Clergy, nor even upon all Presbyterian Ministers but upon those of the latter only, who had held livings under the usurpation of Cromwell, and whatever others they chose to associate with themselves. In this neighbourhood, therefore, all eyes were turned to those, who within the bounds of the Presbytery of Perth, answered to this description. But Presbyterianism was here conspicuous only by its absence, notwithstanding the Toleration granted by King James. Indeed, so as to collect a number, which could at least make some appearance of passing muster as a Presbytery, the whole Presbytery of Dunkeld and half of that of Auchterarder had to be added to the Presbytery of Perth. But, even when these two-and-a-half Presbyteries were united, there were only three Presbyterian Ministers in all the bounds, answering to the requirements of the new Establishment, *i.e.*, those in Rattray, Arngask and the soldiers' nominee in Perth. However, their numbers were soon doubled. There was an Irish Minister, Glass by name, in the district and, though he was under obligation to return to Ireland, whenever wanted, he was added to the rudimentary Presbytery. And then Mr. Alexander Pitcairn, Minister of Dron, and Mr. James Inglis, Minister of S. Martins, both of whom had originally been Presbyterians, but who had changed sides under Episcopacy, once more turned round.

The Presbytery of Perth, therefore, now numbering six names for about 40 parishes, was duly constituted and proceeded in terms of the Act of Parliament of *May 26th* to "purge out all insufficient, negligent, erroneous, and scandalous Ministers," and to "plant" their extensive bounds with Presbyterians. It is so remarkable a coincidence that every single Episcopal Clergyman (with one exception, who turned Presbyterian) should have been discovered to have been either "insufficient, negligent, erroneous or scandalous" that we cannot help suspecting that all these adjectives were more or less synonymous with "Episcopal." But before going on to shew that this was the case in the other parishes, we must relate how Perth (the "purging" of which from its "insufficient," etc., Ministers has already been related) was "planted" with Ministers of an opposite (*i.e.*, Presbyterian) character. This proved not to be an altogether easy matter. For it turned out that the Town Council and a large section of the citizens were in favour of the old Church and they had considerable power to enforce their Episcopal leanings, inasmuch as "since 1616 the Provost and Bailies of Perth were *ex officio* members of Session." This body, therefore, determined to call a Minister after their own hearts and require the Presbytery to admit him. They accordingly presented a call for Mr. James Lundie and Mr. *Robert* Anderson. Also they desired that the latter should preach on the next Sabbath. But the Presbytery declined. Their reasons were (1) that the calling elders were only Prelatic elders and were never admitted elders under the present Government; (2) that Mr. James Lundy was a Prelatic Minister; and (3) that it did not come in the shape of a call but of a presentation. On these grounds they refuse to accede to the request of the Town Council and resolve to proceed to the election and ordination of Presbyterian elders.

It appears probable that this over-riding of the local wishes by the newly-constructed Presbytery was the occasion of the following incident related by Bishop Sage (who as long ago as 1672 had been bringing the younger members of the Drummond family into Perth for educational purposes and had formed a friendship with the afterwards celebrated parish Minister, the Rev. Alexander Rose). "I remember," he says, "that some of the Magistrates of Perth, after both their Ministers were deprived, came to the Earl of Craufurd and insinuated to him that they were hopeful Mr. David Anderson, a good-natured man and a very good pastor, who had been one of the Ministers of the said Town, perhaps might yet be induced to comply and that he would be extremely acceptable to the people, if he were reponed. But presently his Lordship turned huffy and told them that that was not so much as to be mentioned. So they were forced to let fall that design."

They had, however, no intention of at once ceasing their efforts on behalf of the old Church and the dispute raged for the greater part of a year. But the Presbytery, locally feeble as we have seen it to be and representing a party certainly not numbering more than half the Nation, yet was backed by the prestige of having been on the winning side in the late Civil War; by the support of the body which was now able to call itself the Scottish Parliament and by the countenance of a Prince, whose interests happened to coincide with theirs. Under these circumstances, therefore, the excess of force lay with them, and on *June 4th, 1691*, they had the satisfaction of "planting" Perth with a Presbyterian divine according to their own forms. The name of this first Minister of the present Establishment was Mr. *Robert* Anderson.

CHAPTER III.

HOW THE EPISCOPAL INCUMBENTS WERE OUSTED AND PRESBYTERIANS PLANTED IN THE NEIGHBOURING PARISHES, 1688-98.

HAVING "purged" the City itself of Episcopacy and "planted" it with Presbyterianism, the Presbytery now determined to proceed with the utmost rigour of the law to do the same for the extensive district under their supervision. In this and the next Chapter we shall follow them step by step, omitting only a few of the more distant parishes, which lie to the north of the Tay in the region of Dunkeld. These two Chapters may prove to be a little tedious to the reader but, as general statements only carry the authority of the person who makes them, it will be more valuable to give all the particular facts as gathered from the Presbytery Records, on which any general statement must be founded.

At one of the earliest meetings of the Presbytery a bird's-eye view of the state of their jurisdiction is given. They describe the flocks as being " in a desolate condition." The " desolation " consisted in a full supply of Episcopal Clergy and a complete dearth of Presbyterians.

The problem before them was how to reverse the state of affairs : how to create a full supply of Presbyterians and a dearth of Episcopalians. This result shewed no signs of producing itself spontaneously and therefore some more drastic method must be devised. The plan ultimately adopted was that vacancies were to be forcibly made by the help of the Privy Council and then these "vacancies" filled up in the following manner. The existing elders were all to be ignored as being Prelatical. New ones were to be elected according to the forms, which prevailed in the Presbyterian body under the Toleration of King James. The elders, when duly constituted, would call Ministers and appeal to the Presbytery to admit them. If any locality proved refractory and failed to call a Minister within six months, then the Presbytery knew that according to the Act of *May 26th, 1690*, they had the right of themselves nominating and inducting an Incumbent, *tanquam jure devoluto*. In the last resort they could require the Civil Magistrate to support their proceedings.

Let us therefore proceed to follow the campaign. It has been said that Perth itself was the first parish to be captured. This is so far true that it certainly was the first to be "purged" of Episcopacy; but, though, as we have seen, it was "planted" with Presbyterianism tolerably soon, yet there were two parishes, which, having been "purged" later, were "planted" earlier, *i.e.*, Dunbarney and Abernethy. Here follow the particulars :—

DUNBARNEY :—

The Episcopal Parish Minister was Mr. John Balneaves. He was deprived by the Privy Council in *July, 1690*, for not reading the Proclamation of Estates and for not praying for William and Mary. On *January 14th* next year the Presbytery succeeded in taking possession of the parish by the ordination of a Mr. Tullidaph.

ABERNETHY :—

Mr. R. Jenkins, who had been Incumbent under the Bishops since 1672, was deprived along with his brother of Dunbarney and his place taken without difficulty by the ordination on *April 29th, 1691*, of a Mr. Alexander Dunning. An incident, characteristic of the times, is recorded in connection with the change. In order to get the Precentorship, a Mr. James Sibbald " compeared before the Presbytery and declared he was very sensible of his former failing in complying with the late sinful (*i.e.*, Episcopal) times."

Of course the easiest cases come first and the same year saw two more parishes surrender to the attack, *i.e.*,

ABERDALGIE :—

Mr. John Hardie, instituted by the Bishop in 1679, shares the same fate as the two former brethren, and is succeeded by the Presbyterian Mr. Schaw on *September 23rd, 1691*.

DUNNING :—

The Episcopal Parish Minister was Mr. David Freebairn, " a man of blameless conversation and sweet temper; a vigilant preacher and successful physician and one of the kindest of friends."* These qualities, however, were no protection to him, and on *September 20th, 1691*, an attempt was made by the Presbytery to ordain Mr. William Reid in his place. It proved, however, unsuccessful. Mr. Freebairn evidently had friends, and the Presbytery speak of " a party of armed men sent from Tullibardine by the Marquis of Athol," to protect him. But the following week Mr. Reid's ordination was carried through. Mr. Freebairn will reappear in our narrative.†

The next year (1692) saw four more parishes "purged and planted," though not without resistance. They are as follows, the case of Erroll being particularly noteworthy.

* MS. by Mr. Smith of Perth in the Episcopal Chest : O. 9.
† See Chapters XII., XIII., XIV., XV.

ERROLL :—

The Prelatic Incumbent was Mr. John Nicholson, to whom "the Session gave a high testimonial for faithfulness and painfulness." The first sign of trouble came on *September 8th, 1689*, under which date we read that "there was no sermon because the troopers came into the town and dissipat the people with sound of trumpet, and Dr. Nicholson was informed that they would offer him violence." Notwithstanding this threatening omen, the good clergyman was let alone for the next nine months, when sentence of deprivation was passed against him by the Privy Council and the keys of Erroll Kirk ordered to be delivered up to the Presbytery. It was easier, however, for the Revolution authorities to issue than to enforce such orders. Another seven months were allowed to elapse before a serious attempt was again made to dislodge Dr. Nicholson. On *February 4th, 1691*, Mr. John Anderson, who had been sent by the Presbytery to preach the Church vacant, had to report that he was unable to obtain admission.

This, of course, was an unsatisfactory state of affairs for the local Presbyterians, and on *May 10th* Mr. Tullidaph appeared on the scene to carry out that which Mr. Anderson had failed to accomplish. But the other parishioners, having got note of his intentions, convened in considerable numbers and met the Presbytery's emissary and his guards, as he was entering the Church-yard. "One of the two Presbyterian lairds began to harangue and to soothe them, but the resolute clowns were not to be wrought upon by such whining rhetorick, and therefore they told the laird promptly that the preacher would do best to be gone without any further noise, for that day he should not enter the Church of Erroll. The Presbyterians then began to offer blows, but they were soundly beaten and Tullidaph with his friends was obliged to retreat."

Three months later Dr. Nicholson is still in possession and "Lord Kinnaird, Sir John Hay, and several other gentlemen compeared before the Presbytery from Erroll . . . and menaced any that should be sent by them to preach there." This threat was duly fulfilled, for, when, after the lapse of another five months the Presbytery again sent Mr. Reid to preach the Church vacant, "he was stopped by a rabble from preaching in the Kirk but did so in the Kirkyard and served Mr. Nairne's edict." At last on *January 12th, 1692*, the parish surrendered after holding out against repeated attacks since *September 8th, 1689*, and Mr. Nairne entered on his duties as first Minister of the new Establishment there.

MONIEVARD :—

Mr. David Young was deprived by the Privy Council on *September 1st, 1689*, for not praying for William and Mary but for King James. On *May 4th, 1692*, he was superseded by Mr. John Campbell, "who gave satisfaction for complying with Prelacie." This does not mean that he was in Episcopal Orders but that, being a Presbyterian, the Bishops, with the toleration which marked their dealings with the more moderate of his persuasion, had allowed him to continue in his parish after the Restoration.

COLLACE :—

Mr. George M'Gruther, of whom we shall hear more afterwards, had been Episcopal Parish Minister of this place since 1670. He was deprived in 1689 for the usual reasons: was actually ousted on *March 23rd*,

1692, and succeeded on *July 6th* by the Presbyterian, Mr. James Campbell.

TIBBERMUIR :—

Mr. Alexander Balneaves, who seems to have begun his ministerial career under the Episcopate of Charles I.'s time and had been made Dean of Dunkeld by Bishop Hamilton, was Minister here. He had long ago got into trouble with the Presbyterians for giving the Marquis of Montrose a glass of water, and now again on *November 26th, 1690*, he is summoned before the Presbytery. On *December 31st* he is reported as keeping neither fasts nor thanksgivings nor reading the proclamations. This action, however, on his part is not to be wondered at, since the fasts were often appointed on a day which the Church does not allow to be considered a fast, *i.e.*, Sunday, and for the purpose of bewailing the sinfulness of the late Prelatic times. For some time he was beyond the reach of attack but on *July 20th, 1692*, we read that Mr. Balneaves, who had had the artifice to keep himself free from prosecutions during the changes, was now cited before the Presbytery but compeared not. Cited *pro secundo*, compeared not. He was accused '(1) of not residing in his Parish (and, if he had done so, we may be sure that would have been an offence also) but on his estate of Carnbadie : (2) of being guilty of frequent and unnecessary travelling between his home and his Parish and crossing the river thereby twice in boats; a profanation of the Sabbath : (3) of not praying for William and Mary.

He was deprived on *September 7th*.

The Duke of Atholl thereupon obtained Mr. Meldrum, who had served under Episcopacy at Irvine, to be settled. It was at Mr. Meldrum's institution that the

Presbytery of Perth first subscribed the Westminster Confession, not only as the Confession of the Church of Scotland but as their own.

In the following year (1693) there was only one Parish settled, *i.e.*,—

LITTLE DUNKELD :—

March 29th, 1693. Mr. Alexander M'Lagan "renounced" Episcopacy and was continued as Parish Minister by the Presbytery. This was the only instance where the like occurred in our two-and-a-half Presbyteries.

Next year (1694) there was again only one Parish "purged and planted" but it was a very notable case, as will appear from the following narrative drawn from the *Presbytery Records* :—

METHVEN :—

In this case the death of the Episcopal Incumbent, Mr. John Omey, seemed at first likely to render the occupation of the Parish easy. But in fact it did not prove to be so. All *November* and *December, 1693*, the Presbytery's representative, Mr. Anderson, failed to obtain access to the Church. He complained that the Laird of Methven's answers "contained nothing but dilatours."

Mr. Alexander Dunning was then appointed to preach the Kirk vacant. His action was more vigorous but not more successful than that of Mr. Anderson. By the end of January all he could report was that "on Sabbath he went to the Parish Kirk of Methven, where he found a great rabble of people stopping his access and that Mr. Young, late Incumbent of Monievard . . . was within the Kirk at the same time." Mr. Dunning, however, preached to those, who were disposed to listen to him, in the Churchyard, and declared the Kirk vacant. Not satisfied with the progress he had made, he went in March to Edinburgh and prosecuted the matter before the Privy Council.

On *May 2nd, 1694*, the Parish having been vacant for six months, the Presbytery claimed the right of filling it up, *quasi jure devoluto*. This of course was resisted by the Lairds of Methven and Balgowan. Nevertheless the Presbytery persist and select Mr. William Moncrieff but (*June 14th*) "there were uncommon circumstances attending his ordination." When the Presbytery with their Moderator, Mr. Robert Anderson of Perth, went to Methven and were proceeding to the Kirk, they found the Laird of Balgowan, Busbie, David Smyth, brother of the Laird of Methven, and several parishioners standing as a guard before the Church door. Mr. Robert Anderson in the name of the Presbytery desired that he might have access to perform the intention, on which he and his brethren had come there: but he was answered with a positive refusal. He and his fellows thereupon protested and then met together in a house near the Church to consider what they were to do next. There they determined that Mr. Robert should preach in the Kirkyard and should perform there, as they could not get access to the Kirk, the solemnities of the ordination: which was accordingly done."

Such was the solitary victory gained by the Presbyterians in 1694. Their advance in 1695 was no greater but somewhat more easily won :—

FORGANDENNY :—

"Mr. Andrew Hardie, who had been admitted to the Parish in 1667 was deprived very early and the Parish being long vacant and a qualified Session ordained, Mr. William Dick, a preacher in the bounds of the Presbytery of Kirkcaldy was after due formalities ordained and admitted Minister of Forgandenny, *Sept. 4th, 1695.*"

The year 1696 passed without the loss of a single Parish in the district to our disestablished Church. In 1697, however, another was wrested from them by the Presbytery :—

FOWLIS WESTER :—

Of this Mr. John Drummond was Parish Minister under the Bishops. He was deprived by the Privy Council for the usual reasons, and not only so but also committed to prison. He died in 1695. Two years later—*March 31, 1697*—Mr. William Hepburn obtained possession of the Parish in the interests of Presbyterianism.

The Episcopal Church had thus only been deprived of four parishes in the last five years. But the following twelvemonth (1698) saw three more Presbyterianized, *i.e.* :—

KINNOULL :—

Of this Parish, Mr. Thomas Fowlar had been Episcopal Incumbent since four years subsequent to the Restoration of Charles II. After the Revolution he was deprived by the Privy Council for the usual reasons and for thanking God for Viscount Dundee's victory over Major-General Mackay at Killiecrankie. He was, however, a great favourite with the parishioners and held his own till 1697, when he was obliged wholly to leave the Church and to deliver up the box with 500 merks therein. At last Mr. Andrew Darling was admitted by the Presbytery on *February 2, 1698.*

AUCHTERGAVEN :—

Mr. William Aisson (or Easson) described by one, who knew him, as "a good, serious Christian, but weak and credulous," was the Prelatic Incumbent here. He was deprived by the Privy Council on *October 8th,*

1689, for "praying that the Lord would exalt King James's horn above those of his enemies." As usual, however, it was easier to decree than to effect his deprivation; a thing, which Mr. Anderson, who was admitted to the Parish by the Presbytery on *April 25th, 1690*, found to his cost, his position being so insecure that he only remained a few months. For five years after this Mr. Easson and his friend, Mr. William Frazer, continued to officiate unprevented. But on *February 6, 1695*, letters of horning were issued not only against them but also against the Patron, Lord Nairne, as "havers of the keys of the Kirk of Auchtergaven." This second attack also they were enabled to defeat and they remained in possession for another three years, but at last, on *April 26th, 1698*, Presbyterianism gained the Parish and Mr. Thomas Fisher, its representative, was admitted to the living.

The third Parish "purged and planted" in 1698 was:—

KILSPINDY:—

Of this Mr. John Blair had been Incumbent since 1667. On *November 26th, 1690*, he was summoned before the Presbytery but he compeared not and Provost Smith's son, of Perth, a staunch Churchman, brought a commission from him, which the Court refused to hear. One of the crimes charged against him is that he has failed to celebrate "the Protestant victory in Ireland." On *March 29th* of the following year he is summoned before the Synod of Perth and Stirling. He treats them, however, as he treated the Presbytery, and is "deposed." Nevertheless eight months afterwards "he does yet continue to baptize children to the great contempt of the Government and Laws now established. . . . His contempt and disorder being

Review of the first Ten Years. 25

notour, the Presbytery appoint him to be cited before the next Provincial Assembly." Somehow or another that body had no better success with him than the Synod and Presbytery had. For, three years afterwards, we still find him in possession of Kilspindy and it is not till *February 26, 1698*, that, after obtaining letters of horning against him, Mr. William English is ordained to the Parish by the Presbytery. And, when this was done, they must bitterly have regretted their own action, for Mr. English gave them great trouble till at last in 1718 they proceeded to depose him.

The reader will observe that, as the Prince of Orange landed at Torbay on *November 5th, 1688*, and as Kilspindy was only planted on *September 26th, 1698*, about ten years had now passed, and that 14 of the 29 Parishes, with which we have taken in hand to deal, were still in the hands of the Episcopalians. It is evident therefore, that, even if we admit that the mass of the people were rather tolerant of the old Prelacy than intelligent and enthusiastic supporters of it, yet their reception of Presbyterianism was very cold and perfunctory. There was, to say the least of it, no active dislike of the Bishops and no zeal for the Genevan system such as swept the old Church from the south-western districts of Scotland. And, if this is evident from the narrative of the *Presbytery Record*, we may be sure that it would have been still more clearly brought out, if any full chronicle on the Episcopal side had survived the confusion of the time.

CHAPTER IV.

HOW THE PURGING AND PLANTING FARED IN ITS SECOND DECADE, 1699-1709.

THE concluding remarks of the last chapter will be greatly strengthened by the consideration that another is needed before we can complete the story of the purgation and plantation of our district. The new Establishment, which has been working vigorously and systematically for ten years to obtain possession of the (extended) Perth Presbytery, has still a struggle of fully another ten years to come, ere it can call itself master of the field.

One Parish was lost to the Church in 1699, *i.e.:*—
RATTRAY :—

The Episcopal Parish Minister here at the time of the Revolution was Mr. David Rankin. On *October 10th, 1689*, the usual Privy Council formula of deprivation was passed against him. But for many years it was only a *brutum fulmen*. On *July 15th, 1691*, indeed, the Presbytery's representative, Mr. William Reid, attempts to enter the Parish but he is obliged to report that "he can neither have safe access at present to the Church, nor a legal call given him by reason of the disaffectedness of heritors and people." Evidently there was no dislike of Episcopacy here. An opening for the Presbytery at last occurs on *May 10th, 1699*, and Mr. Bowis is then ordained to the Parish.

Special efforts seem to have been made by the Presbytery in 1700, since during its course no less than five additional Parishes were purged and planted. They follow in due order:—

RHYND:—

The Episcopal Parish Minister here since 1678 had been Mr. William Poplay. After the Revolution he "was long kept in possession of his Parish and the exercise of his Ministry by his noble parishioner, who resided at Elcho Castle, *i.e.*, Margaret, Countess of Wemyss."

October 24th, 1694, Mr. W. Poplay is summoned before the Presbytery. He declines its jurisdiction. Here the matter seems to have rested until 1696, when on a new complaint Mr. Poplay was summoned before the Privy Council. He now subscribes a resignation of the Parish but continues preaching in fields and private houses until 1700, when by a special act of the Privy Council he is compelled to leave the district. Mr. Thomas Fisher, who had been ordained by the Presbytery on *October 6th, 1699*, then obtained possession of the Parish.

ROGORTON:—

Of this Parish Mr. Patrick Ochterlonie was the Pre-Revolution Clergyman, having been ordained in 1681. During the years 1690 and 1691 he was several times summoned before the Presbytery and Synod. Sometimes he compeared and sometimes he did not. When he did so, it was to decline their jurisdiction. On one occasion he based his position on the ground that the Synod of Dunkeld had disjoined his Parish from the Presbytery of Perth. The reply to this gives little countenance to the modern theory, held by some, that there was continuity between the Pre-Revolution Episcopal Church and the Post-Revolution Establishment. For the Presbytery's answer to Mr. Ochterlonie's plea was that "the Presbytery may not own the deed of the Bishop and Synod of Dunkeld," *i.e.*, in the matter of the transference of the Parish. On *July 20th, 1691,* Mr. Tullidaph succeeded in declaring Rogorton vacant, but very little was gained by this formality, for Mr. Ochterlonie not only held his own, but is reported to have been administering Baptism in the great Church of Perth. Probably this was due to the influence of that staunch Churchman, Provost Smith, and the Episcopally-inclined Town Council. Five years afterwards the Presbytery's Commissioners to the General Assembly are instructed to report "the great hurt done to the Government by deprived and deposed Ministers, particularly by Mr. Ochterlonie, who continues in office, notwithstanding he is deposed by the Church." At last on *August 30th, 1699,* things begin to look more hopeful for the Presbyterians: no less than two elders and two heads of families sign a call for a Minister of that persuasion, and in the following Spring (*April 25th, 1700,*) Mr. George Blackie is admitted by the Presbytery. Mr. Ochterlonie then retires to the neighbourhood of Brechin, where he acts as Lord Panmure's factor till 1716.[*]

KINCLAVEN:—

Mr. Thomas Murray was the Episcopal Parish Minister here, having been admitted only a year or two before the Revolution. He succeeded in holding his own for many years, and was not dislodged till *April 30th, 1700,* when Mr. Alexander

[*] On *May 16th, 1711,* Wodrow (Letters, I., 223) mentions that an Episcopal Clergyman, Mr. John Achterlony, was ministering with such success at Aberlemno, near Brechin, that the Parish Kirk was deserted. This Mr. Achterlony removed in 1726 to Dundee, and re-appears in Chapter XII. as Bishop of that District.

Glas was admitted to the Parish by the Presbytery. But his dislodgment by no means put an end to Mr. T. Murray's activities, as we shall hereafter see.

TRINITY GASK:—

Mr. James Roy, the Prelatic Incumbent, was cited before the Presbytery on *October 24th, 1694*, but his summons was delayed at that time owing to the bad state of the roads. When, however, he did compear on *December 19th*, it was only to decline the authority of the Court. The latter, therefore, "appoints him to be represented to the next Session of the Commission of the General Assembly, being so rude that by no means he could be persuaded to stay to hear the grounds and reasons of his citation." Whatever these grounds and reasons may have been, they proved inoperative during six years, for it was not till *September 3rd, 1700*, that the Presbytery's representative, Mr. John Murray, was admitted to the Parish.

AUCHTERARDER:—

The Episcopal Parish Minister was Mr. John Rattray, who was in due course deprived for not praying for King William and Queen Mary. On *February 6th, 1695*, the Presbytery obtained letters of horning against him as "a haver of the Church keys." The Presbyterian, Mr. James Mitchell, was substituted for him in 1700.

KINFAUNS:—

Mr. John Gall, the Episcopal Parish Minister, "was according to many traditionary accounts a man of the most respectable and amiable character. He was well affected to the Revolution of civil government, and thankful that the three kingdoms were happily delivered from the apprehensions justly entertained of the intended introduction of Popery. But the utter ruin of the

Episcopal Church and the prosecutions against its Ministers alienated his affections from the new Government, so that he left off mentioning King William by name in the public prayers. He was deposed by the Presbytery on *July 28th, 1697*, and Mr. Schaw was appointed to declare the Parish vacant. On *September 31st*, "it is reported for Mr. Schaw that he went to Kinfauns Kirk and preached in the Kirkyard, and intimated sentence of deposition and declared the Church vacant." In 1698 letters from the Privy Council were procured and executed against Mr. Gall, who then left the Parish wholly and gave no more trouble to the Presbytery. Nevertheless it was not till *September 12th, 1700*, that Mr. Matthew Coupar was translated from Ochiltree and admitted Minister of Kinfauns. "The Moderator gave him institution by delivering him the Church Bible, the keys of the Church doors, and the bell-strings."

After the energy displayed by the Presbytery in 1700, they made less rapid progress for some time. In 1701, indeed, they gained two Parishes, *i.e.*,—

MADDERTY:—

Mr. James Graham, the Episcopal Incumbent, was deprived at the Revolution for the usual reasons, and on *February 5th, 1695*, letters of horning were out against him and others as "havers of the Church keys." The incident ended on *January 8th, 1701*, with the ordination of Mr. Andrew Brugh to the Parish by the Presbytery.

S. MADOES:—

The Pre-Revolution Minister here was Mr. Thomas Hall. He was cited for intruding on *November 7th, 1694*. On appearing before the Presbytery, he declined its authority. The occurrence seems to have had no effect upon his conduct, for he was again summoned three years later. On this occasion he refused to appear at all. In his absence witnesses were examined, one of whom, *Oliver Elder*, deponed "he has many times heard Mr. Hall preach, and that long since he heard him pray for King William and Queen Mary, but he has not heard him do so this long time: knows not whether he kept the last Fast or not!" *James Brown* depones that "he was witness to Mr. Hall's baptising Patrick Donald's child," and there were more witnesses to the same effect. The Presbytery, therefore, "considering his great contumacy at this time, notwithstanding four citations, . . . deposes him from his office of Minister, and appoints Mr. Dick to preach at S. Madoes and declare the Church vacant." The latter gentlemen tried to fulfil his commission, but on *September 21st, 1697*, came back reporting that "he went to S. Madoes, but met with such opposition from the Pitfours, senior and junior, and their associates that he could get no access to preach in the Kirk, Kirkyard, nor ground of the Parish. Nevertheless he intimated the sentence, and declared the Kirk vacant." Notwithstanding these steps, however, the Presbytery could get no permanent entrance to S. Madoes till *March 12th, 1701*. They then ordained Mr. George Blair to the Parish.

The conquest of Madderty and S. Madoes in the first year of the eighteenth century was followed by a truce of four and a-half year's duration. All through this time the Presbytery did not purge and plant a single additional Parish. What can have been the reason? May we not believe that this pause was the local shadow of the following imperial events?—viz., the death of King James on *September 16th, 1701*;

that of King William on *March 8th, 1702*, and the consequent accession of Queen Anne. For it was an open secret that the new Monarch strongly sympathised with the old Church. No doubt the knowledge of this, accentuated by an actual letter of Toleration from Her Majesty, induced men to pause and see how the stream was going to flow. The Revolution arrangements might, for all people knew, undergo serious modification, or even, as many hoped, be altogether upset. However, they held their ground, and so our Presbytery felt it safe once more to proceed with the expulsion of the Episcopalians.

At the same time a local circumstance may have contributed to the same result. For during the years in question the Presbytery had on hand probably the severest ttruggle, which they ever had to undertake, in order to force themselves into an unwilling Parish. This was:—

CARGILL :—

The Episcopal Incumbent here was Mr. William Rattray, "a robust, strong man, and would have made as good a trooper as a minister." This muscular Christian was deprived by the Privy Council in 1689, but 13 years after his "deprivation," we still find him "ordinarily intruding both within and without the Paroch."

On *February 8th, 1703*, a formal attempt was made to gain entrance to Cargill. "The Presbytery finding no access to the Church, the doors thereof being all shut and the Bedell absenting himself, the Moderator and the rest of the brethren went to the most patent door of the Church and after knocking and calling for the keys to get entry and none compeared with the keys to give access, the Moderator in the name of the Presbytery took instruments in the Clerk's hands before witnesses. Then appeared George Rattray, brother to the late Incumbent, and owned judiciall that he had locked the Church door and had the keys, but would not give them up, alledging that he had Blair-drummond and other heritors, their orders, for so doing."

Two more attempts were equally unsuccessful. On *March 31st, 1703*, Mr. Wylie attempted to preach on behalf of the Presbytery, but reported that "he was interrupted by George Rattray and could get no access." On *April 20th* he had a similar report to make:— "Seeing he could get no Nottare Public to go with him but at an extraordinary rate, he went up without any, and finding he could get no auditory though he had gone (*i.e.*, to the Church), he went not."

In view of these failures the Presbytery resolve to bring in the aid of the secular arm. Accordingly application is made to Sheriff-Depute Ramsay, but he replies that he will not meddle with the business. This, of course, leads to an appeal to the Sheriff Principal, the Duke of Athole, but that functionary discovers that Cargill is not within his jurisdiction.

Before, therefore, the Episcopal Incumbent can be coerced, it appears that both the Sheriffs must themselves undergo that process. Accordingly on *May 9th, 1705*, orders are received from the Privy Council to the Sheriff directing him to put the Presbytery "in possession and keeping them in it of the Kirk of Cargill." Having now the Privy Council at their back in the matter, the Presbytery return to the charge. They desire the Sheriff-Depute on *June 27th* "to execute the Council's order and to deliver the keys of Cargill to the Presbytery." The Duke of Athole also undertakes to see that his deputy delivers the keys. But for many months they are not surrendered. Either the Sheriff-Depute did not happen to be at home when the Presbytery's representative called; or else, when

they did have an interview, there was some informality
discovered in the form of their demand. However, without
the proper surrender of the keys, the Presbytery consider
that the Parish is practically purged, and proceed to
plant it. On *June 27th*, by virtue of *jus devolutum*,
they give a unanimous call to a young man, John
Gow by name. The latter finishes his trials on *August
28th*, and on *September 20th* he is ordained to Cargill.
"The Moderator gave him institution by delivering
the Bible and bell stringes and also earth and stone
to him of the Manse and Glebe." Two months later,
however, Mr. Gow reports that "his circumstances in
the Paroch are very grievous to him." Still, supported
by the Presbytery, he holds on, although it now appears
that all that had been already done in order to obtain
access to the Church, must be done over again with
respect to the Manse. Mr. Gow fails to oust Mr.
Rattray from it : the Sheriff and his deputy find that
it too is not in their jurisdiction : the Commission of
the General Assembly thereupon apply to the Queen's
Advocate : that official discovers that he can do nothing
without orders from the Privy Council : his memory
proves treacherous and "the Presbytery therefore
appoint Mr. Darling to writt the Clerk of the Commission to *mind* the Advocate thereof against the first
Council day." But, having got the Presbytery so far
towards possession, we shall leave Mr. Darling writing
to the Advocate and decidedly nonplussed because he
receives no answer.

The year 1707 saw the surrender of another
Parish, *i.e.* :—

ARNGASK :—

The Episcopal Incumbent here was Mr. Gilbert
Melvill. A Presbyterian field preacher ministered some-

Arngask—Scone. 35

what irregularly in the place till 1694, and on *February 27th, 1695,* Mr. John Demster was admitted Minister of the Parish. This, indeed, might entitle Arngask to be classed as planted in the year 1695. But after Mr. Demster had remained only about a twelvemonth, he was translated, and the Parish, once more vacant, was torn by factions. On *May 15th* and *July 31st, 1706,* it is reported that "there is great heat and dissension existing at Arngask." In December it is still the same, but at last on *May 21st, 1707,* Mr. Gillespie is successfully ordained by the Presbytery.

About a year after the "settlement" of Arngask, the keys of another Parish were surrendered, *i.e.* :—

SCONE :—

The new Establishment met with as frigid a reception here as it did in Cargill. The Episcopal Incumbent was Mr. Patrick Walker, who had recently succeeded a Mr. John Liddell. "Purging" operations seem to have been begun in earnest in 1694. No progress having been made, letters of horning against Viscount Stormont and the Beadle of Scone are obtained early in 1695. In *September, 1696,* the Presbytery's commissioners are instructed to lay complaints against his Lordship before the General Assembly, and two years afterwards a Mr. Christie is actually ordained to the Parish. However, he dies after three years, and the whole case is re-opened. On *November 14th, 1705,* the Parish is still "desolate." The Presbytery therefore call Mr. John Kennedy, but on *January 2nd, 1706,* a petition is presented in the name of some small heritors and the whole elders " craving that in regaird Mr. John Kennedy . . . is unacceptable to the whole body of the people of the Paroch, the Presbytery will be pleased to revoke their sentence." This, however, they decline to do. But on *April 10th* Mr. Kennedy himself "refuses his exercises for Scone on account of the opposition of the people, and because the Synod seem inclined to let them choose their own Minister." At last on *January 2nd, 1707*, Mr. James Stewart is ordained to the Parish, but only to resign on *September 10th*. On *January 9th, 1708*, the Minister sent to preach is forcibly prevented by Lord Stormont's servants, but the Presbytery may be said to have triumphed, when the keys were surrendered to them on *April 28th, 1708*, i.e., twenty years after the fall of the Pre-Revolution system.

By one method of reckoning, Scone would be the last Parish to be settled, but there still remains Forteviot to be accounted for. It was, indeed, "planted" with a Presbyterian Minister in 1696; but, as the settlement proved, like some of the former ones, to be only temporary, it seems legitimate to consider it as not finally surrendered to Presbyterianism till 1708. The narrative follows :—

FORTEVIOT :—

Mr. William Barclay (ordained 1651) was the Pre-Revolution Minister here. He is deposed on *October 8th, 1690*, and on *September 9th, 1696*, Mr. A. Chalmers admitted by the Presbytery. He leaves after a year, and is succeeded by a man of bad character, and then ensues protracted agitation. In *1705 (October 3rd)* the Presbytery "take the desolate state of Forteviot into their serious consideration." On *December 5th* they "spend some time in prayer that God would give them light and direction in making choice of some fit person." But a month later a report is handed in from the Parish stating that "it is impossible to reconcile the different and factious humours there." The Synod, the Duke of Athole and Lord Dupplin are all appealed to for their co-operation, and the Presbytery resolve "to compel the Sheriff-Depute to put the law in operation against Mr. John Graham, Intruder (Episcopal) at Forteviot." At last a Mr. Walker is settled, but we cannot pursue his history further than to say that on *March 17th, 1709*, he complains that he cannot get his stipend paid.

Such are the facts, as related almost entirely by the Perth *Presbytery Record*, concerning the purging out of Episcopacy and the planting in of Presbyterianism throughout the district with which we are dealing. From them the reader can now draw his own conclusions as to whether Episcopacy was the intolerable burden it was represented to be in the Act of Disestablishment, and Presbyterianism the spontaneous choice of the People. The truth, indeed, appears to have been far otherwise. From the evidence now adduced, it is evident that, over the extensive region through which we have travelled, Episcopacy, if not universally defended with the intelligence and enthusiasm of the masses, was yet in possession "with the minds of the People." On the other hand it is equally evident that Presbyterianism was regarded as disturbing a very satisfactory state of affairs, and that it owed its triumph to the general prestige it had gained by its support of the Civil Revolution : to the defeat of King James' cause on the field of battle : to King William's astute support of it to serve his own ends : and last, but by no means least, to the forcible and unyielding way in which the Presbytery coerced all who withstood them with the pains and penalties of the law. But every reader can judge for himself from the particulars which have gone before.

CHAPTER V.

HOW THE CHURCH'S BATTLE FOR EXISTENCE FARED IN PERTH FROM 1691 TO 1707.

WE now pass from the long struggle, which the Perth Presbytery had to undertake before they could gain our neighbourhood, to the story of that which subsequently befel the ousted Churchmen. A thoughtless, modern reader might be disposed to imagine that all that the evicted Incumbents would have to do was to organize their followers into a free Church, and live as comfortably as they could with their neighbours of the new Establishment. He might remember the case of the Disestablishment of the Irish Church, in the Nineteenth Century, and think that we had now to describe similar experiences. Or, if it did occur to him that things were done more roughly in times past than now, he might recollect that, even in the bitter times of the "Reformation," the Scottish Bishops were allowed at least sufficient income to provide for their needs till the end of their lives. And so he might now expect to hear that the evicted Clergy were left in a tolerably comfortable position.

But far otherwise was the real state of affairs. It was not only that they were suddenly deprived of house and income for the future, but the arrears of stipend, which happened to be owing them from the past, were to be paid, not to them, but to their supplanters. This was bad enough: it was, indeed, very severe. But worse remained. No worship but that of the Established Communion was now to be tolerated within their bounds by the pertinacious Presbytery, and so (not at present to refer to higher principles) the ejected Ministers were to be prevented from, in any shape, exercising the only profession by which they had been trained to earn their daily bread.

And thus the root of an evil was planted, which was to spring up into a veritable bed of thorns for the disestablished Church in the first half of the eighteenth century. For on its disestablishment during the present period it was never allowed a moment's breathing space, in which to create some organisation suitable to its altered circumstances. Organisation? The moment she had fought and lost the battle of retaining some of her property and former position, and was in all the confusion of defeat ("in the claw of an enraged lion," as Mr. Morer well described it), a second and more serious contest still, that namely for existence in any form whatever, was suddenly thrust upon the afflicted Church. And all that her sons could do under the circumstances was either to fight or fly, each at his own discretion and in his own way.

We must now, therefore, proceed to relate how our Presbytery fell upon the rear of the defeated forces, and endeavoured to exterminate them utterly within their bounds.

At the end of the last chapter we had reached the year 1708. But as this was only in watching our Priests being evicted from their livings, it is evident that, in order to tell the story of how they fared after their expulsion, we must turn back to the year in which the first of them were ejected, *i.e.*, 1691. And, as in the case of the "purgation and planting," the

Presbytery Records are again almost our only source of information: the Episcopal Clergy were evidently in no case to keep methodical diaries of what occurred, or to hand them systematically down to official successors, if they had kept them.

This authority, obviously, will not supply us with any information concerning those who did not remain in this district to fight the battle. "Many of the Episcopal Clergy," we learn, however, from the writer of the Perth MS. in the Advocates' Library, "went into England, where it is said some of them acquired a great reputation by their learning and piety and devotional writings." Archbishop Ross, our Diocesan, moved to Edinburgh. Of Mr. David Anderson, late Minister of the second charge in the City, we are informed that he retired with his young family to the Gowrie House, where he kept a school. Their circumstances compel us to believe of many—and there is evidence to prove it—that were driven into great poverty and distress.

All honour to those who suffered the despoiling of their goods for conscience sake. But we must perforce turn from them and proceed to relate the doings of their more militant brethren, who fought and left a record behind them, and saved a remnant of the Church to descend with blessing to our own day.

It would be an anachronism to suppose that in these early days the Church was already reduced to the "shadow of a shade." That only came about after a century of affliction. From what has already transpired, it is evident that our Presbytery had completely failed to carry the landed gentry as a class with them. These remained faithful to the old Church. The Magistrates of Perth also have been shewn to be staunch in their

Churchmanship, and both from what has gone before and from evidence subsequently laid before the Presbytery, there is no doubt that great numbers of the people both assisted the Lairds in the attempt to keep the Presbyterians out, and also attended the worship conducted by the disestablished Clergy. To take one example of each. In Scone, for instance, we saw that the Presbytery's nominee was "unacceptable to the whole body of the people," and we shall soon hear of "multitudes of people being convened" in the Episcopal Meeting-House of Perth.

It would be manifestly impossible any longer to attempt to follow the fortunes of these Churchmen systematically throughout the large district, which has been dealt with in the preceding chapters. In the times of disorganization, which were now thrust on the disestablished communion, we must be content to obtain glimpses wherever we can. The evicted Clergy evidently exerted themselves to hold their people together in those places alone, where their own capacity and the circumstances of the locality rendered it possible. Since they had no access allowed them to the old buildings of the Church, they were obliged to form make-shift chapels, which they termed by the temporary name of "Meeting-Houses." It is to these Meeting-Houses that we must now attend.

The Presbytery attended to them. What they aimed at was, having ejected the Episcopal Clergy from their Parishes, to put down their ministrations in their humble chapels also. It was to be a matter of life and death. The officiating Clergy were technically styled " Intruders." Perhaps this term was chosen by way of reprisal, since, if human nature was the same then as now, it is not impossible that, when the new

"Intruders"—Perth Meeting-House. 43

Presbyterian Incumbent walked in at one door of the Parish Church and the Episcopalian retreated by the other, the latter might not infrequently have allowed that very word to drop from his lips. Alas! for the bitterness of feeling! but it is for the historian to record facts, not to create ideals. "Intruders," however, the old Clergy were henceforth styled by the new : they were cited as such before the Presbytery : ordered to discontinue their ministrations altogether : on their refusal, deposed from the ministerial office (so far as Orders Episcopally conferred can be cancelled by those, who do not hold the Bishop's office), and handed over to the (generally unwilling) Secular arm to be concussed into obedience, and if the Magistrates on their part hesitated to enforce the law in all its rigour, they too found themselves threatened by the determined Presbytery.

The rest of this Chapter must therefore be filled by transactions such as these, which happened in our district in the earlier part of our time, viz., from 1691 to 1706. They consist of three attempts to suppress the Meeting-House of Perth itself, and of one to do the same for the Episcopal assemblies in Rhynd and S. Madoes respectively. All of these, however, were only very partially successful.

(1) CASE OF THE PERTH MEETING-HOUSE, 1691-1697 :—

Not unnaturally, the information in our possession about this early period is very scanty. But we shall here gather together all that is recorded over and above what was related before with regard to the deposition of the two Ministers, Mr. Adam Barclay and Mr. David Anderson. First let us collect all the notices possible of Episcopalian doings, remembering that they are the beginnings of our disestablished congregation. To begin with (as has already been stated for a different purpose), the Rev. David Anderson continued to reside at the Gowrie House within the City, and although he did not come actively enough forward to be summoned before the Presbytery, it is yet to be presumed that he did what little he could in a quiet way to help the good cause. In *June, 1693,* he had a daughter born to him, and procured the services of the ousted Incumbent of Kilspindie, Mr. Blair, to baptise her under the name of Elizabeth ; and again, on *September 24th, 1696,* the Rev. Adam Barclay, late Minister of the first charge, baptises another of his daughters, called Margaret. At last, in 1697, Mr. Anderson died* about the age of 50, having lived " piously and inoffensibly." This is all we know of him subsequent to his deposition. Of Mr. Barclay all that can be said is that the friendly service he rendered to Mr. Anderson shews that he remained true to the Church. But, while the two late Incumbents of the City seem to have lived so quietly, a couple of their country brethren made more stir. "Mr. John Blair," say the Presbytery, " late Incumbent of Kilspindy, and Patrick Auchterlonie, late Incumbent of Rogorton, both lawfully deposed from the Ministry by the Synod of Perth . . . yet continue in other places and baptise children within the Town of Perth and the great Church thereof, to the great contempt of the Government and laws now established, and of the Ministers now settled in that place " (*December 25th, 1691*).

These are all the definite acts of Episcopalian Clergy, which have come down to us from the period 1691-97.

*This Rev. David Anderson of Perth is an ancestor of J. R. Anderson, Esq., Convener of the Church's Foreign Mission Board (1894).

But that they are only examples of a greater number, which are unrecorded, is to be presumed from the following hostile action of the Presbytery. On *December 25th, 1691*, they pass the following resolution against the Revs. J. Blair and P. Auchterlonie :—"Their contempt and disorder being so notour not only to all the members of the Presbytery, but to all the town of Perth and country about, the Presbytery appoint them to be cited to the next Provincial Assembly, to be holden *January 15th, 1692.*" It does not appear from the *Presbytery Record* what the result of this move was, but those in authority evidently felt that they were not yet armed with sufficiently drastic powers to suppress the disestablished Clergy, for in 1695 an Act was passed through the Scottish Parliament "prohibiting and discharging every outed Minister, under pain of imprisonment, ay, and to find caution to go out of the Kingdom, and never to return thereto, from baptizing and solemnizing marriages betwixt any parties in all time coming." The passing of such an Act implies that the ejected Clergy were pretty active, and we know that they were at least as zealous in Perth as elsewhere.

(2) ATTEMPT TO FOUND A MEETING-HOUSE AT RHYND, 1696-1700 :—

After this imperfect glimpse of the beginnings of a Meeting-House in Perth, following immediately on the Disestablishment, we have an equally imperfect glance at a less successful attempt to found one at Rhynd. The ejected Incumbent, the Rev. William Poplay, "continued after 1696 to preach in fields and private houses until 1700, when, by a special Act of the Privy Council, he was compelled to leave the district."

(3) NEW DEVELOPMENTS AT THE PERTH MEETING-HOUSE, 1698-1700:—

After the Rev. D. Anderson's death at the Gowrie House in 1697, there were new developments in the Perth Congregation; and this strengthens our conclusion that, though little is recorded of Mr. Anderson, he must have had a say in the management of local Church affairs, and that his influence was used on behalf of a quiet and unobtrusive policy. Messrs. Barclay, Blair, and Auchterlonie also disappear from view—the last probably to his factorship at Brechin. But their places are taken by two very vigorous clerics, *i.e.*, Mr. Thomas Murray, late Parish Minister of Kinclaven, and Mr. George M'Gruther, late Incumbent of Collace.

In order to preserve the aroma of the time, what followed will be related chiefly in the words of the Presbytery :—

This body, having (*December 13th, 1698*) been appealed to by the Kirk Session "anent suppressing the disorderly preachings and meetings in this town, appoint the Moderator (*December 14th*) *first* to apply to the Magistrates, in the Presbytery's name, and crave remedy thereof according to Law, and in the meantime appoint Mr. Thos. Murray and Mr. Geo. M'Gruther . . . to be cited to the next Presbytery day for their intrusion." When the brethren reassemble on *January 11th, 1699*, the two recalcitrant Incumbents fail to appear before them. They are summoned *pro secundo*, and a deputation appointed to wait on them and demand the surrender of the Session-books in their possession. Moreover, it appears that the Presbytery have been attempting, but unsuccessfully, to call in the aid of a powerful ally against the Episcopalians :—

"The Moderator and Mr. Nairn reported that they went to the Provost of this Burgh, as appointed, and represented the irregularity of the Meeting-House, and the dangerous consequence in such a place as this town. The Provost answered he supposed the Presbytery had power within themselves to suppress it, and, they once doing their pairt, he would assist, as is incumbent on him as a Magistrate."

At the two subsequent Meetings of the Presbytery, our friends still fail to put in an appearance. Provost Davidson is "loth to meddle with them," and so the Presbytery begin their trial in the absence of the accused. Although the Provost shelters the two Clergy, he yet commands the witnesses against them to be present. They, having had their duties explained to them, are ordered to appear before a Committee at 7 a.m. next morning. When that early hour arrives, only a few of them keep the engagement. Their evidence is interesting:—"After prayer, . . . all present being purged of prejudice, etc., *Walter Moncrieff* deponed as to the haill interrogaters that he hath heard Mr. Thomas Murray preach within his own dwelling-house in this town of Perth within this half-year byegone: likewise Mr. George M'Gruther preach once or twice within the said Mr. Murray's house, and within the said time, but did not hear Mr. Patrick Auchterlonie, and depones *negative* as to marriage and baptism, and this to be veritie as he shall answer to God." *James Rioch* depones that "he has heard Mr. Thos. Murray preach in his own house often: Mr. George M'Gruther only once, and it was at Mr. Murray's also. And both of them preached on the Sabbath day and at the ordinar preaching time," etc. *Joseph Taylor* depones the same, adding "and resolve to hear him (*i.e.*, Mr. Murray) again." On *March 22nd*, some more of the witnesses are brought forward and give similar evidence, and one "Patrick Coupar, Flesher," adds the interesting circumstances that "*since Martinmas last there was great multitudes of people convened to hear Mr. Murray*," and that "an offering was collected at the door." On *April 10th*, a few more reluctant witnesses are examined and give similar evidence, both as to the fact of the services and the numbers attending them. *Henry Hardie* confesses "he *could* tell several times against them, but *would not* tell or depone anything."

The Presbytery now have the case in formal shape, but how are they to bring matters practically to a head? The supineness of the local Magistracy must be superseded or reinforced by a little energy from head-quarters. And so, on *July 5th*, "the brethren appoint Mr. Andrew Harlaw to go to Edinburgh and represent the case of the Meeting-House at Perth . . . to the Commission or to the King's Advocate," and the Moderator is to write to Mr. G. Meldrum to assist him. On *July 19th, 1699*, the deputation reports "that he went to Edinburgh, as appointed, and brought ane letter from the King's Advocate directed to the Magistrates of Perth, advizing them to discharge the Meeting-House in this town." But even this does not bring matters to a head; for, next year (1700), we still find the Presbytery expostulating with Mr. M'Gruther for performing "irregular baptisms," which shows that he had not been suppressed. And here, for a time, the case seems to have remained stationary.

(4) ATTEMPT TO PRESERVE AN EPISCOPAL CONGREGATION AT S. MADOES, 1699-1705.

It appears that Mr. Poplay, while trying to keep together a remnant of Church-people in the Parish of

S. Madoes—Perth Meeting-House. 49

Rhynd, as related above,* also crossed over into S. Madoes, until he was expelled in 1700.

But Episcopacy by no means disappeared from the Parish along with him. For, in *1705* (*March 15th*), Mr. George Blair arrives from Edinburgh, and reports to the Presbytery "that Mr. Walker has got advice to rease Council letters against Mr. Hall, who was 'intruding' at S. Madoes." On *June 13th*, "the Presbytery appoints the Clerk to write to Mr. Hall that they have gotten the Council's sentence against him, and, if he will live peaceably, without making encroachments upon the Parioch where he lives, they will proceed no further against him; but, if he transgresses, they will proceed as far as the Law will allow." On *June 27th*, the same message is repeated, but evidently without effect, for on the 11th of the following month letters of denunciation are produced against Mr. Hall.

(5) ATTACK OF PRESBYTERY ON REV. H. MURRAY OF
PERTH MEETING-HOUSE, 1703-6 :—

But we must once more return to Perth. The Rev. Messrs. T. Murray and M'Gruther no longer appear in the matter. Whether it was that the Presbytery had succeeded in suppressing them, or whether they departed on account of a new arrangement, which was now entered upon by the Perth Church-people, is uncertain. But, at any rate, a very important step was now taken by those in authority at the Meeting-House. On her accession to the Throne, as we have seen, Queen Anne issued a letter of toleration, in which the following sentence occurred :—
"It is our Royal pleasure that they (*i.e.*, the Scottish Episcopalians) should be directed to live suitably, etc., and that in so doing they be protected in the peaceable

* Page 45.

exercise of their religion, and we recommend to the Clergy of the Established discipline their living in brotherly love and communion with such dissenters." Availing themselves, as it would appear, of the new Queen's friendly disposition, the Churchmen in Perth decided that the time was come when they must organize their congregation on a more regular basis, suitable to their disestablished position. Accordingly, a contemporary* informs us that "the Rev. Henry Murray, who had been licensed by the Presbytery of Auchterarder in 1685, appointed Chaplain to the Marquis of Athole and Minister of Dunkeld in 1688, and deprived 1701, was in 1703 chosen to be Minister of the Episcopal Meeting-House in Perth."

This was too much for the Presbytery. At first, indeed, their hands seem to have been too full of other similar matters to allow them to do anything† effectual but on *July 6th, 1704,* "the keeper of the Baptisms obtains powers from the Presbytery to exact baptismal fees from those baptised in the Meeting-House." This was all for the present, but on *March 13th, 1705,* the Kirk Session began to move again. "George Threipland, George Wilson, and John Gourlay . . severally compeared before them . . and confessed that they were married to their wives by Henry Murray." This roused the activities of the Presbytery once more. Their first move was (*April 24-25, 1706*) that their "Moderator and Mr. Jamieson repaired to the personal presence of Mr. John Ramsay, Sheriff-Depute, and in the Presbytery's name by way of instrument, required him to put the law in execution conform to the late proclamation of Her Majesty's Privy Council, of date *March 21st, 1706,* anent intruders upon Churches and

---

* Mr. Smith of Perth. MS. in Episcopal Chest.
† See pp. 31-2.

Parishes." But the Sheriff-Depute succeeded in evading their demand, and in bringing them into collision with his Principal, the Duke of Athole. His Grace "is much incensed that the Presbytery should have instrumented his Depute to put the late Act of Council in operation against the Intruders in their bounds, without acquainting his Grace first and desiring that the Presbytery should send some of their number to commune with his Grace before they proceeded furder against his Depute. The Presbytery having heard the representation, appointed brethren to go to Dunkeld and wait upon his Grace, and represent to his Grace that before the Presbytery did instrument his Deputy, they sent two of their number to commune with his Grace, but that his Grace had gone to Hamilton before they could reach him. And also to complain to his Grace that his Depute has not obeyed the Council's will, and . . . withall they appoint them to tell his Grace that they cannot delay that affair any longer, but if nothing be done effectually betwixt and next Presbytery day they will be necessitate to proceed and also to complain to his Grace that his Depute does much countenance the Meeting-Houses." Nothing, evidently, was done, and so an application to the authorities in the Scottish Capital was resolved upon. Accordingly, on *April 25th* "a letter to the Queen's Advocate anent the affair of the Perth Meeting-House" was sent to Edinburgh. Then Mr. Darling is appointed to accompany the Perth Magistrates thither. But on *May 29th* he reports that "according to the appointment he was in readiness to go with them, but when he came to wait upon them, could find none of them to go with him." The Presbytery, however, is not a body to be turned back by a few difficulties, and (*May 29th*) "it being represented that some of the Magistrates in Perth are just now in Edinburgh, the Presbytery appoint their Rev. Brethren, Mr. Jamieson and Mr. Stodd, to go to Edinburgh and use their endeavours to get Perth rid of the Meeting-House . . ."

They came very near, indeed, to doing so. The secular Government was now intent on bringing about the Union of Scotland and England. Doubtless the Queen herself would have liked it to be in Church as well as in State. But her advisers judged that to bring in a purpose of ecclesiastical amalgamation would have proved disastrous to the scheme in any form, owing to the temper of the dominant faction in Scotland. They not only, therefore, dropped all idea of the union of the two Churches, but in their zeal for that of the two States, became actively hostile to all idea of encouragement of Scottish Episcopalians. Indeed, they resolved that, in order to win the Presbyterians to the project of civil union between the countries, they must humour them in their hostility to the disestablished Church. Accordingly a Royal Proclamation was issued against the Episcopal Clergy, and the Duke of Queensberry wrote to the Privy Council, in harmony with the address of the Commission *"to let loose the laws against the dissenting Clergy."* It was accordingly proclaimed to be *high treason* to speak or to write against Presbyterianism!

"In pursuance of the above-mentioned Act of Privy Council, the Ministers of the Meeting-House of *Perth* and ·Elgin* were both put up in jail by the Magistrates of these respective Burghs, though they daily prayed for the Queen, and were ready to qualify themselves to the Government." This crisis was reached in the year 1706 or 1707.

* Also five of the Edinburgh Clergy (*Stephen IV.*, p. 32, and *Case of the Episcopal Church of Scotland*, 1707, p. 137).

CHAPTER VI.

HOW A NEW BISHOP WAS APPOINTED, AND THE PRAYER-BOOK INTRODUCED IN PERTH.

WE shall avail ourselves of this interval of ominous stillness to deal with two matters, one of which occurred slightly earlier and the other slightly later than the point reached at the end of the last chapter.

(1.)—On *June 13th, 1704,* the Prelate in whose Diocese Perth lay, *i.e.,* Ross, Archbishop of S. Andrews, died in Edinburgh. The deeply-important question therefore comes up :—" How was our first Post-Revolution Diocesan appointed?" The following remarks will answer this question. Just as the Stuart Dynasty had, in 1660, risen superior to the *Rebellion* and been restored, so now the followers of the same line of Princes very naturally and reasonably hoped that it would ultimately regain its own from the *Revolution.* Now, of course, the Scottish Bishops were of those who entertained this anticipation. Inasmuch, therefore, as they held very strongly that it was the mutual duty of the Church and State to co-operate with one another, they came to the decision : *first,* that in order to preserve the *esse* of the Church they would confer the Episcopal character on new colleagues, in order that the Apostolical Succession might be continued, *but* that they would best be consulting the *bene esse* of the Church if they delayed assigning particular Dioceses to the new Prelates, until such time as they could carry the State along with them in their arrangements. Pending, therefore, the collapse of the Revolution, and the restoration of the old *régime*, the new Bishops (although Bishops) should not share in the active government of the Church, and, whenever a Diocese became vacant, it would fall to be administered by the senior surviving Diocesan Bishop. Strange as this expedient undoubtedly was on so large a scale as was then accorded to it, yet it is to be remembered *first* that the Bishops confidently hoped that it would only have to be resorted to on a small scale and for a brief time; and *secondly*, that the Church still acts upon it on occasions. For, when a Diocese is vacant, it falls to be administered by the Primus; and, between the time of the Consecration and the Collation of a new Bishop, we have the same state of affairs on a small scale as the Post-Revolution Prelates resorted to on a larger, *i.e.*, a Diocesan Bishop, the Primus, actively administering a portion of the Church, while a Non-Diocesan Bishop stands beside him. It is a necessary, though essentially temporary, state of affairs.

Archbishop Ross then, being dead, our Diocese naturally came under the jurisdiction of the Senior Bishop, until the Church, having consulted the (soon to be restored) secular Power, saw its way to confer the permanent jurisdiction on a new Prelate. And the Senior Bishop, to whom our Diocese now fell, and fell for a much longer period than was probably contemplated at the time, was Dr. Alexander Rose, Bishop of Edinburgh, who now claimed precedence as Vicar-General of S. Andrews. Of this Prelate it is recorded that he was the nephew of the deceased Archbishop. He took his M.A. degree at King's College, Aberdeen, and studied Theology under Bishop Burnet at Glasgow.

His first appointment had been as Parish Minister of Perth. In 1684 he had been nominated by the Crown to the Principalship of S. Mary's College, S. Andrews. The Royal Warrant for his Consecration to the See of Moray was dated *March 8th, 1687*, from which he was translated to Edinburgh before he had visited his northern Diocese.

Through the absence of documents on the disestablished side, and owing to the fact that it was the policy of the Bishops at this epoch to keep as quiet as possible, we cannot say what part either Archbishop Ross or Bishop Rose played in our local history. What is certain is that they were our Bishops, and we may presume that they took what measures seemed most advisable to them for the welfare of the Perth Congregation. Certainly Bishop Rose proved himself a very wise and able administrator as head of the whole Scottish Church.

(2.)—The other matter alluded to at the opening of this Chapter was a most important modification in the conduct of public worship, which was introduced into our neighbourhood at this time.

It is, of course, an historical commonplace that from the time of the Restoration of the Episcopate in 1661 to the date at which our narrative has arrived, neither the *Book of Common Prayer* nor anything similar had been used in the religious assemblies of the Scottish Church. There were certain points, indeed, and these not unimportant, in which the Episcopal differed from the Presbyterian forms. There was the systematic reading of Holy Scripture, the repetition of the Creed, the Lord's Prayer, and the *Gloria Patri*, and the keeping of some of the Festivals to distinguish the Episcopal from the Presbyterian worship. But apart from these points, some of which were not universal, the general structure of the one worship was much the same as that of the other, *i.e.*, *ex tempore* forms were used. So moderate were the Restoration Bishops, ecclesiastically speaking! They probably reflected that it was the introduction of the Prayer Book in 1637 which led to the total overthrow of the Church in 1638, and concluded that their proper policy was to remain content with the restoration of the Apostolic authority to the Ministry, without attempting a premature introduction of liturgical forms.

But now that the Bishops were loosed from their bond with the Nation, they felt themselves no longer tied by that excessive moderation which had characterised them while they had been "established." Everywhere throughout the Kingdom by a spontaneous impulse the *Book of Common Prayer* began to be used. And, if it be asked whether it was the *Scottish Book* of 1637, or the *English Book* that was now being adopted, the answer must be as follows. The *Scottish Book* was undoubtedly reprinted at Edinburgh in 1712: (the Communion had already appeared in 1707) and doubtless used to a limited extent. But there was a grave difficulty in the way of re-publishing the *Book* of 1637 on a large scale, and that was that it would have been necessary either to print the name of King James VIII., or else that of Queen Anne in it, and to do either would have led to disastrous results. To do the former would have been to court the wrath of the "powers that be," and to do the latter would have been to raise dissension in the Church. This was enough to make the re-issue of the old *Scottish Book* hang fire. But the same difficulty did not lie against the *English Book*. Friends sent down 19,000 copies of it from the

Prayer Book first used in Perth.

south. No doubt the Revolution Monarch's name appeared in them, but then it was the *Book* of the English, and not formally of the Scottish, branch of the Church. To borrow it and adapt it to their own use did not commit Scottish Churchmen to either of the two Sovereigns. Moreover, there was to some minds a positive reason in favour of the *English Book*. The Scottish Church was in an afflicted condition: a Treaty of Union was being signed between England and Scotland, and was it not prudent to court as close an alliance as possible with the great Church of the great Nation to which they were now being united? And so, as has been said, the English *Book of Common Prayer* was being introduced by common consent on all sides.

Were Perth Churchmen to be backward in so good a cause? Certainly not. The actual date on which the Liturgy was first used in the neighbourhood is not recorded. But, though we cannot actually lay our finger on the happy day itself, yet there appears to be little doubt that it occurred some time in the year 1709. At all events the following extract from the *Presbytery Records* is the first notice of the use of the Liturgy in post-Reformation times in these parts.

November 3rd, 1709.—" The Presbytery are informed that some of the Episcopal Incumbents living within their bounds did in their gowns perform a number of superstitious ceremonies altogether foreign to this Church and Kingdom, at the interring of the corps of Mr. Patrick Strachan (sometime Incumbent of the Parish of Mains) in the Burial Yard of Perth, before a confluence of people."

There were also two other places where the *Prayer Book* was introduced, *i.e.*, the Parishes of Methven and

Scone. As for the former, we have the following evidence :—

November 3rd, 1709.—" The Laird of Balgowan said that he had only the worship of God in his family according to the English form, and herein he apprehended that he did nothing contrary to the law."

And, as for Scone, there are reported to be "Innovations" there. This came to be the usual way of describing the introduction of the Prayer Book. They, who considered that a Revolution in Church and State was "glorious," were scandalized at the subversive rashness of those who, in their own religious assemblies, changed *ex tempore* for written forms of worship, and "Innovator" became a term of reproach on these men's lips!

CHAPTER VII.

HOW THE REVS. MESSRS. SMITH, RHYND, AND WALKER WERE SENTENCED BY THE PRESBYTERY, 1709-10.

EPISCOPACY without the Prayer Book had been bad enough, but Episcopacy with the Prayer Book was far worse. Its adversaries were more than ever exasperated. Where was the completeness of the victory over Charles I. and Archbishop Laud, if the seed which they had sowed was to be allowed to strike even a few permanent roots in Scottish soil? And so we have the Rev. Alexander Dinning, Minister of Abernethy, thundering, on behalf of his friends, against the "Innovation." At the conclusion of a sermon, he exclaimed, "by way of syllogism," that "those who read their prayers worship the Devil." "For," he continues, "if the Scripture had not commanded us to sing Psalms and we did sing Psalms, then were we worshipping the Devil. And, if the Scriptures had not commanded us to pray and we notwithstanding did pray, then were we praying to the Devil. But I defy all the world to shew me where the Scripture commands us to read Prayers; therefore, they who read Prayers worship the Devil!"* In vain did that staunch Churchman, Mr. James Smyth, Apothecary in Perth, on hearing these sentiments, cry out :—"Mr. Alexander Dinning makes all the venerable members of the Church of England, the Queen's Majesty not excepted, worshippers of the Devil!" The current of events was

* MS. in Episcopal Chest.

too strong for him, and the Presbytery determined to make once for all a supreme effort to suppress both Episcopacy and Prayer Book within their bounds.

The following is the story of this attempt as drawn from their own Records :—

It was determined to prosecute certain Churchmen for their conduct in three different places. (1) The Revs. William Smith and Thomas Rhynd had been keeping the Episcopalians together in the Parish of Methven and introducing the Prayer Book there. (2) The same two Priests had publicly interred the remains of the late Rev. Patrick Strachan in Perth Burial Ground, and used the English Service at the solemnity. And (3) the Rev. Patrick Walker had been officiating in the Parish of Scone.

We shall briefly deal with the last case first. On *December 2nd, 1709*, the *Rev. Patrick Walker*, Chaplain to the Viscount of Stormont, was formally reported to the Presbytery as practising "Innovations" in the Parish of Scone. On *February 14th, 1710*, his libel was prepared. Omitting much that is formal, we extract the two following points from it:—(1) He has "intruded in a most disorderly and irregular manner into the Paroch of Scone, where there is a fixed Gospel Ministry," and "has introduced a sett form," etc. (2) And "particularly you baptized a child to John Stewart, living in the Paroch of Scone since Whitsunday, 1709," and three other children likewise. He is to be summoned *pro tertio* to the next Presbytery. At this meeting *(March 8th, 1710)* he does not appear, and is declared contumacious. On *April 5th* some witnesses give evidence as to Mr. Walker preaching, baptizing, and making use of the English Book. Others were called to prove drunkenness against him. But concerning

Three Divines Prosecuted. 61

this last charge it is to be remarked that the Committee appointed to consider the matter reported that on this head there was "nothing proven." On *September 13th* sentence was passed for the ecclesiastical "offences"; but with regard to the drunkenness, while it was mentioned in the Preamble, it is not repeated, as the ecclesiastical matters are later on, as one of the grounds of the sentence.

The other two cases, *i.e.*, those of the *Revs. Messrs. Smith and Rhynd* (who had "intruded" together both in Perth and in the Parish of Methven), we shall describe at some length and together. They afford us a very vivid glimpse into the doings of the time.

On *November 3rd, 1709*, the Presbytery resolve to process the "intruding" Clergy, and order the Clerk to find out who they are and to summon them. At the next meeting this official reports that the "Innovators" are "Mr. William Smith, sometime Incumbent of Moneydie; the other Mr. Thomas Rhynd, Chaplain to the Laird of Balgowan, . . and he had given order and warrand to the officer to summond them." Nevertheless "they compeared not." Hereupon they are summoned *pro secundo* and again *pro tertio*, but "compear not," both on *January 10th*, and on *February 14th, 1710*. However, on the last of these dates the Presbytery go on with the case. Meeting at 7 a.m., they called for the libels which the Committee had prepared :—

LIBELL BY THE PRESBYTERY OF PERTH AGAINST MR. WILLIAM SMITH, INCUMBENT UNDER THE LATE PRELACY IN THE PAROCH OF MONEDIE, AND FOR THE PRESENT RESIDING WITHIN THE PAROCH OF METHVEN.

Primo. That whereas the purity of religion and particularly of Divine Worship and uniformity therein is a signal blessing to the Church of God, and that it hath been the great happiness of this Church ever since our reformation from Popery to have enjoyed and to have maintained the same in great measure, yet it is a verity that you, the said Mr. William Smith, have not only in a most irregular and disorderly manner intruded upon the Paroch of Methven, where there is a settled Gospel Ministry, but also by an avowed discharging of the several parts of the ministerial function, you have intruded a set form of worship, and that in direct opposition and contrary to the known principles of this Church, contained in the Confession of Faith (which is that God should not be worshipped according to the imaginations and devices of men, or any other way not prescribed by Holy Scripture) contrary to the constant practice of this Church, yea and which was not so much as attempted under the late Prelacie, and likewise in contempt of the standing acts of the judicatories of this national Church peremptorily forbidding these and the like innovations, particularly the *15th Act* of the General Assembly, held at Edinburgh, *April 21st, 1707*, entitled "*An Act against innovations in the worship of God*," which further declares such attempts to have been and still to be of fatal and dangerous consequence to the Church, and visibly tending to corrupt the puritie of religion, mar the uniformity of worship, and to foment schism and division to the disturbance of the peace, both of Church and State, and that, notwithstanding the doctrine, worship, discipline, and government of this Church, is ratified by good and laudable laws made since the late happy Revolution establishing and securing the same (particularly *5th Act of Parliament, 1690, and 23rd, 1693,*) which Acts are most expressly ratified and confirmed by the *6th Act* of Parliament, 1707. As also by the Act ratifying and approving the union of the two kingdoms of England and Scotland it is expressly provided that the form, puritie, and uniformity of worship, as now established in this Church, is, in the terms of the foresaid Acts, to continue to the people of this Church without any alteration in all succeeding generations, and this to be held as a fundamental and essential condition of the said Union without any alteration or derogation thereto in any sort for ever.

Secundo. Upon the (blank in MS.) day of November last you did in a most disorderly way in and about the Burial-place of Perth assist at the Funerals of Mr. Patrick Strachan, late incumbent in the Parish of Mains, in performing such rites and ceremonies as are condemned by the Constitutions of this Church in the First Book of Policie and her constant practice consonant thereto, being altogether foreign and strange to the people of this Church and Kingdom since the Reformation from Popery, which is likewise of most dangerous consequences as manifestly tending to grieve the godly, lay a stumbling-bloke before the weak, and to harden Papists in their superstitions, and fostering the same among Protestants, such superstitious practices at Burials being also condemned in the Directory for Public Worship.

Tertio. That you in the like disorderly course have taken upon you to administer the Sacrament of Baptism, cross to the constitution and practice of this Church, and that notwithstanding the known law of the land against irregular Baptisms, and particularly you baptized several children, within these five or six years immediately bye-past, to John Stewart, sometime living in the Milne of Pitcairn, in the Parish of Rogorton, where there was a settled Minister at the time. Witnesses, etc.

Such was the libel against Mr. Smith. That against Mr. Rhynd ran in very similar terms, and need not be given *in extenso;* but the following first head of it is both peculiar to himself, and interesting as showing that the Episcopal Church was actually making converts to herself from the educated classes at this time:—

"Notwithstanding, he, the said Mr. Thomas Rhynd, was trained up and educat at the charge of the present Established Church, having been Bursar to the Synod of Merse, and also was further encouraged by the Commission of the General Assembly to enter upon tryals in order to the Ministry to the service of the Church, he then professing a great zeal for Presbyterian Government, yet he has not only renounced his former principles, but in a most daring and presumptuous manner in a well-constituted Church has invaded the Office of the Holy Ministry [*i.e.*, been Episcopally ordained] without a lawful and orderly call thereto."

March 8th, 1710.—Report having been made of serving summonses, etc., on the "Innovators," the

Presbytery then proceeded to call them to answer to their libels. "Which having been done, none compeared; but one, Mr. James Smith, Apothecary in Perth, compeared, and said he had a commission from Mr. Smith and Mr. Rhynd." The witnesses also were called, and they compeared in considerable numbers. The Meeting having been adjourned to 3 p.m., "Mr. James Smith produced two papers, which he called commissions, to answer for Mr. W. Smith and Mr. T. Rhynd, which were both read. The tenor whereof follows:—"I, Mr. William Smith, Minister of the Gospel, being cited to appear this day before the Presbytery of Perth for intrusion, baptizing, etc., as the libell bears, and, not inclining to attend myself, I do hereby grant full power and commission to Mr. James Smith, Apothecary, etc., and decline them as no ways judges competent in the matters libelled against me, conform to and for the reasons mentioned in a Declinator and Protestation subscribed by me of this date, which he is to present and produce to them, and thereupon take instruments and to do every other thing, as if I were present.—*March 8th, 1710.*"

"Then the said Mr. James Smith produced two other papers, which he called Protestations and Declinators, and offered them to the Presbytery, and urged to have them read." Here follows the Declinator as taken from a copy in the Episcopal Chest. We give it *in extenso* as being the fullest explanation of the views on the Episcopal side which has survived :—

DECLINATOR AND PROTESTATION OFFERED BY MR. WM. SMITH, MINISTER OF THE GOSPEL, TO THE PRESBYTERY OF PERTH.

It may be thought strange that one in my circumstances, who have lived so many years among you, without giving disturbance to any person, should be processed before you for intrusion,

Mr. Smith's Declinator. 65

baptizeing of children, and innovation in worship, as your libell against me bears, since it is notably known to you all that I am a Minister of the Gospell of the Episcopall Communion, and, as I have hitherto lived, so I hope to continue in the unity of the Catholick Church and its Government descended with Christianitie itself from the days of the Apostles. And therefore I cannot, without schismatically separating from that great and venerable body, own any spiritual jurisdiction in you ; for, *first*, albeit the present laws have empowered you to prosecute such Episcopall Ministers as continue in their Churches, or desire to be assumed by you into the Government of the Kirk, and have subjected such to your discipline and cognisance, in so far as they are really scandalous, erroneous, negligent, and inefficient, yet I am in neither of these cases and the laws have not subjected such as I am to your discipline, who, without possessing any Church, Manse, or Benefice, or keeping any Public Meeting-House, do only worship God in my own family. (2) As to the crimes of intrusion and baptizeing, these are purely civill and only cognizable by the Judge-Ordinary, such as the Privy Councill, and therefore, as I am noways subject to your jurisdiction on this account, so you are not judges competent therein. (3) As to the English Liturgie, which you call innovation, contrary to the puritie of the Gospel, and worshipping God according to the devices and imaginations of men, I think it is agreeable to the Word of God and the practice of the Primitive Church, and is no innovation, being universally practised at the beginning of the Reformation, as Buchanan in the nineteenth book of his History affirms, saying— " *Scoti religionis cultui et ritibus Anglis communibus subscripserunt,*" and has been likewise continowed in many places and families both before and since the Revolution, neither is there any law against useing it by any of a different communion from the Presbyterian, but every person may worship God with or without book, by conceived or extemporary prayers, as they please. However, you having declared yourselves against the English Service are parties, and therefore cannot be judges in this matter, nor I any wayes obliged to account to you for the same. And therefore I do decline your authority and jurisdiction in the premises for the reasons foresaid, and protest that you proceed no further therein, otherwise to be lyable for cost, scaith, and dammage, and thereupon I take instruments.

Such was the document. But, though " Mr. James

Smith earnestly insisted to have the papers, which he called Declinators, read, the Presbytery utterly refused." Nay, they "simpliciter reject the pretended proxies," and declare Messrs. Smith and Rhynd contumacious.

Witnesses were now examined. *Mr. Rhynd's libel* first came up: several gave evidence of his having performed clerical duties within the Parish of Methven. One of them heard him preach: also read prayers out of a book, and saw him make use of the *Book of Common Prayer*: "likewise the deponent said that some of his hearers do speak in time of Divine Service." Another "heard him preach very good orthodox doctrine, etc.:" He said, "In time of preaching the hearers do not speak, but in time of prayer they do." Again he has "not only vilified that form of sound words contained in the Confession of Faith of this Church, . . but in conference with people has most profanely called the said Confession a bundle of nonsense, and the compilers thereof a pack of rogues." As to *Mr. Smith's libel* several witnesses testified to seeing him perform ministerial functions; and as to the *two libels combined:—Nathaniel Fife* "saw Messrs. Smith and Rhynd" at the Burial of Mr. Strachan in Perth. Mr. Rhynd did officiate as Priest or Curat. Mr. Smith did no more than he did, only he had the distinction of a gown. He further deponed that he heard and saw them do according to the Rubrick of the Book, which he presented to the Presbytery, which was the *Book of Common Prayer*, at the interment of the corps of Mr. Patrick Strachan." *John Alexander* "saw an old man and a young man there in canonical* gowns, but knew

*Would he have described the gowns, which the Presbyterian Ministers wore, as "canonical"? and have we, therefore, a hint here that the Episcopal and Presbyterian Clergy used different vestments at this epoch?

not who they were." He deponed that Mr. Patrick Strachan was buried after the English form. *Charles Wilson* "saw them in black gowns, and the *Book of Common Prayer* in their hands, from which they read from the entry of the Burial Yard of Perth to the grave." Several more witnesses gave similar evidence, and then the Presbytery resolved to adjourn. More witnesses were examined on *March 22nd.*

The Committee appointed by the Presbytery to revise and report upon the whole case found it proved that both the Innovators were guilty in all points according to the evidence. On *April 6th* the Presbytery put the affair in shape for bringing before the Synod, and on *April 19th* the latter body "ordered the Presbytery of Perth to lay the whole matter before the General Assembly." Accordingly they enjoin their commissioners to the Assembly "to be very careful and diligent about that matter." On *May 31st* the Meetings of Assembly being over, the Commissioners reported to the Presbytery that "they had laid that matter before the Committee of the General Assembly for Overtures, and they, having taken it into their consideration, gave it as their advice that this Presbytery should proceed to declare them Intruders and Innovators in the Worship of God, and require the Magistrat to make their sentence effectual, and, if he shall refuse to do it, that they instrument him, and send over their instrument extended to the Church Agent, that criminal letters may be raised against the said Innovators." The Presbytery, having heard the report of their brethren, . . "resolved to bring that affair to a period by proceeding to a sentence against the Innovators the next Presbytery."

This they did on *September 13th, 1710.* The

"*Sentence of the Presbytery of Perth against Mr. Wm. Smith, late Incumbent of Moneydie,*" is far too long a a document to be given here in full. The first paragraph recites the warnings given by the General Assembly and the Acts of Parliament passed against Intruders and Innovators. The second gives a detailed narrative of the case against Mr. Smith. The remainder of the sentence runs as follows :—

"And the Presbytery of Perth, having given him time to reflect upon his former way, and to reflect upon the dangerous and dismal course he is engaged in ; as also they being called by the above named Act to give an account of their diligence to support ecclesiastical judicatories, withal being desirous to consult with the same in whose bounds the like innovations are found, that there may be the greater harmony in these measures and methods that may be judged most expedient for suppressing and preventing the growth of such scandalous and innovating courses, which the abettors thereof are bestirring themselves with so much vigour on all hands to advance, have for some time sisted their procedure, *but now*, after all, finding that any further delay is not likely to be profitable, but rather prejudicial to such, whom, by their restless endeavours, they are labouring to seduce, and that by our silence we may not be found guilty in not doing at present what we judge incumbent to us, in giving our joint testimony against the shameful defection, which he hath made from the puritie and simplicitie of Gospel ordinances, and the divisive courses that he is still cleaving to, *therefore, we*, being now met in the name and by the Authority of our Lord Jesus Christ, sole Head and King of the Church, do, by virtue of that said power committed to us, *discharge*

the said Mr. William Smith from intruding any longer
upon the Paroch of Methven, or any other Paroch
within the bounds of this Presbytery; as also from
introducing ceremonies and innovations not warranted
by the Word of God, and contrary to the purity of
doctrine confessed, and uniformity of worship at present
practised in this Church, least he meet with that
challenge, 'Who hath required these things at your
hands? In vain do ye worship Me, teaching for
doctrine the commandments of men.' And, providing
he would suffer the word of exhortation, then, if either
he tender the Glory of God, the success of the preached
Gospel and the quiet of this Church and Kingdom; or
if he have any regard to his own peace, either now or
at a dying hour, we would, in the fear of the Lord,
obtest him seriously to consider what such innovating
and divisive courses, if not timeously prevented, will
terminate in to him and those seduced by him. But,
if to his former contumacy he shall superadd this, to
despise our faithful warning and authoritative prohibi-
tion, *then*, as he may tremble to be found among those
by whom offences come, and cause divisions contrary
to the doctrine we have received, and of the dreadful
doom of evil men and seducers, their waxing worse
and worse, deceiving and being deceived, so we must
proceed according to our duty and his merit."

The sentence against Mr. Rhynd was of a similar length
and character.

These sentences were read from all the pulpits on the
24th of the month, and accompanied by exhortations
to the people "anent the danger of being seduced,
and of . . . forsaking the Assemblie of the Saints
. . . that we be not again entangled in the yoke
of bondage."

But they had not the desired effect, for the entry in the *Presbytery Record* of *October 25th, 1710*, runs as follows:—" With respect to the Innovators that are under process at this time, the Ministers of those Pariochs where they reside told they had made enquiries anent them, and are informed that they continue to contemn the sentences that were intimated against them. Further, the Presbytery having sought advice from the Synod how to proceed with respect to them, they advized that they apply to the Civil Magistrat, and require him by Law to make their Sentences effectual." On *May 12th* an Act of Synod was read before the Presbytery exhorting them to be vigorous in putting down the Innovators.

What became of Messrs. Smith* and Walker after the appeal to the "Civil Magistrat" does not appear; but on *September 26th, 1711*, we discover the result with regard to Mr. Rhynd, for on that day the Presbytery of Dundee apply for a copy of his sentence, as "he has set up the English Service there."

* But see page 87.

CHAPTER VIII.

HOW THE REVS. HENRIE AND THOMAS MURRAY AND WALTER STEWART WERE DEPOSED BY THE PRESBYTERY, 1711-12.

THIS struggle for bare existence, following upon their defeat as Ministers of the Establishment, must have been a trying one for our Priests. But there was a constant succession of them prepared to go on contending for the right without regard to temporal consequences. And so the trials described in the last chapter were followed by others, which must be related in this. It is hoped that a full narration of all that occurred will not be considered unimportant. In the various *Libels*, *Declinators*, and *Sentences*, the principles, on which the two parties acted, are clearly brought out, and Churchmen at least have the satisfaction of seeing that they, who so prominently contended for their cause in Perth, laid due stress on the fundamental principle of the Apostolical Succession. In the last chapter, for instance, we saw Mr. Smith expressing his resolution " to continue in the unity of the Catholic Church and its government, descended with Christianitie itself from the days of the Apostles." And now the Clergy, about to be implicated in the trial, which is the subject of this chapter, assure us that it was not merely for non-essentials, but for the preservation of the unbroken line of historical continuity that they were contending in opposition to the Presbytery :—Their words are : " We cannot separate . . from the Catholic, Christian Church, whose government—namely, the Episcopal—has descended to us from Apostolick days."

Understanding, therefore, that the struggle was maintained in defence of a principle of vital importance, we proceed the more willingly to trace its course, still availing ourselves of the all but exclusive aid of the *Presbytery Record*.

Under the date *September 27th, 1711*, we find the following entry:—" The Presbytery now resolves to do something in the affair of the Innovators. And, having taken the matter into their serious consideration, and after some communing thereon, and finding that there are some more of the Episcopal Clergy besides those whom they formerly prosecuted, who are guilty of intruding into Pariochs within the bounds of this Presbytery, that are planted, publicly practising innovations in the worship of God that have no foundation in Holy Scripture, and are contrary to the present established order of this Church, and are guilty of several other irregular practices, viz. :— Mr. Henrie Murray and Mr. Walter Stewart, both in the Burgh of Perth, and Mr. Thomas Murray, in the Parioch of Kilspindy, the Presbytery hereby appoints the aforesaid persons to be summoned to compear before the next Presbytery . . ."

October 24th, 1711.—The officer reports that he has summoned the Intruders : the Presbytery order him to call them at the most patent door : which having been done, none of them compeared. " Then the Committee was enquired at if they had met and prepared draughts of libels against the said Innovators ? They told that they had met and done something in that matter, but have not got the Libels fully compleated."

November 21st, 1711.—The accused send Mr. James Smith to " decline the Presbytery as no ways judges competent in the matter we are cited on." After a vigorous discussion, the Moderator makes a counter protest to the effect that the Proxy has declined a judicatory of Jesus Christ, authorised by law. The paper of the accused is then read :—

DECLINATURE AND PROTESTATION OF MR. HENRIE MURRAY, MR. WALTER STEWART, AND MR. THOMAS MURRAY, MINISTERS OF THE GOSPEL, TO THE PRESBYTERY OF PERTH, NOVEMBER 21, 1711.

Having expressed surprise that they should be proceeded against after the expression of the Queen's wish for toleration, they go on :—

1. However, we cannot own any spiritual jurisdiction in you, without separating from the Catholick, Christian Church, both ancient and modern, whose government—namely, the Episcopal—has descended to us from Apostolick days. And, as we have hitherto lived, so we hope to continue in the unity of the Church.

2. But that, albeit the present laws, from which you derive all your authority, have subjected such Episcopal Ministers as continue in their Churches, or are really scandalous, erroneous, negligent, or inefficient to your cognizance and censure, yet, since we are in neither of these cases, we cannot submit to your jurisdiction.

3. As to the charge of intrusion, we answer that they are properly intruders in the Scriptural sense of the word, who thrust themselves into the Ministrie without a legal mission or canonical ordination, and by the acts and laws of the Church of England no ordination is valid but which is originally Episcopal. Neither can we be charged with intruding in the legal or parliamentary sense of the word, because intruding is properly *in vacuam possessionem*, as the Act of 1695 expresses it, "intruding into vacant Churches possessing Manses and Benefices," which cannot be charged on us, who only preach in a Meeting-House, and to willing people. However, if this be a crime it is purely civil, and therefore cognizable by the Judge Ordinary, and therefore ye cannot be competent judges in this matter.

4. As to the English Liturgy, which you mean by innovations, we think it is agreeable to the Word of God and the practice of the primitive Church, and likewise of our own Reformers, for Buchanan tells us in the 19th Book of his *History* that the

Scotch, being delivered from the French slavery by assistance of the English, did thereupon subscribe to the same worship in Religion and the ceremonies in common with England. So that the using of the *Book of Common Prayer* and English Liturgy is no innovation in this Church, but rather a retrieving or reviving of that regular worship, which was professed and practised at the Reformation, and we are fully persuaded that it is necessary to the peace of the Church that all Churches or Congregations, at least under one Prince, should use one form of Liturgy or of Divine Worship. The Queen and Parliament have lately declared in Mr. Greenshields' trial* that there is no law in this nation against using the English Liturgy, and "where there is no law there can be no transgression." However, you, having declared yourselves against the English Service, are parties, and therefore cannot be judges in the matter, nor we any ways obliged to account to you for the same.

5. As to what may be meant by disorderly practices, for which you charge us in your summons, we are not conscious to ourselves of any that can subject us to your censure. And, therefore, for these and other reasons to be added, if we see cause, we decline your authority and jurisdiction, and protest that you proceed no further therein, otherwise to be liable for cost and damage, and whereupon we take instruments thereon."

This Declinature being read, as said is, the Proxie was desired to remove until the Presbytery should consider if they should deliver libels to him for his constituents. And he being removed, and the Presbytery taking the matter into their serious consideration, they agreed not to give libels to the Proxie, especially after he had declined them. The Proxie being called in, the premises were intimated to him (whereupon followed protests and counter-protests).

After this the Presbytery adjourned till 3 p.m., when the libels were read. As it will be necessary only to give one of these, we reproduce that of Mr. Murray at full length. It exhibits to us the mind of the Presbytery :—

MR. HENRIE MURRAY'S LIBEL.

"Whereas, by the blessing of God upon the pious endeavours of our worthy and renowned ancestors, it hath been the mercy

---
* This was another case in Edinburgh very similar to their own.

and happiness of this National Church to be at first purely reformed, according to the Word of God, in Doctrine, Worship, Discipline, and Government, as is evident from our *Confession of Faith, Books of Discipline,* and *Acts* of many General Assemblies, Likeas the puritie of Gospel Ordinances, free from the dregs of superstition, idolatry, and will-worship, together with a beautiful uniformity of dispensing the same, hath in a great measure been hitherto preserved, and that by the countenance the Lord hath given to the zealous wrestlings of others since, in contending for the " Faith once delivered to the Saints," in opposition to attempts for corrupting thereof by ceremonies and inventions of men, as clearly appears from many *Acts* both of Assembly and Parliament made for establishing the same to us, especially since the late happy Revolution ; which laudable laws are expressly confirmed by (such and such *Acts,* etc.).

Yet it is a veritie that you, Henrie Murray, notwithstanding all this, and the faithful warnings that the General Assembly and Commission have given to all persons of the dangerous consequences of such innovations, as some by their restless endeavours are labouring to introduce into the Worship of God at present in this Church, together with the fatal tendency thereof both to Church and State, ordaining withal inferior judicatories to take tryal and prosecute such as shall be found guilty, which you could not be ignorant of, yet, for all this, we say, casting off all regard to the peace, order, and edification of this Church, you do in a bold manner fly in the face of all authority, both civil and ecclesiastical, in several lawless and irregular practices. As 1*mo* That within the ancient burgh of Perth, where there have been of a good time and now are two Ministers of the Gospel settled in a legal and orderly way, you presume to exercise the several parts of the Ministerial Office, without any legal call thereto, while in the meantime you have not owned the *Confession of Faith,* established by Law, nor so much as qualified yourself in terms prescribed by Law, in order to share in the benefits of that protection allowed by our gracious Queen to such of your persuasion that are thus qualified.

2*do* That in the Administration of the Holy Sacrament of the Lord's Supper you oblige communicants to kneel in the act of receiving, which hath always been condemned by *Acts* of the General Assembly and the practice of this Church as not agreeable to our Blessed Lord's practice in the Institution of the same ; as a gesture symbolizing with idolators in their idolatrous worship, and a manifest breach of the foresaid puritie and uniformitie of Worship.

3tio You observe the festival days, and not only those pretended to be kept in honour of our Blessed Saviour, but also such as are dedicated to Saints. and Angels, and that cross to *Acts* of Assembly and *Books of Discipline*, which condemn the same as idolatrous and superstitious, and ranks them among the abominations of the Romish Church.

4to You have intruded a *Liturgy* and set form in the public Worship of God,* not only without any warrant from any law of the land establishing it, but also such as was not so much as attempted under the late Prelacie, nor practised by yourself since your intrusion till within these few months, upon what motives or views you yourself know.

5to You follow the order prescribed by the said *Liturgy* in burying of the dead, particularly on *November 6th, 1711*, or one or another of the days of the said month, in and about the burial place of the Burgh of Perth, at the funerals of Bethia Omay,† late spouse to Alexander Conqueror, merchant in the said burgh, which rites and ceremonies are condemned by the constitution of this Church in her first *Book of Policie* and *Directorie for Public Worship* as being of most dangerous consequence, and her constant practice consonant thereto, in the performance whereof you assisted at the foresaid burial, which gave no small offence, these ceremonies being altogether foreign and strange to the people of North Britain ever since their Reformation from Poperie.

6to After the like disorderly manner you have taken upon you to administer the Sacrament of Baptism, cross to the constitution and practice of this Church, notwithstanding the known law of the land against irregular Baptisms. And this you have been frequently guilty of, and among others you baptized the children of John Mordoch, junior, Glover in Perth; James Walker, Maltman there; Laurence Chapman, Messenger there; Daniel Cameron, Teacher of a Private School there; John Crockatt, Maltman there; John Cuthbert, Tailor there; and Alexander

* Whether is it with the Presbytery or the Episcopal Clergy that the present Established *Church Service Society* and authors of the *Euchologion* sympathize?

† Probably, I should think, a relative of the evicted Parish Minister of Methven.

Much, a person to whom the Ministers of the place refused the privilege of Baptism to his child, and all these within these few years bye-past." Witnesses, etc., to prove this, etc.

MR. WALTER STEWART'S LIBEL.

It is the same as Mr. Henry Murray's, *mutatis mutandis*, with the exception of the following:—

6to All this is more highly aggravated, because, though you formerly upon all occasions professed great zeal for the present Church Establishment, yet you have not only apostatized from and renounced your former principles, but in a most daring and presumptuous manner in a well-constituted Church, invaded the office of the holy Ministrie without a lawful and orderly call thereto, at least without any legal document warranting you to enter upon the said sacred function.

Although the Presbytery were in so much doubt as to the validity of Mr. Stewart's claim to exercise the functions of the Ministry, and although he did not enlighten them, it will be convenient to interpolate here the following quotation from the Dunkeld *Diocesan Register*:—"The Rev. Walter Stewart was ordained Deacon by Bishop George Haliburton of Aberdeen at Denhead, *February 16th, 1711.*"

But to return to the trial. Mr. Thomas Murray's *Libel* was in similar terms to the other two, and therefore need not be reproduced in these pages.

After summoning the accused *pro tertio*, the next step was the examination of witnesses on *December 19th, 1711*. Their depositions will not be given in full, because they simply go to prove the statements in the libels, without throwing any new light on the subject. Two little points, however, are interesting. One man, for example, "minds he was in the Meeting-House on All Saints' Day, and particularly he saw Mr. Murray keep Yule Day." It is also interesting to observe what a plentiful supply of local tradespeople there was, qualified by attendance at the Church

Services to serve as witnesses. None of the witnesses against Mr. Thomas Murray compeared.

On *January 9th, 1712*, the Committee appointed to consider the whole process report that "they find Mr. Henrie Murray's and Mr. Walter Stewart's Libels clearly proven, but have not got an Overture prepared." The matter is accordingly delayed till 11 a.m. next day "*that they may bring the whole matter to a period.*" Accordingly next day at 11 a.m., "the Presbytery took the whole affair into their serious consideration, and, having reasoned thereon at some length, they agreed presently to pass sentence on them, and, having made application to God by prayer, a vote was stated *simpliciter : Depose* Mr. Henrie Murray from the Ministerial office, and authoritatively discharge him from exercising any part thereof within the congregation of Perth or any parioch within the bounds of the Presbytery? The rolls being called and the votes marked, it was carried unanimously *Depose*. Therefore the Presbytery did and do hereby *simpliciter* depose the said Henrie Murray from the Ministerial office." The same is also done with regard to Mr. Walter Stewart.

Then follow copies of the sentences, of which we shall only give the important part of Mr. Stewart's.

The first paragraph of this recites the Process before the Presbytery, and describes the accused's Declinator as "a displayed banner against the order and government of this Church; to be fraught with insolent and disdainful speeches in his own avouching the said innovations, and adducing such reasons in defence of the same as do not only sufficiently evidence his virulent and schismatick temper and disposition, but also such as . . . will be found to the disgrace of a Protestant Profession." . . . "They do find the the following Articles sufficiently proven, viz.:—His intruding upon the said Congregation and Burgh of Perth; his observing of Festival Days; his using a *Liturgy* in the worship performed by him; his following the order prescribed in the said *Liturgy* for the Burial of the Dead; his taking upon himself to administer the Sacrament of Baptism, cross to the constitution and practice of this Church . . . : they must hold him *pro confesso* as guilty of invading that sacred function [*i.e.*, of the Ministry] . . . which is highly censurable . . . Upon the whole they judge him a person unworthy of claiming any interest in the office of the Ministry of the Gospel, and therefore, being moved with a zeal to the Glory of God and a sincere desire to prove faithful in contending for the Faith once delivered to the Saints, and consequently to purge the Church of all such dangerous innovations, especially of invasions on the office of the Ministry itself, *We*, being met in the Name and by the Authoritie of our Lord and Master, Jesus Christ, sole King and Head of His Church, do, by virtue of that Power and Authoritie committed to us, *Depose the said Mr. Walter Stewart from the Office of the said Holy Ministrie*, which he has assumed, and deprive him of all pretensions thereto, and consequently discharge him from the exercise of any part thereof." This Sentence is to be intimated throughout the bounds of the Presbytery.

And they, "judging it to be their duty in this juncture to signify to the neighbouring Presbyteries an account of their procedure in reference to Innovators within their bounds, which they have under process, as to the length they are come in that affair, and of the above-named Sentences, which they have passed against them and appointed to be intimated; and withal in a brotherly way to represent to them that, as they humbly conceive their former Sentences were not without success, so they are of opinion that a vigorous prosecution of others and as much harmony in sentencing the same as can be obtained, may be a means (through the Blessing of God) for strengthening one another's hands and putting a stop to the Innovations that like a flood are coming in upon this poor Church."

Such were the processes against the Rev. Henrie Murray, his young Deacon the Rev. Walter Stewart, and the Rev. Thomas Murray of Kilspindie. But in the case of the last of these there is an entry ominous of coming change: a change which must be more largely set forth in the next chapter. The entry is as follows:—

February 20th, 1712.—"The brethren that were at the Commission of the General Assembly *reported that they had gotten no advice* anent summonding witnesses that were given up to prove Mr. Thomas Murray's Libel that were contumacious."

CHAPTER IX.

HOW THE PRESBYTERY SUCCEEDED IN "BRINGING THE WHOLE MATTER TO A PERIOD," 1712-15.

YES! the prosecutors "could get no advice" at this juncture of affairs, and consequently (as Wodrow wrote to his friend, the Rev. Alexander M'Crackan), "our brethren there (viz., of the Perth and other northern Presbyteries) are in a very sad taking, and need your sympathy very much." Sympathy indeed, for "mighty changes in the posture of our Church affairs" were occurring and rendering it impossible for them any longer to go on treating the Episcopal Clergy as they had been treating them for the last twenty-three years!

On *March 3rd, 1712*, a Toleration Bill passed through Parliament and received the Royal assent. Its title was as follows:—"An Act to prevent the disturbing of those of the Episcopal Communion in that part of Great Britain called Scotland in the exercise of their religious worship, and in the use of the *Liturgy* of the Church of England; and for repealing the *Act* passed in the Parliament of Scotland intituled *An Act against irregular Baptisms and Marriages*." And the Bill itself opens in the following manner:—"Whereas, since the abolishing of the Episcopal Government in Scotland, those of the Episcopal persuasion there have been frequently disturbed and interrupted in their religious assemblies, and their Ministers prosecuted for reading the English Service in their congregations, and for administering the Sacrament according to the form and manner prescribed in the *Liturgy* of the Church of England—Be it therefore enacted, etc., that it shall be free and lawful for all those of the Episcopal Communion in that part of Great Britain called Scotland to meet and assemble for Divine Worship to be performed in their own manner," etc., etc.

What had brought this great change in the posture of affairs about ? That, on the one side, the Churchmen of Perth might congratulate themselves on their patient endurance and brave struggles for liberty having seriously contributed to enlist public sympathy ; and, on the other, that the Presbytery of Perth might assure themselves that it was largely their conduct, as described in the preceding pages, which had thus succeeded in "*bringing the whole matter to a period,*" is evidenced by the following quotation from Wodrow :—" I hear," he says, "of no (Presbyteries) but those of Perth and Aberdeen that raised processes against these Innovators ; and the first went on and deposed one for contumacy and bringing in a foreign Liturgy. *This was made the introduction to the bringing in the bill for protecting those of the Episcopal Communion in Scotland.*" This passage, indeed, shews that he was very imperfectly informed as to the number of Presbyteries in which Episcopal Clergy were prosecuted, for there were cases of this sort not only in Perth and Aberdeen, but also in Crail, S. Andrews, Orkney, and Edinburgh. It also shews that he was very imperfectly informed as to what had been happening even in Perth, when he merely says that there they " went on and *deposed one* " Episcopal Clergyman, for the preceding pages shew that they prosecuted and sentenced at least six, viz., Messrs. Smith, Walker, Rhynd, H. Murray, T. Murray, and Stewart, not to speak of their attacks on Messrs. Blair, M'Gruther,

Poplay, and Auchterlony. But yet, that a contemporary, like Wodrow, should positively affirm that the doings in the Perth Presbytery were made the introduction to the bringing in of the Toleration Bill, is pretty conclusive testimony that public opinion had approved the conduct of our Perth friends and condemned that of their prosecutors. So then, although the Episcopal Church had lost the first great contest, and had been altogether driven from her "established" position, she had (though not without loss and confusion) gained substantial victory in the second battle,—that, namely, which she waged for Toleration. A new epoch had dawned, and the Disestablished Communion found itself in a position which, compared with all that had gone before, was enviable. There were drawbacks, indeed, which must be presently described, but the following benefits were now well assured, viz., there was "ample room and verge enough" allowed by the law, and a very considerable proportion of the nation still adhered to the "ancient paths." Granted that things were to continue in their present state, there was every reason to believe that Episcopacy would form one of the most prominent elements in the religious life of Scotland during the newly-begun century.

There is another thing besides the prosecution of the Clergy of the Perth Meeting-House, to which "*a period was put*" by the present turn of affairs, and that was the full entries concerning the Episcopalians in the *Presbytery Records*. And so the materials for this *History* become for a time sadly diminished: we enter upon an obscure period. Nevertheless, sufficient notices remain to enable us to give at least an outline of the happier time, which had at length dawned for the Church in Perth.

To illustrate the bright side of this nearly recordless time, the following six notices are available :—

(1.)—The first is from the *Presbytery Records*, and, as it were, formally marks the cessation of the long series of prosecutions, which have been already recorded. The tone of the entry seems to prove the justice of Wodrow's remark that our Presbytery and their friends were "in a very sad taking and needed sympathy very much." (It is dated at the end of the period with which we are dealing) :—

August 31st, 1715.—" The Presbytery being asked by the Commission to make a collection for defraying the expenses the Church has been at in commencing processes for removing Intruders into Churches and suppressing other disorders, this Presbytery finds themselves in case to do nothing in that matter, they having been at great charges already in processing Episcopal Incumbents and getting them removed, and planting of Churches in their bounds since the late happy Revolution, without any reparation."

That they did not like being forced to tolerate Episcopacy is further evidenced by the following quotation from Wodrow. Writing on *July 12th, 1713,* the latter says that Mr. Addison, a Presbyterian Minister, "fell foul of the English ceremonies in the Church of Perth, and disgusted many of the officers of the soldiers there."

(2.)—The next little memorial of the time, which we shall bring forward, consists of two extracts, the first from our *Presbytery Records* and the other from a *Proclamation* by the Synod of Perth and Stirling. As the extract of *August 31st, 1715,* given above, marks the present freedom of the Church from persecution, so these have reference to its internal growth

Spread of Episcopacy.

and prosperity. The *Presbytery*, on *June 9th, 1714*, "take into their serious consideration the threatening aspect of affairs, the pernicious influence of erroneous doctrine, the great prevalencie of Popish and superstitious worship, the bold encroachments upon our Constitution, the lamentable defection of many from our Covenanting principles, and the restless endeavours both in Church and State." The *Synod*, on *June 25th*, after lamenting "the many heinous sins of all ranks; gross atheism and ignorance, great barranness and unfruitfulness under a pure and plentiful Gospel Dispensation; high contempt of the precious ordinances of Jesus Christ; all manner of immoralities, as horrid prophanation of the Lord's Day, cursing and swearing, drunkenness and uncleanness," go on to mention, as it were, in a climax, "the woful defection some have made from the true doctrine of Christ and worship of God, since a door has been opened for introducing Errors in doctrine and Innovations in public worship, and the great danger many are in of being carried away . . from the purity and simplicity of the Gospel to a form and mode of worship not warranted by the Word of God." Evidently the main drift of these passages is simply that Episcopacy was now in a comparatively flourishing condition within the district, as well as elsewhere, and in fact they only present us with the Presbyterian way of describing that, which an Episcopal Historian relates thus :— "About this time the Liturgy of the Church of England was almost universally received and introduced in all the Episcopal Churches of Scotland. . . . Meeting-Houses were set up in several towns and villages, where both pastors and people manifested the greatest forwardness for embracing the English liturgy; . . . Church principles and communion began to be now better understood by the generality of the people."

(3)—And we are in a position to add a few particulars concerning the welfare of our Congregation itself. "At this period the ejected Bishops were held in the greatest respect and veneration during their lives by the members of the Church. Even the descendents of some of their predecessors in the Episcopate were highly esteemed in their localities. The *Perth MS.* in the Advocates' Library supplies an illustration of this. It describes the case of the family of Dr. W. Lindsay, who had been one of the Incumbents of Perth, and died Bishop of Dunkeld in 1679. His wife had died a short time before him, and his surviving children were placed under the care of a relative in Perth. The old women of that town used to stroke the heads of his little grand-children, and bless them for their grandfather's sake, who, they were sure, was a good man."

(4).—Our fourth group of notices give us a glimpse of the Clergy of the Perth Congregation. The son of the Rev. W. Smith (whose trial by the Presbytery was related at some length in chap. vii.) informs us that Rev. H. Murray "continued in the Meeting House till 1716" (he had been, we remember, formally appointed to the charge in 1703). "He was," adds Mr. Smith, "in the habit of praying for her Majesty (Queen Anne), but after her death never complying nor praying for the King (George I.)."

His young assistant also, the Rev. Walter Stewart, whose acquaintance we have already made as a Deacon, "was now (*i.e.*, *March 11th, 1712*) promoted to the Presbyterate by the said Bishop of Aberdeen (*i.e.*, George Haliburton), and was thereafter three years

Lawson, II., p. 125.

The Perth Congregation.   87

officiating in the Meeting House of Perth and at Auchterarder." The reason why it was the Bishop of Aberdeen, who performed the Ordinations of Mr. Stewart, is probably to be found in the fact that, after being driven from his northern Diocese, this Prelate took up his abode so near at hand as Denhead, Coupar Angus. And, indeed, it may be conjectured that, although the Dioceses, as they fell vacant, passed under the formal jurisdiction of the Bishop of Edinburgh, he, who ordained Mr. Stewart, performed other Episcopal Offices for the Perth Church-people, until his death on *September 29th, 1715*.

Also "in the year 1712" (says Mr. Smyth, junior), "the Rev. Wm. Smyth, late of Moneydie, came to Perth to his son's house, where he always read Prayers to as many as pleased to hear him, when the Minister of the Meeting House" was prevented doing so.

(5).—And, not only have we the above information with regard to the clerical arrangements, but we know also that there was a Constitution of some kind drawn up for the Congregation, and that the chief lay officials were entitled "Managers," who, on certain occasions, summoned a general meeting of the Congregation, or at least had the power to do so.

(6).—Lastly, we are informed* that our friends turned their attention towards obtaining a more suitable place of Worship. The name, "Meeting House," on the lips of Churchmen, was, of course, allowable enough, when deliberately applied to a temporary and makeshift Chapel, such as had hitherto been in use since their ejection from the old Church of S. John; but it was a different thing to acquiesce permanently, either in the name or the thing itself.

* Fittis's *Gleanings*, p. 182.

Accordingly they proposed to furnish themselves with a more satisfactory edifice, and the actual proposal, which they made, shews what an extraordinary change had "come o'er the spirit of the scene" since the passing of the *Toleration Bill* in 1712. "It consisted of nothing less than an application for leave to adopt the unused *East Church* (*i.e.*, the Choir of S. John's) as their place of Worship. The Perth Presbytery, however (so we are told), took steps to frustrate the attempt." It is not recorded what arrangement was actually made upon the occurrence of this disappointment. Perhaps a hall was hired and properly fitted up. One consequence was that the temporary term of "Meeting-House" had to be acquiesced in for some time longer, and, as a matter of fact, for so long a time that at last its temporary nature was forgotten.

Altogether, then, things were looking to a wonderful degree brighter than probably the most hopeful for many a long year had expected. But there were shadows as well.

Amongst these was the wretched state to which many of the evicted Clergy appear to have been reduced at this epoch. Thomas Stephen says that there were about 200 of their families "totally destitute." Many of them sought their daily bread in England, and "many were obliged to apply themselves to mean secular employments." Doubtless, if we had records on the Episcopal side, we should find that the sacrifices which our Clergy made, were of no trifling character. It is not likely that the Presbytery would think it their duty to record the sufferings, which they (no doubt conscientiously) felt obliged to cause ; but it does so happen that at least two local notices are extant, which illustrate this feature of the time. In the one case we have a pathetic notice of Mr. George M'Gruther, the ousted Parish Minister of Collace, whom we have already seen, struggling hard on behalf of the Church in Perth. Scott, in his *Fasti*, says of him:— " Getting into poverty, he received aid from the Kirk Sessions of S. Madoes, Scoonie, and Kettins." Now, this evidently implies that he had been reduced pretty low. It would naturally be hard for a Parish Minister to be driven to depend on any one's charity; but to be compelled to wait on that of the very people who had despoiled him, unjustly, as he believed, argues considerable suffering on his part. Also in the *Kirk Session Record* of Forgandenny there is the following eloquent entry : - *March 29th, 1713*.—" It being represented likewise by the Minister that, since the last Session, he had ordered two shillings for an abdicate Episcopal Minister, whose name he had forgot, the Session allows the Boxmaster to give the said two shillings to the Minister, and this to be stated."

This was a shadow thrown by the past upon the brightness of the present period of Toleration. There was also another shadow cast by the future. For, strictly speaking, the benefits of the *Act* were only to be extended to those, who took the oaths of Abjuration and Allegiance. And, though many of the Clergy (the Rev. Henry Murray amongst them), were ready to swear positive allegiance to Queen Anne, yet they could not conscientiously take a negative oath that, in the event of the death of this Stuart Princess, her brother, King James's son, would have no right to the succession. Nor can the Presbyterians plead that the refusal of this oath put our friends out of the pale of legitimate toleration, for they themselves, although for a different reason, scrupled at the same oath. Their insuperable difficulty was that they could not bring themselves to swear that the future King of England must be a member of the Church of England. Still, the case of the Presbyterians does not concern us. What is evident is that, notwithstanding the present Toleration, there will be a serious contest between the two parties over the succession, as soon as the now childless* monarch shall be removed by death.

* In Dean Stanley's "Westminster Abbey" there is a description of the finding of 15 little coffins of this Queen's family.

BOOK II.

Penal Laws and Divisions.

CHAPTER X.

HOW THE CHURCH IN PERTH WAS INVOLVED IN A SECOND DISASTER, 1715-1719.

ON *August 1st, 1714*, Queen Anne died, and the anxious crisis had arrived. It is preposterous (as is so often done) to describe Prince James, the late Queen's brother, and oldest son of her father, King James VII., as a *Pretender*, when he now claimed to be heir of the Throne. It is a simple fact that he had considerable weight of reason on his side, and this even though it is granted that there was considerable weight of reason on the other side also. The Jacobites, therefore, as the Stuart party now began to be called, were not irrational fanatics.

We are not called upon, indeed, to discuss the rising of 1715 in all its bearings as a national question; but a few general words from a Church point of view may here be allowed. While, therefore, we hold that all, who then considered that the balance of argument was in favour of continuing the old Dynasty, were perfectly justified in making a determined effort to cause their views to prevail, we also hold that there were certain considerations, which might justly have given Churchmen pause before joining in the enterprise actually undertaken. In the first place, just as Pope Leo XIII., in A.D. 1892, commanded Royalist French Churchmen to give their support to the Republic, on the ground that the Church cannot undertake to set forth any form of secular government as a necessary article of the faith, so our friends might have acted on a similar principle at this crisis. They might have said:—"As citizens we believe in the doctrine of a hereditary monarchy in opposition to that of one based on parliamentary election ; but, ecclesiastically, we cannot presume to stake the Church's existence on either the one or the other of these political theories, and, therefore, we prefer to play a passive part during the present secular changes." Such a point of view, however, was but little known to the Churchmen of that day, amongst whom Archbishop Laud's theory of alliance between Church and State was more prevalent. Even those, however, who felt pledged by every principle of loyalty to draw the sword for the defeat of an attack upon their ancient, national Dynasty, might still have hesitated on another ground as Churchmen to join the actual enterprise of 1715. Seeing that the failure of this political movement would mean the ruin of the Church, they might fairly have stood aloof until they were satisfied that the rising was not foredoomed to failure by incapacity on the part of its promoters ; inadequacy of design and lack of means.

This reasoning, however, though sound, partakes too much of the nature of wisdom after the event. At all events it weighed little with men, whose late success in the matter of the *Toleration Act* had rendered them sanguine : most of whom imagined that the Church did commit herself to the principle of a hereditary Monarchy, and whose loyalty to the Stuarts had been raised to white heat by the persecution, which they had lately been compelled to endure at the hands of their rivals. And so, there being much real weight of reason, and an inexhaustible supply of generous feeling (not to speak of lower incentives) in favour of the enterprise, a vast number of Scottish Churchmen espoused the cause of the exiled Prince.

In this undertaking the City of Perth played a conspicuous part, and it would greatly enliven these pages if we were to transfer to them an account of Lord Mar's occupation of the Town in favour of Prince James, and of the Chevalier's own visit to the same. We must not, however, stray too far into the region of secular history, but confine ourselves to whatever bears upon the local fortunes of the Church.

While Mar's troops held the City, there can be little doubt that our local Episcopacy would enjoy a brief moment of importance, greater than had fallen to its lot since the Disestablishment. But military and political questions seem so to have absorbed men's minds that little has been chronicled concerning ecclesiastical affairs. The *Presbytery Records* throw no light on the state of the Church in Perth at this time, and, if the Rev. H. Murray kept any register, it has perished.

The Commander-in-Chief soon found that the Presbyterians as a whole regarded the cause of him, whom they called "The Pretender," and that of Anti-Christ as identical.* He therefore laboured assiduously to overcome the bias of the popular mind. For this purpose he imported a valuable possession, of which the Fair City had hitherto been devoid. He brought in a printing-press, which was managed by a Mr. Freebairn. Jacobite publications (at least one of which still survives in the Episcopal Chest in Edinburgh) were put forth, and urged that King James VIII. had not the remotest desire to disturb the Protestant settlement of the Kingdom. Recourse was also had to the pulpit as well as the press. In pursuance of the General's orders,

* Fittis's *Sketches*, p. 160. [I am indebted to the same work for several other statements in this chapter.—*Author.*]

suitable sermons were preached by non-juring Divines on texts selected by Lord Mar himself.

One of these discourses delivered (probably) in Perth contained the following passage:*—"I shall now consider you as Protestant, and apply myself to the deluded populace, who are bugbeard out of their duty by two terrifying scarcrows and ugly vizors: the one is the King's religion: the other his education at the French Court. As to the first, it is an old maxim '*Si vis fallere plebem, finge Deum;*' that is, 'The best way to buble people is to pretend religion. . . .' Did any of you make exception against the Duke of Hannover for being a Lutheran? We all know that we of the reformed religion are as disgustful to those of that profession as Papists themselves are: witness the reception of the poor English reformers at Lubeck, when they fled from Queen Marie's persecution. Witness also your own now reigning Prince, who has built Churches to the Jesuits (reputed the worst of Papists) in his capatall of Germany: yet there the reformed have not the least allowance for the exercise of their religion. . . . Ar their errors small? What think you now of consubstantiation, picturs, and images in Churches? What would many of our Presbyterians say to be obliged to swear backword as to many heads of their profession of faith by the Lutherans, who are all of them Arminians? *How grossly partial are we in this matter! to except against the religion of our native Prince, and yet to set up a stranger lyable to the very sam objections!* . . . Is there but the remotest probability that the King will venture his crowns by trusting to any Popish potentate for help, considering how regardless all of them have been of him?"

* Oliphant's *Jacobite Lairds of Gask*, p. 38.

Notwithstanding, however, both the real argument and also the assumption of a maximum of zeal for Protestantism contained in the above, the preaching and the printing proved to be unproductive work, and when Lord Mar set himself to compel Parish Ministers to cease praying in public worship for the Elector of Brunswick (George I.), he was equally unsuccessful. One potent reason, no doubt, why he found it so difficult to enlist Protestant sentiment on his behalf was the fact that, however sincere the Prince may have been in his assurances that he did not intend to coerce his subjects into Romanism, it was evident that he was equally determined that he, a Romanist, should not be coerced into Protestantism by his subjects. When he arrived in Perth, he could with difficulty, if at all, be persuaded to darken the door of a non-Roman Church there. Nor was a Royal Proclamation from Scone, so far recognizing his subjects' religion as to enjoin a general thanksgiving for his arrival, and the offering of prayers on his behalf in the Churches, more successful.

We must not follow the march of the army from Perth to the indecisive battle of Sheriffmuir; nor must we linger over the subsequent meeting of the Council in Scone, at which it was decided that the Prince must retreat; nor must we retire with him and Mar across the frozen Tay and listen to his desponding witticism "*See, my Lord, how you have led me on to the ice!*" But, considering that Churchmen in Perth were, as a whole, involved in the dismay which followed upon the Prince's withdrawal and the utter collapse of all their hopes, we may well pause to describe the state of the deserted City. When the fiat of the Council was promulgated, it produced much dissatisfaction, which became intensified at the news of

Argyle's approach. The Jacobite burghers were in a dreadful plight. "The Clergy," says Sinclair, "the inhabitants of the City; the Magistrates in the country; the merchants, tradesmen, and the like, who, though they had not taken arms, had yet publicly discovered themselves; had received the Chevalier; had owned him; had assisted in proclaiming him, and perhaps signed addresses to him, or in some other way had distinguished themselves against those into whose hands they were now to fall; these were all in an inexpressible consternation, enquiring every moment what was determined on at Scone, and visibly preparing to get out of the way even before the army left Perth" *(January 31st, 1716)*.

Of course the sum-total of these events constituted a disaster to the Church, as notable as its Disestablishment and Disendowment in 1689. In Perth, the Town Council on *May 21st* passed a resolution depriving those concerned in the late "rebellion" of their freedom. But that was comparatively little. A *Bill* was carried through Parliament discharging the Episcopal Clergy, who had not taken the oaths required by the *Toleration Act* of 1712, from officiating to any number of persons above eight, and the family in which they performed any part of their office. During the year 1716 this Act was used with crushing effect. The Presbyterians in various parts of the country, but especially in the north, where Episcopacy was strong, used it as a potent weapon wherewith to strike Churchmen down. Those of the latter, who had already been driven out of the Parishes, had to look on while their "Meeting-Houses" were demolished, and those, who still retained their Parish Churches, were expelled, and many of both classes were thrown into prison.

Rev. W. Smith's Ministry.

Amongst other misfortunes, both Mr. Murray and Mr. Stewart had to leave Perth. The latter retired to Doune, where he ministered for some time, but the name of the place to which the former betook himself is not recorded. Their congregation, however, though it must have received a deplorable shaking, was not wholly deserted. For (says the Rev. W. Smith's son) "when Mr. Henry Murray was obstructed by the Magistrates, my father, who had settled in the Town, was accustomed to conduct service in his own house for all who chose to come."

During, therefore, at least the earlier part of this obscure period, Mr. Smith may be said to have been Incumbent. And whatever incidents or notices of these years are extant may here be grouped together. Surely the fragmentary records of a Ministry exercised under such discouraging circumstances will be perused with sympathetic interest by Churchmen of a happier epoch.

Mr. Smith, then, we may be certain, often used the prayer issued by Bishop Rose for those troubled days, the invocation of which ran thus:—"O Eternal God! who in Thy righteous judgment hast covered many of us with a cloud in the day of Thine anger, and hast broken us sore in the place of dragons."

It would seem probable also that the same Presbyter is referred to in the following narrative:[*]—When the troops of what was now settled as the Government had possession of Fingask in 1716, and some of the soldiers quartered in the house, one of the family relates that "the good lady became alarmingly ill, and in the midst of much anxiety and care (her husband and sons being at a distance, and uncertain of their

[*] Fittis's *Sketches*, p. 213.

fate, and the cause on which they were embarked giving way on every side), my father, Sir Stewart Threipland, was born. It was thought that, under the distressing circumstances of her situation, she could not survive, and a Clergyman of the Episcopal Church in Perth was sent for privately—the Clergy of that persuasion being marked men at that period as known adherents of the Jacobite cause. He, having administered the Holy Communion, proposed, as so favourable an opportunity might not occur again, to baptize the child. This suggestion, communicated in a whisper to the nurse and others, was at once assented to by them, But the difficulty consisted in knowing by what name the infant should be called, his father having left no directions, and his poor mother being thought to be much too weak to be consulted on the subject. The good lady, however, heard a little of what was passing near her bed, and drawing back the curtain she called in a faint voice, 'Stewart, Stewart!' This was enough, and by that name was my father christened before the Clergyman left the house."

Before quoting the extracts from the *Presbytery Records*, which relate to these years, we may remark generally that, while our Presbytery surpassed others in their zeal against Episcopalians between 1689 and 1712, they appear to have allowed others to surpass them in this respect subsequent to 1715. The reflection that all their former efforts had only led up to the carrying of the *Toleration Act* of 1712 seems always to have haunted them. That they were determined, however, to shew to the Episcopal Clergy within their bounds that the brief day of Toleration was over, appears from the following entries:— Evidently some of the more distant parishes had continued even to this time in possession of the Pre-Revolution Clergy. "But," say the Presbytery on *May 2nd, 1716*, "we have a prospect of getting more churches in our possession : the most part, if not all the late Incumbents and Intruders having complied with the Rebellion."

They go on to mention the names of some Clergy, who attempted to "gather up the fragments that remained" to the Church at this melancholy period, in the country districts :—

May 2nd, 1716.—A Mr. Adamson is reported to be "intruding" in various parishes, and not praying for the King and the Royal Family. It is not said, indeed, that he was an Episcopalian, but the probability is that he was so.

November 21st, 1716.—"Mr. James Mercer, Minister at Forteviot, having represented to the Presbytery that one, Ninian Niving, an Episcopal Preacher, who intruded on the Church (of Crail*) in Fife in the time of the late Rebellion, and prayed for the Pretender under the designation of King James VIII., has intruded of late upon his parish, and preaches in the Laird of Invermay's house on Sabbath days, the Presbytery, taking the affair into their consideration, appoint the Clerk to write to the Laird that, if he do not remove the said Mr. Niving, the Presbytery will take notice of him, which will be nothing to his advantage."

December 19th, 1716.—A letter is written to the Laird of Invermay anent Mr. Niving.

The vigilance of the Presbytery was still active a year later.

December 13th, 1717.—"There being a letter sent up from the Presbytery of Dundee directed to this

* Wood's *East Neuk of Fife*.

Presbytery, which was read, shewing that the said Presbytery of Dundee have had several complaints laid before them anent illegal and irregular practices committed by Mr. Thomas Murray, who was lately deposed by this (*i.e.*, Perth) Presbytery, such as his intrusion into several Churches within the bounds of this Presbytery during the late Rebellion, and since that time continues ordinarily to preach, baptize, and exercise other parts of the Ministerial Office within congregations belonging to this Presbytery; therefore, the said Presbytery of Dundee do hereby signify that, seeing that the most notour of these irregularities were done within the bounds of the Presbytery of Perth, that they may please take some effectual course against the said Mr. Thomas Murray, and what assistance and concurrence the Presbytery of Dundee can give will not be wanting." The brethren, "having read and considered the foresaid letter, and after communing anent these irregularities committed by the said Mr. Thomas Murray, do recommend to all the brethren to bring in particular information anent these irregularities . . against next meeting in this place, and in the meantime appoints the Moderator to write a return to the Presbytery of Dundee."

January 15th, 1718.—Mr. T. Murray is reported to have intruded on the parish of Kilspindie and Kinfauns during the time of the late Rebellion. Further enquiries to be made.

October 9th, 1718.—Episcopal Clergy reported to be baptizing, and the matter is referred to a Committee.

December 10th, 1718.—"Anent irregular baptisms by Episcopal Incumbents, the Committee recommend the Presbytery to apply to the Sheriff to take effectual methods for restraining this abuse by calling the

Intruders before them, or any other manner of way, as they shall think fit." The report of the Committee is accepted, and the Sheriff to be approached.

There are no further entries concerning these cases, which seems strange. Perhaps the reason is to be found in this, that while before the Rising the Episcopalians could count on an immense amount of latent sympathy in the public, and thus be enabled to fight the Presbytery vigorously, after the late misfortunes the populace were afraid to shew themselves on the defeated side, and so the Clergy were obliged to yield more speedily, when attacked by the Presbytery and the Sheriff.

Bad, however, as things had been in the three years subsequent to Sheriffmuir (1716-1718), they were still worse by 1719. In the first place the Rev. W. Smyth died in 1718, and it does not appear how his place was filled. Possibly the Congregation may have been reduced to depend on the occasional ministrations of visitor Priests. But there would be serious difficulties even in the way of this. For, not having learnt by their late experiences that if the Throne of Britain were to be regained for the Stuarts, a very large, well-supported, and well-conducted movement must be organized, the Jacobites were foolish enough to land a paltry force of 400 Spaniards in Ross-shire on *March 6th, 1719.* These having been easily disposed of, the penal laws, the administration of which had been shewing some signs of relaxation, were rendered more severe than ever. In April an *Act* was passed by which every Episcopal Minister performing Divine Service in any Meeting-House within Scotland, without having taken the oaths, ... is to suffer six months' imprisonment, and have his Meeting-House shut up for six months; and every house where nine or more persons, besides the family, are present at Divine Service, is declared to be a Meeting-House within the meaning of the *Act*.

CHAPTER XI.

HOW PERTH FARED IN THE COLLEGE AND USAGE CONTROVERSIES FROM 1720 TO 1726.

WHEN things were thus at their darkest "the valuable pilot, who had so ably steered the helm of the tossed vessel" of the Scottish Church, was removed by death. In the beginning of *March, 1720*, Bishop Rose had a fainting fit. From this he recovered, but on the 20th he went to his sister's house in the Canongate, and died there of another fainting fit in the 74th year of his age.

This was the end of an old and the beginning of a new era in the Scottish Church. Hitherto, or at least up to the failure of the enterprise of 1715, the restoration of the Stuarts had been sincerely believed to be an actually impending event. In view of its occurrence, as we have seen, the organization of the Church had taken a peculiar form. It is important to remember at this point what the actual shape, which things had assumed, was. Up till now, as we have seen, it had not been considered necessary to make any permanent and regular arrangements. When, indeed, the Secular power was once more on a proper footing by the Coronation of Prince James, then it would be worth while for the ecclesiastical authorities to place their organization on a lasting basis, and to complete the *bene esse* of the Church by the assignment of Dioceses to the Post-Revolution Bishops; but, in the meantime, a temporary arrangement had been acquiesced in. The Pre-Revolution Bishops, as Diocesans, retained the actual government of the Church in their own hands. When a Diocese became vacant it was *pro tempore* administered by the senior of these Diocesans, of whom Bishop Rose was the last survivor, and the Prelates, consecrated subsequent to the Disestablishment, were content that an undefined interval should elapse between their Consecrations and Collation to their Sees.

Naturally the death of Bishop Rose, following upon the late disastrous overthrow of the Stuart Prince, changed the whole aspect of affairs. The rest of this chapter will be taken up *first* with giving a general description of two great controversies, which sprang up in the Church at large out of the situation; *secondly*, with weaving together into a narrative such fragmentary notices of local Church affairs in Perth as have come down to us; and *thirdly*, with relating how far Perth was involved, through the succession of the Bishops, in the controversies described in the first section.

(1).—Owing to late events, therefore, as we have seen, the Church had now to face the problem of providing for its permanent existence as a disestablished Communion, and to do so in the light of its past stormy history. What was the proper policy to pursue under the circumstances?

Alas! the Church as a whole was unprepared to answer this momentous question. Owing to the rude manner of her disestablishment and disendowment; to the severe contest for bare existence which she had had to wage between 1689-1712; to the irregular Episcopal organization, which had been adopted as a supposedly temporary expedient; and finally to the disaster of 1716, and the penal law of 1719, our

Communion found herself in such a confused condition that she had no Prelate or Assembly recognized as endowed with authority to give an answer. The melancholy circumstances of the case brought it about that everyone had as good a right to speak for the Church as any one else. And, therefore, a large charity is needed in judging the conduct of individuals, who now found themselves plunged, whether they would or not, into a serious controversy. One comfort is that, while the centrifugal forces, which almost contemporaneously developed themselves in Presbyterianism, have proved too strong for those of a centripetal character even to the present day, the centripetal forces of Episcopacy have ultimately proved vastly stronger than the centrifugal.

With these preliminary remarks we may now proceed to describe the substance of the controversies which sprang up at this time. They were two in number.

(a).—To begin with, one arose in connection with the question :—"What policy of *Church Government* are we to pursue now that the last of the Diocesan Prelates is dead?" The answer proved to be a discordant one, and two opposite courses were advocated. *On the one hand* were ranged the majority of the Bishops and the exiled Prince, as represented by the royal delegate, Lockhart of Carnwath. The southern Clergy also, who looked to Edinburgh as their centre, were of this party. Their views seem to have been prompted by a somewhat superficial conservatism. Without making any deep study of the past of Christendom, they were satisfied to continue what an ordinary, commonsense layman would take to be the organization of the Scottish Church, as it had been under Bishop Rose. Roughly speaking, when that

Prelate was the sole Diocesan remaining, and was himself as such administering all the Dioceses in the country because they happened to be vacant, and was surrounded by a group of non-Diocesan Bishops whom he used to consult, the appearance of things was that of an Episcopal Committee with a Chairman governing the Church as a unit. Let this state of things, therefore, said our friends, be continued; let the Church be still regarded as one Diocese, and governed, not by local Bishops, each in his own Diocese, but by the Episcopal bench sitting conjointly as a committee under its chairman, and called the *College*. Hence they were known as the *College Party*. Undoubtedly the holders of this view were animated also by the Erastian spirit. For, while it would have been very difficult for the (exiled) secular power to control a number of Diocesan Bishops, it would evidently be easy for the banished monarch to control the Church, when he had it under a single committee, the members of which were to be nominated by himself, and that committee under a Primate of his own appointment.

On *the other hand*, there were those who took a very different view. Such were Bishops John Falconer and Gadderar; Dr. Rattray of Craighall, and, generally speaking, the northern Clergy, who looked to Aberdeen as their centre, and not a few Laity. These held that the "College" view was an entire mistake. They did did not, indeed, object to the conservatism of the theory, but to the superficiality of its conservatism. They must go further back and deeper down. (*a*) There must no longer be such utter dependence on the Civil Power as had hitherto prevailed. No doubt there must not be a breach between the Church and the (exiled) Monarch : the latter must have his ecclesiastical rights,

but the Church must learn far more to live her own
life and do her own work, trusting chiefly to her own
apostolical commission. (*b*) Again, it was quite a mistake
to suppose that Bishop Rose had superseded the Diocesan
principle, and governed the Church as the Primus of
a College. Doubtless he had consulted his non-diocesan
brethren, but the very ground on which he administered
the whole of Scotland was that he was a Diocesan
Bishop, and that not only permanently, as Bishop of
Edinburgh, but also temporarily, as Bishop of each of
the vacant Sees. In accordance, therefore, both with
the underlying principle of Bishop Rose's administration
and the customs of antiquity, the Church must be
governed by Diocesan Prelates. Hence they formed a
Diocesan Party. (*c*) Again, having resolved on independent action on the part of the Church, and the
re-organization of the Diocesan system, they must be
able to tell their rivals by what authority they proposed that local jurisdiction should now be conferred
upon those who had already been consecrated Bishops
before Bishop Rose's death. And the answer to this
was ultimately found in an appeal to antiquity. The
visible Church derives its "*esse*" and its powers from
the Apostolical Commission handed on from generation
to generation through the Episcopate. This Commission
is conferred in all its fulness at Consecration. Whether
regular or irregular, the ministrations of a consecrated
Bishop are always valid. And this essential endowment the present Scottish Prelates had. But it was
not enough that there should be Bishops anyhow. The
"*bene esse*" of the Church required that the principle
of order should prevail amongst the Prelates: to each
should be assigned a definite local sphere or Diocese,
beyond which the exercise of his powers should be

restrained. And it is this practical limitation to a particular district of the theoretically universal commission conferred by consecration which is called jurisdiction. The latter is thus not a Divine essential of the Church, like Consecration, but simply an ecclesiastical arrangement for its "*bene esse*." Obviously, therefore, a Church possessing the Apostolical Commission could take whatever steps seemed good to it with regard to the assignment of jurisdiction. Hitherto in Scotland the Civil Power had been, even too largely, allowed to regulate this point, and Bishops had allowed it to assign them their particular Sees. But now the Civil Power was in exile, and so the Church must resume the power, which she had delegated to it, and take order herself for the assignment of jurisdiction to her already consecrated Prelates. And what order should it be? Of course, the primitive mode of *election*. Such was the "Diocesan" party which opposed that of the "College."

There was a certain amount of right on each side. On the one hand the essential view of the Diocesans was the more orthodox, but they were at first led to push the theory of Diocesan independance to such an extent as to render unity in the Scottish Church almost impossible. On the other hand, although the "College" party were even more inclined to push their idea also to an extreme, yet it was necessary that, for the sake of unity, at least partial expression should be given to their views.

(*b*).—But, besides this constitutional question, into which the course of events had plunged the Church, there was another controversy of equal seriousness. Its nature was as follows. It will be remembered that before the Disestablishment the all but universal rule

Usagers and Anti-Usagers. 111

was that, except for the use of the Creed, the Doxology, and the Lord's Prayer, the general *ex tempore* character of *the worship of the Church* was the same as that of the Presbyterians. It will be remembered also that after the Revolution "liturgical forms" began to be everywhere adopted. In general, it was the English *Prayer Book* that was used, but while some old-fashioned people still retained the *ex tempore* method, there were also instances of the Scottish Eucharistic Service of 1637 being revived. As time went on, however, the study of antiquity and the appeal of the English non-jurors to the Scottish Prelates concerning their Liturgy of 1718 led many of our most learned northern Divines to see that the Scottish Office of 1637, especially if the order of the prayers were modified, was an altogether more satisfactory Eucharistic Service than that contained in the English Book. Ultimately it came about that, while the "College" party as a whole were contented with the superficially conservative policy of being satisfied with the arrangements for public worship, as they then happened to be in Scotland, the Diocesan party as a whole now felt that there was really no further call on the Church to conciliate a Presbyterianised public opinion. The latter therefore advocated an appeal to Antiquity, not only for Episcopal organization, but also for liturgical forms. As a matter of fact, besides Immersion in Baptism, the restoration of Confirmation, and the use of Chrism in that Sacramental Ordinance, the chief points upon which they insisted were—(1) The express Invocation of the Holy Spirit in consecrating the Eucharist ; (2) The Oblation of the same during the Consecration ; (3) The change of the Prayer for the Church militant into one for the whole Church, including the faithful departed ; (4) The mixture of water with the wine, and to these may be added (5) The restoration of the component parts of the Altar Service to the order in which they occur in the ancient Liturgies. In 1735 an edition of the Eucharistic Service embodying these points (which had already become customary) was printed, and was substantially identical with the "*Scotch Office*" now in use amongst ourselves. Such was the nature of the "*Usage*" controversy, as it was called.

(2).—We have occupied considerable space in giving a general outline of the two great controversies which now shook the Church to its centre. Our excuse is that, unless the reader had some clear notion of their character and importance, the subsequent history of the Church in Perth would for many years be unintelligible to him.

We may now, therefore, return to the Fair City itself. And, first, we must combine the few and scattered local notices which have been preserved to us in such a way as to shew that our Perth Congregation had a continuous existence during this period. We left our friends in the last chapter at the year 1719 (the twelve-month succeeding the death of the Rev. W. Smith), but we are unable to state how they were providing for the carrying on of Services under the difficult circumstances of the time. It seems pretty certain that one of the great weaknesses of a "voluntary" and disorganized Church began to shew itself in our Congregation, and that is that the Clergy, being wholly dependent on their flock for their subsistence, the Lay Managers became Managers indeed. The first Presbyters, whom we come across after Mr. Smith's death, are two old friends still in distress. On *January 24th, 1721*, the Revs. Thomas Murray and

George M'Gruther receive respectively from the Bishop of Edinburgh's fund for the relief of indigent Clergy, ten and seven-and-a-half crowns. Whether or not they were in Perth, however, is not recorded; but in the same year Bishop Falconer speaks of "the Presbyters in and about Perth." He does not, indeed, give their names, for our Clergy were then very cautious about committing their designations and places of residence to paper; but clearer information comes with 1722. It appears that previous to this time negotiations were in progress to bring a certain Rev. Mr. Irvine* to fill the vacant charge, but for some reason they failed. In the year in question, however, a settlement was made. Mr. Smith, junior, tells us that now, "by invitation of the members of the Episcopal Society, Mr. Henry Murray returned (to Perth, which he had left in 1716) and officiat, never complying nor praying for the King but in general terms." The next glimpse we have of this Presbyter is on *February 22nd, 1726*, when the Rev. George Sempill (of whom more anon) writes to a friend:—"One, Mr. Wingate, brought Dr. Stirling's letter to Mr. Murray at Perth." That this Mr. Murray is our Incumbent seems certain, because, in the same letter, Mr. Sempill describes him as "our Moderator," which both shews that a cleric is referred to, and also gives us an interesting glimpse of the survival of Pre-Revolution arrangements long after Disestablishment. Mr. Smith, junior, also informs us that the Rev. H. Murray continued in charge of the Perth Congregation till his death. Now, as this did not occur till much later, we can be quite sure of the existence of our flock during the present period.

* Perhaps Mr. Irvine of Doune, a College Bishop.

Having settled this point, let us now collect our fragmentary notices of Episcopacy in the country districts at the same time.

The *Presbytery Record* informs us that in *January, 1725*, "Mr. Foord, Schoolmaster at Kilspindy, is complained against by some of the heritors as being unfit for his post." Summoned before the Presbytery, he compeared, and "told he was in the Paroch of Kilspindy in the time of the Rebellion, and that there was an Episcopal preacher, Mr. Thomas Murray, who preached at Kilspindy at that time, and that he sat as Precentor to the said Mr. Murray, and that he read a paper emitted by the Earl of Mar's order." Mr. Foord is therefore now dismissed from his office "*as being disaffected to the Church* and State." Churchmen, it appears, were still called upon and willing to suffer for their principles.

On *September 23rd* of the same year we have our first glimpse of an ecclesiastic of great learning and power, who was destined to play a very important part in our local Church affairs. This was the Rev. Robert Rattray, D.D., Laird of Craighall, near Blairgowrie. Having been born in 1684, we find him at the age of 29 (in 1713) requesting Bishop John Falconer to baptize him by immersion, and confirm him by Chrism. Probably this was in view of his Ordination. Now, in 1725, he was in the prime of life, being 41 years old. It is Mr. Sempill who gives us our glance at him. "Craighall," he says (referring in the Scottish manner to Dr. Rattray), "came to Duplin when Mr. Gray and I were there. . . . He went off on Saturday, and held forth in young Balgowan's house on Sunday." His discourse on that occasion is not recorded for us, but Mr. Sempill gives

The Laird of Craighall. 115

us a (not very appreciative) outline of one delivered five months later, probably at Dunsinane. "I heard,' he says, "Craighall deliver my Lord Nairn's funeral harangue. He was as cautious as he could be with respect to his darling (doctrine of an Intermediate State). He told the chief way we could perpetuat the memory of the righteous was by commemorating them at the Altar. And for the separate state I observe he took the cautious way Divines take with the question, '*Where was Lazarus' soul the three days he was dead ?*' He told not if the separate souls were in Heaven or Hades, but that they were in God's hands."

On *April 17th, 1726*, the *Presbytery Record* leads us to suppose that there were some Episcopal assemblies in our neighbourhood, for one of the instructions with which the Presbytery charges its delegate to the General Assembly is, "to beg the Assembly to take such methods to suppress such meetings for worship that are nurseries of disaffection to His Majesty's Government."

(3.)—Having now explained the nature of the controversies, which agitated the Scottish Church at large, and produced the evidence, which shows the continuance of Episcopacy in our city and neighbourhood, it remains to prove in what manner our district was involved in the "College" and "Usage" disputes. And, in doing this, we shall reap the further benefit of tracing our Episcopal succession.

On the death of Bishop Rose the Church was divided as follows, between the "College" and the "Diocesan" parties. The College remained everywhere in possession, except in the following important districts, which fell to the "Diocesans." The Clergy of the Diocese of Aberdeen elected Bishop Archibald Campbell (whose place was, in 1722, taken by Bishop Gadderar, because he himself lived in London). The Clergy of Angus, Mearns, S. Andrews City and its immediate neighbourhood, and those of that part of the Diocese of Dunkeld, which consists of Perthshire east of the Tay (excluding Perth itself), elected Bishop John Falconer, of Carnbee in Fife. The new Bishop of Aberdeen was so staunch a "Diocesan" and "Usager" that he accepted his See in complete independence of the "College." Bishop Falconer, however, though a convinced member of the same school of thought, was eminently a man of peace and conciliation. On the one hand, he satisfied his own friends by acquiescing in his election; but, on the other, he was so happy as to induce the College also to concur in his appointment, by representing to them that it was the Clergy of a new "District" and not of an old "Diocese," who had elected him! Would that this good Prelate's tact had been shared in by all!

Seeing, however, that Perth was expressly excluded from his jurisdiction, why do we bring in Bishop Falconer? For this reason: that, though our city adhered to the "College" and "Anti-Usage" party, this Prelate, so far as can be judged from the scanty information at our disposal, appears to have been a *persona grata* in our neighbourhood, and not to have been unwilling to represent the College beyond the limits of his own District. And it is probable that, in this capacity, or perhaps in no regularly defined capacity at all, he performed Episcopal acts in the Fair City. The evidence on which this conclusion is based is as follows. Writing on *October 7th, 1721*, he first mentions "the verie long expedition I have made throughout that too vast district, which is assigned me," and then adds :—"And not only that, but I launched out farther *through a great part of Perthshire*, but this at the importunitie of parents and children, and of the Clergy, who has the care of them." It seems all the more likely that this "launching out" beyond his own District included Perth itself, because he goes on to say that "the Presbiters in and about Perth petitioned for a Bishop." The position of our Congregation, therefore seems to have been this, that, while taking the "College" and "Anti-Usage" side, they were, in the days of Bishop Falconer, so skilfully treated that they both allowed him, in some capacity or another, to confirm the children belonging to them, and also begged him to use his influence with the "College" to assign them a particular Bishop for their neighbourhood, in something of the same way in which they had assigned Bishop Fullarton to the (not Diocese! but) District of Edinburgh.

Confident, therefore, that Bishop Falconer was to a certain extent officially connected with our City, we give the following glimpse of the worthy Father's Episcopal attire. It is interesting, not only for its extreme quaintness, but also for the light which it throws upon the subject of the vestments of the Scottish Prelates at this period. When, indeed, Archbishop Sharpe and his colleagues were consecrated in Westminster Abbey in 1661, they wore the Rochet and Chimere, and again when the rest of the Scottish Prelates were raised to the Episcopate at Holyrood in 1662, the Archbishop and his assistants were similarly habited. Moreover (if we may argue from a portrait reproduced by the Rev. J. B. Craven in his *History of the Church in Orkney*, 1662-89), Bishop Honeyman used to wear the Surplice and Scarf. It is certain also that a Mitre and Crosier were conspicuous objects in the funeral procession of Archbishop Sharpe after his murder in 1679. So that we must conclude that it was not objection to the Episcopal attire, as such, that caused the Scottish Bishops to lay it aside, but their policy of moderation and conciliation in strictly non-essential ecclesiastical affairs. Still they did for the greater part allow it to fall into disuse, and the black gown became the mark of the Episcopal Clergy of all ranks, as blue seems to have been that of the moderate Presbyterians, and brown that of the extreme Covenanters. The Bishops, however, as was becoming, retained a distinctive habit for themselves in addition to the black gown, and this was the Cassock. Here, therefore, we find Bishop Falconer, who had hitherto concealed his Episcopal rank, waxing bolder, and on *March 11th, 1719*, saying:— " I now have taken the courage again to wear a Cassock, which is not excepted against by any (for ought I know), and approven by many: but, though I want not a girdle, yet it is so heavie that I cannot easilie travel (walk) with it, and therefore Mistress Berrie, I suppose, will project some convenient easie one for mee; it might be some strong, broad, black ribband, which may surround mee twice, and then have knobs, or some such ends, which I cannot express, through want of the terms of art. . . . *Sober pageantrie wants not its usefulness.*"

Unfortunately our Prelate did not long survive to fill the position, which he held after the death of Bishop Rose. Forty years after his ordination as Priest (*May 19th, 1683*), fifteen after his secret elevation to the Episcopate in Bishop Douglas's house at Dundee, and scarcely three years after his election to the District, he departed this life. The *Postboy* of

A Contested Election.

July 25th, 1723, contained the following notice :—*
"On *Saturday, 6th* inst., died John Falconer, D.D., much lamented. He was a gentleman well born, being a descendent of Lord Halkerstoun's family. . . . He was made Rector of Carnbee in Fife. . . . He was a gentleman endued with great meekness, moderation, and charity, . . of good natural parts, and great learning. He always applied himself more particularly to the study of the Holy Scriptures and the writings of the early Fathers : in both he was a great proficient. . . . He was calm, serene, and uniform under the pressure of very narrow circumstances."

His death was the letting out of waters. With great tact he had been able to keep the controversy in its initial stages within bounds throughout, and even beyond, his District. But now, the person who united them being gone, the two parties came into open conflict. The crux, of course, was found in the appointment of a successor. The "College" party, acting in obedience to the exiled Prince's agent, Lockhart of Carnwath, submitted to the Rev. Robert Norrie, "an ancient Presbyter of Dundee," as their nominee. Probably a more unsuitable choice could not have been made. Here was a district, in which quite one-half of the leading Clergy and Laity were "Diocesans" and "Usagers," and, of all people to force upon them, the nominee of the Prince, a man, who had resisted not merely the Usages but the English *Prayer Book* itself, and had long held out for the retention of *ex tempore* forms, was the most unfortunate. On their side, the other party put forward the Rev. Dr. Rattray of Craighall, who was not only a man of

* See *Scottish Ecclesiastical Journal*, 1853, p. 78 (Article by Canon Bright, D.D.).

position in the District, but the most learned and respected theologian then serving in the Scottish Church. He was the very Achilles of the "Diocesans" and "Usagers." When the matter came to the vote, each side was practically equal to the other. The case was argued out before a meeting of the Bishops in Edinburgh. Dr. Rattray, backed by Lord Panmure, made a very powerful defence of his claim, but the decision was given in favour of Mr. Norrie, he being the Bishops' own candidate. He was, therefore, consecrated about the beginning of winter, 1724.

It was one thing, however, to consecrate him, and another to settle him in his District against the protests of an influential half of the Clergy and people. Accordingly we learn from Mr. Sempill that "Craighall has declined his Ordinar's authority. . . . Bishop Norrie indeed meets with a great many provoking things" (*September 23rd, 1725*). Dr. Rattray himself writes on *October 29th, 1726*, about "the hardship of endeavouring to impose Bishops upon a Clergy against their consent." And, besides his theological bias against the Collegians, he gives a very good commonsense ground for opposing Bishop Norrie's party, and writes thus :—"It is surprising to think that they will not consider how much they are at the mercy of the present Government, who, though otherwise they seem willing to overlook them, yet cannot but be provoked at their acting so openly and avowedly by authority from abroad. And, if by this way of doing they shall pull down a persecution upon the Church, how can they answer it to God ?"

Perth, indeed, seems to have recognised Bishop Norrie, but his cause did not make way, and Dr. Rattray's did. The former was probably already in bad health and unfit for the struggle; and the latter, as appears from a letter of Mr. Sempill's (*May 9th, 1726*), gained the adhesion of Lord Strathmore, or at least detached him from Bishop Norrie's side. Already, on *February 22nd, 1726*, Mr. Sempill makes a suggestion that a meeting should be held in Perth to consider a new election, and, after the meeting was over, he wrote in April:—"At the Perth meeting, Logie Drummond said: 'There was a necessity to take in Craighall.'" And before the year was out, or at least in the beginning of 1727, the position was simplified by the death of Bishop Norrie.

CHAPTER XII.

HOW THE LAST YEARS OF THE REV. H. MURRAY'S INCUMBENCY WERE PASSED, 1727-1735.

SOLELY by virtue of Prince James's nomination, and without any election, the College Prelates consecrated John Ochterlony (Presbyter of Aberlemno),* and proposed to thrust him into the vacant See. But what were Dr. Rattray's thoughts upon the subject? He considered it a matter of life and death that another Collegian and Anti-Usager should not be forced upon the District. Bishop Gadderar of Aberdeen was now the only Usager Prelate in Scotland.† If he were to be taken away the "Diocesans" would be absolutely unrepresented amongst the Bishops. At all costs a "Usager" must be elected and consecrated. Then, perhaps, there might be some hope of rescuing the Church from absolute subservience to the (exiled) civil power; some hope of restoring the Catholic system of Diocesan Episcopacy; of asserting the elective power of the Clergy ; and of adopting a Liturgy agreeable to primitive models. With two Diocesan Prelates the attainment of these things would at least not be hopeless.

A favourable omen preceded the election. Fullarton, Bishop of Edinburgh, and successor of Bishop Rose as Vicar-General of S. Andrews, died at the age of 87. Now, he was a "Collegian"; but the Presbyters of Edinburgh, contrary to the Prince's wishes, elected Bishop Millar to succeed him. And, consequently, the latter saw fit to abandon the College and join the Diocesan

* See page 28.   † Bishop Campbell lived in London.

Election of Bishop Rattray.

party. Our election was therefore proceeded with at a time, when the quasi-metropolitan Bishop of Edinburgh and the Bishop of Aberdeen were Diocesans. These two were almost immediately joined by Bishop Cant. If a Usager, therefore, were carried, there was the canonical number of Bishops willing to consecrate.

And so our election was proceeded with. On *May 12th, 1727*, Dr. Rattray writes:—"I conclude Bishop Millar will cheerfully concur in consecrating the elect of Murray, and the person who shall be elected to *this* district, which they are just now going about, and will in a few days be finished." On *May 17th* he announces the result to his friend Mr. Keith:—"The election in this district is very near finished, and a *considerable majority of the Presbyters have been pleased to make choice of me*; the rest, who are but a third of our number, having only taken it into further consideration, three, or at most four, of them only excepted, who were for referring it to what they call the College." Of the three or four who thus declined to vote for Dr. Rattray, Mr. Murray of Perth was evidently one, but how far he acted on his own views, and how far on those of his Lay Managers, is not so certain.

The election of his friend, Mr. Dunbar, to Moray, and of himself to Angus, Mearns, and that part of Perthshire which lies to the east of the Tay,* was described by our Bishop-elect as "a great opportunity for the peace of the Church." There was thus at last the prospect of the "Usagers" being a powerful minority on the Episcopal bench.

On *June 4th, 1727*, though not without protests from the College party, Dr. Rattray was consecrated

* *N.B.*—From this time Bishop Rattray called himself *Bishop of Brechin*.

in Edinburgh by Primus Millar, assisted by Bishops Gadderar and Cant. They then proceeded, by rather a stretch of their authority, to nominate and consecrate the Rev. Robert Keith as Coadjutor* to the Primus, and so the *Usagers* now numbered five Prelates in their ranks, as against seven *Anti-Usagers*.

Dr. Rattray at once returned to his district in the character of its Bishop. For some years, indeed, he was unable altogether to make good his position. As far as our scanty records allow us to judge, the Perth managers were the chief thorn in his side. On *July 7th* he writes to Bishop Keith :—" I visited several worthy families in that country (Strathearn), and endeavoured to state our case in a true light to them, which I hope may not want its effect in due time. As to the Clergy there, I thought it to no purpose to speak to Mr. Murray in Perth . . nor to Mr. Drummond, who is with Sir John Moncrieffe." The latter Presbyter was, not only with Sir John Moncrieffe, but also, either now or else a year or two later, became Mr. Murray's colleague in Perth. The Bishop goes on to say that there were only three more Clergymen, who followed the Perth example of opposition to him, and refers to other three as doubtful. This gives five clerics opposing, three doubtful, and the rest favourable. What the actual number of the latter was does not appear, but the total was probably much the same as at the election of Bishop Falconer, which was 27. This would give the Bishop a majority of at least 19 against 8, which was more than ample. Mr. Charles White of Dundee informs us that our Prelate had "a great

* But down even to the middle of the present century it used to be thought that Bishops had the right of nominating their own Coadjutors.

majority of the Presbyters of the District." Compared, therefore, with the reception given to his predecessor, Bishop Norrie, his entrance upon his Diocese may be called triumphant. The attempt of the College to thrust in Bishop Ochterlonie was thus a failure.

For some years after Bishop Rattray's settlement as successor to Bishop Falconer and Bishop Norrie, there is almost a complete dearth of local Perth records. Almost but not quite. One suggestive assertion in the *Kilmavœnig MS.* remains to us. It is there recorded that a Committee of those in the Town who, we know, were favourable to the new Bishop (and these included some of the Managers themselves), was appointed in 1728 "*to receive the rights of the Meeting-House from Corbs.*" This does not appear to be a very illuminative statement at first sight : but, as a matter of fact, a good deal may be inferred from it. It shews *first* that there were two parties in the Perth Congregation. And what two can they have been but Usagers and Anti-Usagers ? *Secondly*, that the title-deeds of the Chapel were in the hands of Mr. Blair of Corbs, as representing the " Collegians " and " Anti-Usagers." *Thirdly*, that at this time the " Diocesans " and " Usagers " were making an effort to obtain the official custody of the documents. And, if we ask why they were trying to do so at this period, it is clear that their object was the recognition of Bishop Rattray. Probably they thought that after both preceding Prelates had obtained at least some kind of recognition in the City, it was wrong to make such an opposition to their successor, as that it was useless for him to call on Mr. Murray when he was going the round of his District. Most likely also they wished for the complete recognition of Bishop Rattray as Bishop of the Diocese, and not only the incomplete recognition which had been accorded to his two predecessors. And the mere fact that an influential section of the Congregation were advocating submission to our Bishop, viewed in connection with the other fact that the meetings concerning a successor to Bishop Norrie were held at Perth in 1726, seems to shew that our Congregation by taking part in the election had practically admitted that this City was to be in the District of the new Bishop. Thus Bishop Rattray, besides being welcomed by "a vast majority of the Presbyters," had also a certain hold over Perth, where two out of the five Clergy who actively opposed him lived.

Mr. Blair, however, did not give up the title deeds, and there is no record surviving to show that the Bishop pressed his claims further at present. But he exercised his office in the neighbourhood of our City, as the following extract from one of his letters shews. On *July 16th, 1727*, he writes to Bishop Keith :—" You may remember I told you the Laird of Balgowan spoke to me at Edinburgh to provide him in a Chaplain. He renewed his desire, when I saw him the other day. I must therefore beg of you that you will do your utmost, as soon as possible, to look out a right one for him. A young man might live very easily there, and have the advantage of a pretty good collection of books. I think I may procure a £15 for him, which, though but small, is better in the country and in a family than much more in a town, where he had himself to maintain. That, which makes me so pressing with you to assist me in this, as soon as you can, is that a lad of tolerable prudence and right principles would do more service in that country, if got in time, than you may imagine." This

The Concordate.

last remark probably has reference to the Bishop's relations with Perth.

At last the unhappy disputes, which for nine years or more had been dividing the Church, received a settlement in 1731. It was a settlement, indeed, which nearly broke down more than once in the Church at large, and actually did so in the case of Perth; but it was so far successful that it preserved the "Usager" and "Anti-Usager" Prelates in union, until the latter were all removed by death. It came about thus:—The Bishops, "seriously laying to heart the great danger they were in by their unhappy divisions," determined to come to an agreement amongst themselves. A meeting was accordingly held in Edinburgh, at which a *Concordate* was signed with practical unanimity. We must not occupy our space by giving a complete account of it; but, as regards the "College" question, the Collegians yielded, so as to allow Scotland to be divided into ten Dioceses, and to recognize the principle of election, while the "Diocesans" yielded so far as to agree that the Presbyters were not to proceed to elect without a mandate from the Primus, and no one was to be consecrated without the consent of a majority of the Bishops. All metropolitical claim was to be dropped, and the office of *Primus* substituted. As regards the "Usage" controversy, the compromise arrived at was that "only the Scottish or English *Liturgies* should be used." If we lament the differences that distracted the Church in the second quarter of the eighteenth century, let us at least note this *Concordate* with thankfulness. That no such agreement was come to amongst the Presbyterians is evident by the still separate existence of the U.P. Church.

But, besides these widespread effects of the Compromise, it had particular results in our neighbourhood, Bishop Rattray agreed to yield up his title "Bishop of Brechin" to Bishop Ochterlonie; and it was arranged instead, that the Diocese of *Dunkeld*, together with the whole Presbyteries of Meigle and Forfar, *the town of Perth*, and parish of Methven, shall be under the inspection of Bishop Rattray." Thus our Prelate now had a position recognized by the unanimous voice of the Episcopate,—and not only by theirs, but also by that of the locality, which had been assigned to him. To begin with, a meeting of three Bishops (Rattray, the great Usager; Ochterlonie of Dundee, the staunch Anti-Usager; and Gillan of Dunblane, who now inclined to Bishop Rattray's views) was held at Perth in 1732. At this meeting a satisfactory understanding was come to between the three Prelates concerning the outlines of their Dioceses and other subjects. And it is pleasant to relate that Bishop Rattray undertook an expedition into Bishop Ochterlonie's district, in order to persuade the "Usagers" there to submit to their "Anti-Usager" Diocesan. For this Bishop Ochterlonie thanked him.

"Then," says Bishop Rattray, "I must take the properest method I can think of for getting myself as regularly settled in my own District as possible." This must be taken as an allusion more particularly to Perth. A section of the Managers there were almost the only people who had not submitted; but now they felt themselves at last obliged to do so. In a paper, written some years later for the purpose of explaining away the Bishop's authority, they are obliged to speak thus concerning the present time:—"The Bishops were prevailed upon to restore (*sic*) to him his Episcopate, *and the gentlemen of Perth thought themselves likewise*

Bishop Rattray Leads the Church.

under some obligation to follow the example, and in some measure *acknowledged his authority.*" And ensuing acts shew that they acknowledged him not only theoretically, but practically also.

Dr. Rattray was now therefore recognised by the entire Episcopate of the Scottish Church, the Presbyterate of the Diocese, and the Congregations of the same, as Bishop of Dunkeld. The disputes, which had raged in our neighbourhood since good Bishop Falconer's death in 1723, were thus terminated by a definite treaty of peace.

For a year or two things seem to have gone on with tolerable quietness. In 1735, however, the latent differences again revealed themselves. All the Bishops continued, indeed, to be loyal to the Concordate; but, when Bishop Gillan of Dunblane died, and the Rev. Robert White was elected by the Clergy to succeed him, there was a misunderstanding as to whether the Primus (Freebairn of Edinburgh, an Anti-Usager), whose office had been established by the Concordate, and who was supported by Bishop Ochterlonie, or the majority of the Bishops (Rattray, Dunbar, and Keith, who were Usagers), ought to manage affairs. In the end the majority visited Pitscandly, near Forfar, and consecrated the Bishop-elect in the Rev. Mr. Guthrie's neighbouring Chapel at Carsebank. This controversy had, before long, some bearing upon Perth. Meantime our Prelate's position was certainly becoming a strong one. There were now four Usager Bishops, and only two Anti-Usagers, and he was the leader of the Usagers. In Perth itself also his authority was acquiesced in quietly —at least from the time of the Concordate (1731) to the end of the period embraced in this chapter (1735). The only local notice of these years which has come down to us, is of a sufficiently peaceful character, and runs as follows :—"I will, by no means," writes the Bishop, "have the shares of the Presbyters under my inspection remitted to me; but, so soon as I am informed what each of them is to have, and I receive a form of the receits they are to give, I shall acquaint them to send up their receits to the place required, and call for their money there."

Amid these circumstances the Rev. Henry Murray died in 1735. He had been Incumbent of Perth between 1703 and 1716. Between the latter year and 1721 he disappeared from our City; but from 1721 till his death he was again Incumbent here. It speaks well for him that he should have been invited to return to the City after a residence of thirteen years there, and an absence of five. We have scarcely materials whereby to form an estimate of his character. On the one hand he seems to have played a very courageous part on behalf of the Church previous to 1712. On the other, Bishop Rattray speaks of him in his latter years, in terms which lead us to suppose that he was then entirely led by the Managers of the Congregation in their extreme Anti-Usager attitude. Perhaps circumstances beyond his own control rendered him too dependent on them for his means of subsistence. Upon the whole he appears to have rendered very faithful service to the Church in extremely difficult times.

CHAPTER XIII.

HOW THE REV. ROBERT LYON WAS SETTLED IN PERTH, 1735-39.

THE Rev. Laurence Drummond was now by the death of his colleague left in sole charge of the Congregation in the Fair City. Unfortunately, as we are told, "he was but a valetudinary man." It was considered necessary, therefore, that he should be provided with an assistant. Without consulting the Bishop, the "gentlemen of the Meeting-House" bestirred themselves in the matter. During the long and unself-assertive Incumbency of Mr. Murray, they had evidently come to absorb a good many of the Episcopal prerogatives, and now it is evident that the Anti-Usagers amongst them were eager to make such an appointment that there would be no chance of these prerogatives reverting to the Bishop. They, therefore (in their own words), "grant commission to Mr. Drummond to look out for a pious, discreet, and peaceable man to supply the vacancy." Fortunately for Mr. Drummond's repose of mind (for he seems to have been a very quiet, retiring man), he received a commission from the Bishop to exactly the same effect. "Accordingly," continue the Managers, "after some days' deliberation he proposed Mr. John Graeme of Souterton, who was very well known to all the gentlemen concerned, and readily approven by them." This Presbyter was the Anti-Usager Incumbent of Dunning, and what follows leads us to suppose that, like the Rev. H. Murray in Perth, his private views were not of a very pronounced character, but that, owing probably to being dependent on his Lay Managers for his living, he was a docile instrument in their hands. We know exactly how he felt when the offer from Perth arrived, for the Rev. Mr. Erskine of Muthill writes thus to the Rev. John Alexander of Alloa :—" My neighbour, Mr. Graeme's, congregation at Dunning are still unanimous in standing out against their Bishop (White), but I'm told himself is now determined to acknowledge him, and having both Leith and Perth in his offer, he is difficulted which to accept, but certainly, as he gives out, one of them." Accordingly, on *December 10th, 1735*, a letter was received from Mr. Graeme intimating his willingness to come to Perth. Seeing that he was now ready to submit both to his present and intended Bishops, and also agreeable to the Managers, Bishop Rattray was ready to accept him. This appears from a letter which he wrote privately to Bishop Keith, *December 20th, 1735* :—" He is a sincere, good man," he says, " but timorous, and has no courage to stand his ground even in what he thinks to be right, when he sees himself likely to meet with any opposition ; however, I have very prudential reasons for acquiescing in their choice of him." No doubt the Bishop was delighted to accept a man acceptable to both himself and the Managers. However, this promising arrangement was upset by Mr. Graeme's "timorousness" and the overbearingness of the Dunning Managers. They brought pressure to bear on him, and induced him to withdraw his intended submission to the Bishops, and to remain where he was. "So," says Bishop Rattray, "he gave the Perth people the slip."

Whereupon our Managers, evidently labouring under the false idea that the Bishop had wilfully baffled them, "pitched on Mr. David Fyffe of Glenboy, and invited him to Perth. He preached, and gave entire satisfaction." However, the negotiations with him also miscarried, and with a view to understanding the real motives of the actors in our drama, and of estimating the share of each in the serious result, to which these events were leading up, it is important that we should relate Mr. Fyffe's affair. In a long letter (*February 22nd, 1736*) to Bishop Keith, Bishop Rattray explains what occurred. It appears that it did not please the Managers to send any intimation to the Bishop that they had opened correspondence with Mr. Fyffe. Now, it so happened that at this very time he received an application from Lady Mary Lyon to allow Mr. Fyffe to add Glamis and Eassie to his present charge of Glenboy. Of course, along with the application an offer of a substantial increase of salary was also made. Having had no intimation from the Perth Managers of what they were doing, the Bishop acceded to Lady Mary Lyon's request, and promised her that effect should be given to her proposal. Thereupon he was at last informed that the Perth Managers had fixed upon Mr. Fyffe for themselves. It was most unfortunate, but he could not break faith with Lady Mary Lyon. He says distinctly that he "apologised" to the Managers. And there is every reason for believing that his apology was sincere, for what ground have we for supposing that he should be manœuvring so as to prevent the settlement of one of his own Clergy in the important but semi-disaffected Congregation of Perth? Nevertheless, he received a "saucy" reply to the effect that "no landward parish whatsoever was to be put in competition with" the Fair City, and much more to the same effect.

So far was the Bishop from wishing to gain an open triumph over the Perth Managers in the matter of the appointment of a colleague to Mr. Drummond, that on *April 24th* we find him writing to his confidential friend, Bishop Keith :—" I shall be very well pleased to have Forbes* at Perth, but I must not be seen in it." By this he seems to imply that he would rather accept a nominee of the Managers, than try to force a candidate of his own upon them.

Coming now to the year 1738, the latter, in their " Narrative," go on to say :—" A gentleman occasionally passing through the town proposed to some of the Managers to take a trial of Mr. Robert Lyon, who had been a short time before Deaconat ; and, as Mr. Drummond was but a valetudinary man, they were easily induced to do so. But they previously wrote to a Reverend and very worthy Clergyman to know his character, and particularly with regard to the Usages, whose answer left them no room to suspect him, and accordingly we took him to Mr. Drummond's assistance." It was the Managers, therefore, and not the Bishop, who brought Mr. Lyon to Perth, and it was " a Reverend and very worthy Clergyman," a friend of their own, and not Mr. Lyon himself, who induced them to believe that he was not inclined to the Usages. This is their own account of the matter.

Who was this Deacon that now steps prominently forward in the Church affairs of Perth ?† The individual

* Possibly Rev. Robert Forbes, afterwards Bishop of Ross.

† He must not be confused with another Rev. Robert Lyon, who was also a friend of Bishop Rattray: Incumbent of Crail at least as early as 1732 ; appeared as Bishop Dunbar's proxy at the Edinburgh Synod of 1738 ; subsequently went to reside in Stretton at Bedfordshire ; saw Bishop Rattray's *Liturgies* through the press, 1744 ; corresponded with Bishop Alexander in 1750; sent that Prelate money from Mr. Bowdler ; and died in 1764.

Settlement of Mr. Lyon. 135

who best answers to the description which he gives of his father, is the Rev. James Lyon, a native of Forfarshire, who was ordained under the patronage of the Earl of Strathmore ; appointed to the Charge of Kirkwall ; wrote a vigorous pamphlet in defence of Episcopacy there, which is still extant ; and was finally ejected from his living subsequent to the Revolution. But it is only a conjecture that he was really the father of the Clergyman who now settled in Perth. A ring in possession of Miss Christian Bruce of Dunimarle, containing some relic of Mr. Lyon, gives us to understand that he was 29 years of age on his appointment, and therefore he must have been born in 1709 or 1710. We learn that he had no brothers, but two or three sisters. Cicely seems to have been his favourite of these, but the whole family appear to have lived happily together. He gives the following account of his early years :—" I have the honour," he says, " to be descended from one of those Clergymen who unhappily survived our flourishing Church and prosperous Nation at the late Revolution (1688), by which means it was my lot, through the wise providence of God, to be early trained up in the school of adversity, inasmuch as my father underwent the common fate of our other spiritual pastors and dear fathers in Christ, who were by merely secular and, what is worse, unlawful force, thrust away from their charges, and deprived of that maintenance to which they had a general and divine right, as well as a legal title by our constitution. . . . . Into this once glorious but now declining part of the Church Catholic, I was, through the care and loving piety of my loving parents, entered by a holy Baptism. . . .
I received a liberal and pious education through the

goodness and care of Heaven, manifested in the wonderful
support and preservation of our family, though my father,
worn out with sufferings, lived not to see it half completed."
Under the calamitous circumstances of the Church, and
after observing his parent's fate, it would have been ex-
cusable in young Lyon if he had prudently selected to
enter upon another line than that of the Ministry of the
afflicted Church; "but," says he, "it clearly appeared upon
impartial enquiry that this Church, for purity of doctrine,
orthodoxy in the faith, perfection of worship, and her
apostolic government, equals, if not excels, any other
Church on earth. Therefore, I persisted by the Divine
Grace, an unworthy member in her faithful communion
till . . . at length arrived at that age,* when, by
the Canons of the Church, I could be admitted to
Holy Orders, which I received at a time when no
earthly motive could influence me but a sincere intention to serve God, and to my power to do good
offices to men." This was the individual who, now
with the Bishop's consent, was settled in Perth by our
Managers as Mr. Drummond's colleague. On *November
15th, 1739*, we find him present at a general meeting
of the Congregation. The final arrangements for his
stipend are not without interest. "At the earnest desire of
the Rev. L. Drummond," we read, "that Mr. Lyon, his colleague, ought to be gratified for the extraordinary trouble
he has got, and may get hereafter, through the said Mr.
Drummond's infirm state of health, the meeting do unanimously appoint James Bayne, their Treasurer, immediately
to pay to the said Mr. Lyon the sum of £5 sterling,
and agreed and resolved that hereafter his salary shall
be £30 sterling yearly, to commence from Martinmas last.

* It is difficult to harmonize this statement of his age with the
inscription on the Dunimarle Ring.

CHAPTER XIV.

HOW THERE WAS A SCHISM IN THE PERTH CONGREGATION, 1740.

IT was now evident that a crisis was approaching in our Congregation. The *Concordate* of 1731, indeed (strained as it was at times), availed to keep the "Usager" and "Anti-Usager" Bishops together, and so the unity of the Scottish Church at large was always successfully preserved. But the two parties were still facing one another in Perth with jealous feelings. On the one side were ranged seven of the Managers, *i.e.*, Messrs. Davidson, Blair of Corbs, Dr. John Murray, James Oliphant, Wood, Keir, and Young. These were the "Anti-Usagers." Confirmation itself seems to have been regarded by them as one of the Usages, since Mr. Davidson had never received that Apostolic ordinance. They looked upon the distinction between the Church and the Presbyterians more as one of taste than of principle, and their conduct leads us to suppose that they rather viewed Bishops and Clergy as the *employés* of a religious society managed by themselves, than as persons inheriting a spiritual commission derived from Christ. The leaders on the other side were the Revs. L. Drummond and R. Lyon; four Managers, *i.e.*, Dr. Carmichael, and Messrs. Smith,* Stirling, and "Dowhill;" also Lady Stormont, and James Bayn, the Treasurer. These were the "Usagers," that is, as a party they looked upon Bishops of the Apostolical line as essential to the visible Church, and while satisfied

* Probably the son of the late Rev. W. Smith.

to confine themselves to the English *Book of Common Prayer* for the sake of unity with the others, would prefer that the *Scottish Eucharistic Office* should come into use. A *modus vivendi* might, indeed, have been found between these two parties in Perth, as it was amongst the Bishops, but unfortunately it appears that the personal equation was allowed free scope in the situation here.

If we regard this combination of parties in the congregation as a heap of fuel, then we may take the Rev. Robert Lyon as the spark which set them all ablaze. His first offence seems to have been that he obtained Priest's Orders from the Bishop without previously receiving the consent of the Lay Managers. Then, Mr. Drummond being very infirm, the practical work of the Congregation was gathered up more and more into his hands. Then it was discovered that the Communion tokens were marked with "R. L." instead of "L. D." He next began to vent some of his Usage doctrines, though he "often couched them, being afraid to be too plain at first." Worst of all, he is said to "have advocated private Confession. This most of his hearers took (but mistakenly, as Mr. Lyon would, no doubt, have said) to be the same with the auricular Confession of the Church of Rome." And there were more such accusations.

Hence sprang a conflagration. We need not follow all the windings of the dispute. It is evident that in Mr. Lyon the Managers found that they had not the same pliable material to deal with as they had been accustomed to in Mr. Murray and Mr. Drummond, and, though nothing whatever to the real discredit of Mr. Lyon emerges, it is not improbable that in his youthful enthusiasm, he may not always have displayed that consummate tact, which his difficult position required, and of which we had so eminent an example in Bishop Falconer. On the other hand, the Managers were overbearing and most unecclesiastical in their views. They certainly displayed fully as much want of tact as Mr. Lyon, in that they were absolutely intolerant of a little unbalanced enthusiasm (if it was so) in a young man only recently admitted to Holy Orders.

It is consoling to find the Bishop playing a firm and dignified part. His conduct is thus described by the disaffected Managers:—" Craighall now came to Perth and called a meeting of the gentlemen of both sides, to whom he communicated himself in terms to this purpose; that he was sorry to hear of the divisions that had for some time prevailed amongst us, and he should think himself lucky if he could be the happy instrument of removing them. To compass which, he made a proposal that both parties should submit their whole disputes to two or four gentlemen to be mutually chosen, and become obliged to adhere to the determination of these arbiters." Nothing, surely, could have been juster or more becoming his Episcopal character under the circumstances. In an ordinary case, of course, he himself ought to have been the arbiter, but, seeing that he might be supposed to be biased on the particular question at issue, it was a wise thing to waive his own right, and propose to hand the matter over to umpires chosen equally by both sides.

Mr. Lyon's friends were, of course, willing to abide by the Bishop's ruling, but the seven Managers, as if thinking that they would belie their title, if they allowed the supreme control to slip in any degree out of their own hands, scornfully rejected the proposition.

A very awkward problem now came up. "Esther" (Easter) was at hand, and it was out of the question that the two warring factions should approach the Altar together, without the re-establishment of mutual charity. The Bishop therefore ruled that "only those should be admitted, who were willing to accept his peaceable mediation." The Corbsites, who had already repudiated both their Priests, threw their Bishop over for the second time, and never so much as hinted of appealing to the Episcopal bench. However anxious we may be to do them justice, it is difficult to see wherein their Episcopalian principles lay. It was, at any rate, impossible for them to receive the Holy Sacrament at the hands of those, whose authority they defied. And they did not. The Schism was complete! Whatever was wanting to consummate it, was speedily supplied by the seceding party. "They were so lucky," they say, "as to prevail upon the Rev. George Sempill to accept the charge." This Presbyter, who came from Newtyle, was, as we have already seen in Bishop Norrie's time, an extreme partisan on the Anti-Usager side. It is not easy to understand how he could imagine that Mr. Blair of Corbs and his partners could give him spiritual mission in opposition to the Bishop of the Diocese. But, indeed, he adopted their schismatical situation with zeal. It appears that Mr. Lyon, thinking, most likely, that in the present exasperated state of feeling, some one other than himself would be more acceptable, exchanged duty temporarily with the Rev. David Lindsay of Dunning. When, however, the latter presented himself at the Perth Meeting-House with a view to officiating, the door was locked in his face.

What was it becoming for the Bishop to do under the circumstances? Here was Mr. Sempill, a Presbyter, coming without leave into his Diocese; joining with those who had recently defied his jurisdiction; officiating without a license, and locking the door of their Chapel upon one of the regular Clergy! Would he have been fulfilling his duty, if he had let all this pass? He, at least, did not think so. On the contrary, he characterised Mr. Sempill's conduct as "such an encroachment on the rights of his brethren, such a violation of order, and such an insult on the authority of the Church, as, if it should be allowed to pass unpunished, would render us despicable in the eyes of men of all persuasions." His own opinion was that sentence of deposition should be pronounced. But, before proceeding to such an extremity, he wrote to consult the other Bishops, *i.e.*, Keith, Ochterlonie, Dunbar, and White. The second (who was now, since the death of Bishop Freebairn in 1739, the only surviving Prelate of the "College" party), characteristically replied that he recommended a trial before the College of Bishops. The other three strongly recommended Bishop Rattray to depose Sempill on his own authority.

He therefore summoned the erring Presbyter to appear before him at a certain place and hour in Perth. Instead of preparing a proper defence, the course, which the latter took without apprizing his Diocesan, was to obtain a promise from the Town Council that they would have officers in waiting to disperse the Bishop's meeting. Having heard of this plan, and ascertaining from the Provost himself that he had not been misinformed, our Prelate took pains that Sempill should receive a second summons, this time to Scone. "Indeed," he says *(August 18th, 1740)*, "had not my Lady Stormont offered us the use of the house of Scone, we had been very much put to it." The accused, however, did not appear, and on the next day the Bishop writes to Bishop Keith :—" I was obliged yesterday to proceed to the deposition of Mr. George Sempill. I would most willingly have taken a milder course, but you will see by the whole process . . . . that there was a necessity for doing it, and that without further loss of time." The Presbyters of the Diocese, with hardly an exception, approved of the course taken by the Bishop.

And it is difficult for us not to endorse their opinion. That in the complete break down of Church organization, which followed the Disestablishment and the rising of 1715, and that during the period of controversy concerning the form in which the Church was to be re-habilitated (1720-1731), the lay Managers of a particular Congregation should have gathered the supreme ecclesiastical power into their own hands, is not to be wondered at, and may be excused. Far be it from us to judge men hardly, who lived in such difficult times. But that, after Bishop Rattray had been not only received as Diocesan by the Clergy and Congregations of the District, but also unanimously recognised as such by the bench of Bishops in 1731, and submitted to by the Managers themselves,—that, after all this, rebellion should be declared against him, appears to be plainly inexcusable. There is no misconduct recorded on his part sufficient to justify such a course, and, therefore, we are forced to the conclusion that the disaffected Managers and the Rev. George Sempill were guilty of Schism.

"Remember not, Lord, our offences, nor the offences of our forefathers, neither take Thou vengeance on our sins, but spare us, good Lord, spare Thy people, whom Thou hast redeemed with Thy most precious blood, and be not angry with us for ever! Spare us, good Lord!"

CHAPTER XV.

HOW BISHOP RATTRAY BECAME PRIMUS, DIED, AND WAS SUCCEEDED, 1738-44.

THE local Schism, described in the last chapter, reached its crisis, as we saw, at Easter, 1740, and was rendered irrevocable a few months later. In the next chapter all that is known of the two congregations, between 1740 and 1745, will be related. Meanwhile, we must anticipate part of the time to be subsequently dealt with, and give our attention to events which, though seriously affecting Perth, relate rather to the Diocese at large.

(1).—In the year 1738 an Episcopal Synod was held in Edinburgh. Since 1735, when Bishop Rattray, as leader of the majority of the Bishops, had, without the concurrence of Primus Freebairn, consecrated the Rev. R. White as Bishop of Dunblane, the situation had been uncomfortable. To have one man officially Primus, and another, who was the strongest and ablest on the bench, leader of the majority, was an unsatisfactory arrangement. It was the object of the new Synod to find a solution of the problem. When it came to be held, the decision actually arrived at, though not without difficulty, was that Bishop Freebairn should be superseded as Primus by Bishop Rattray. This decision, which was supported by Bishops Rattray, Keith, and White, who were present, and Dunbar, who voted by proxy, and was opposed by Bishops Freebairn and Ochterlony, was based on a reference to the terms of the *Concordate* of 1731, wherein the office of Primus had been substituted for that of Metropolitan. It is possible that the action of this majority may have appeared a little masterful, since the terms of the *Concordate* were not absolutely beyond doubt on the point, and we can hardly be surprised that Bishop Freebairn protested. But, on the other hand, practical necessity required that the vigorous leader of the majority of the Bishops should no longer find himself hampered at every turn by the resistance of the aged and infirm Primus, acting on the instigation of the Erastian Bishop Ochterlonie. The spirit of the *Concordate*, and the discussions which had taken place at its ratification, seemed to contemplate such action as had now been taken. And, we may add, the present *Code of Canons* (that of 1890) substantially supports the proceedings of Bishop Rattray's upholders on this occasion (see *Canon XXXI.*, § *4*).

In any case the matter was soon settled by the course of Providence, for Bishop Freebairn died the very next year, at the age of 84. Bishop Rattray then demitted the office of Primus, but, of course, his resignation was not accepted. In 1742 Bishop Ochterlonie also died. For the last three years or so he had been the sole remnant of the "College" party on the bench. The "Usagers" considered that he was "notoriously secular," and it was rather he than Primus Freebairn, who had kept up the opposition to Bishop Rattray and the Usagers since 1731. By his death, therefore, every obstacle was cleared out of the way of our Primus. The position in which the latter now found himself must have been the cause of much legitimate satisfaction to him. His career had been one long struggle against the Collegians and Anti-Usagers. But in that long struggle he was constantly gaining a step, and whenever he did so, he did not again withdraw his foot backwards. At first he appears upon the scene as the supporter of Bishop Falconer (1720-3); on that Prelate's death he comes forward in his room as leader, against Bishop Norrie, of the cause which the former had so ably championed; on this second Prelate's death he is elected to succeed him in Brechin by a majority, though still opposed by a minority of his Clergy and a majority of the Bishops; in 1731 he is unanimously recognised as Diocesan of the Dunkeld District; then in 1733 he becomes the leader of a majority of the Bishops; next, in 1738, he has a disputed election to the Primus-ship; afterwards, in 1739, an undisputed claim to that office; and now the last of his opponents is carried off by death, and he is left master of the situation. It is the career of a strong man, who, in difficult times, knows his own mind and how to give effect to it. But was it the career of an honest man aiming at the good of the Church, or that of an ambitious man scheming for his own exaltation? There is nothing in the preceding narrative, nor in his remaining MSS. letters, to favour the latter supposition, but everything to prove of the former.

Bishop Rattray's inspiring motive is, in fact, clear enough. For he was a man well versed in theological lore, as well as a practical ecclesiastic. His *Essay on the nature of the Church ;* his *Review** *of the Election of Bishops in the Primitive Church ;* his *Essay on the Nature of Man ;* and his *Instructions in the Christian Covenant,* are learned and powerful treatises, which well repay study, and would have brought him great reputation had he belonged to a more popular Communion. His liturgical work also, especially in connection

*In answer to a work entitled *A View of the Election of Bishops.*

with the *Liturgy of S. James*, cannot (according to so high an authority as Bishop Dowden) "be considered as yet superseded, and deserves even now a place in the library of every liturgical student." It may be considered as beyond doubt, therefore, that Bishop Rattray's leading motive was not personal ambition, but the earnest longing of a deeply read theologian to give effect to sound ecclesiastical principles at a time, when an important work of reconstruction was forced upon the Church.

Moreover, he succeeded in realising these high aims. His opponents, indeed, may have thought that he hit them too hard at some critical turning points. It must also be allowed both that he was a Jacobite (if that is a fault), and also that he left the legislative privileges of the Presbyterate unrecognised. But it is unfair (especially when we remember that he never had a free hand till the death of his last Collegian opponent in 1742) to blame him for not accomplishing everything in the disorganised Church. And in several directions he was an invaluable benefactor to the distressed Communion. *First*, it was greatly due to him that the Erastian plan of Royal nomination to vacant Bishoprics was abandoned. *Secondly*, he did not only destroy the wrong, but also contributed largely to the substitution of the right system, namely, election by the Church. *Thirdly*, the vicious College system found in him a victorious adversary, and the primitive Diocesan arrangement a successful champion. *Fourthly*, he conferred a priceless boon directly on the Scottish (and indirectly, therefore, on the American) Church by his labours and studies on behalf of the *Scottish Office*. And *lastly*, although the opportunity of supplying the fatal want of a recognised collection of laws, which necessarily prevailed at that period in the Scottish Church, never came to him during his lifetime, yet he left behind him a proposed *Code of Canons*, which was adopted after his death, and became the basis of our present system.

Alas! this great Prelate was not long spared to enjoy the triumph of his policy. It was in *May, 1742*, that Bishop Ochterlonie died, and on *May 9th, 1743*, the Primus himself took ill in Edinburgh, and passed away on the 12th (*Ascension Day*), in the 60th year of his age. A contemporary poet, Dr. Thomas Drummond of Logicalmond, gives the following account of his end:—

> With unconcern he views th' approaching gloom
> Of sudden Fate, sudden to all but him,
> Whose soul was ever plumed for ready flight
> And longing to depart. With unconcern
> He views the gaping tomb, the coffin, and the shroud,
> (The bugbear fright of infant minds appall'd
> With cowardly pannick). Now with unconcern
> He leaves this giddy world and bids adieu
> To every social tye. And now the scene
> Begins to close. Each wandering thought attend!
> Fancy, be still! Profaneness, drop the page,
> Or read with awe! See there with holy hands;
> His eyes upraised with reverential joy;
> His soul intent on Heav'n; in rapture high
> Of mental pray'r, th' unbloody sacrifice,
> Soul-strengthening food, he takes,—
>
> .   .   .   .   .
>
> He takes, he wonders, he adores, he dies!

"He was a man," says his contemporary, Skinner of Linshart, "whom the Episcopal Church of Scotland will long look back to with a mixture of pleasure and regret: with pleasure in the grateful remembrance of having had such a Bishop, and with a deep regret for having been so soon deprived of him."

(2.)—This eventful Episcopate of sixteen years having been thus concluded, it was necessary for the Clergy to fill the vacant Chair. On *June 28th, 1743*, therefore, "by the invitation of the Very Rev. Mr. William Seton, in Forfar, Dean of the District, a Synod was held in Meigle, in the house of Mr. Peter Laird, to consider the situation." A sense of bereavement is very strongly expressed on the part of the electors in the Minutes of the Meeting. There were ten Clergy present, of whom two, the Revs. Robert Lyon, Perth, and George Innes, Balgowan, were from this immediate neighbourhood.

The Dean having opened proceedings, Mr. Lyon produced a letter from the Rev. Laurence Drummond, nominating him to appear and vote as his proxy. It was addressed to the Dean, and ran as follows :— "Yours* of the 14th I received, and you may believe none is more willing to meet and unite with you and the rest of my Rev. Brethren in such measures as shall be thought proper in our present destitute state. I am very sensible of the great loss the whole Church, as well as we of this District, sustain in the death of the good and the great Bishop Rattray, our late Ordinary, and of the great necessity of having a fit person again set over us as our centre of unity. But I hope the great weakness of body I have long laboured under, will be a sufficient excuse for my not meeting with you and my brethren at the time and place you appoint. Therefore, as I cannot personally attend, I hereby declare that I think it proper that we should, without delay, address the Bishops of this Church for a mandate to elect a proper Bishop for ourselves, and as my brother and colleague, Mr. Lyon, is to meet

* Dunkeld MS. *Diocesan Register.*

with you, who sufficiently knows my mind, so I hereby nominate and appoint him my proxy, and in my name to give his vote for me, as he shall do for himself, in everything that shall come before you. I pray God direct you all, now and at all other times, with His Holy Spirit." Mr. Drummond's suggestion was the finding of the meeting, and a mandate was applied for.

This having been obtained, there was a second meeting held at Meigle on *August 9th*. Here, too, Mr. Lyon was accepted as Mr. Drummond's proxy. The latter wrote :—" I beg you . . . to give my vote for Mr. John Alexander in Alloa, to be our Bishop, he being, as far as I can judge or inform myself, a person eminent for piety, learning, and Catholic principles." This Priest was unanimously elected, and " the Bishops of the National Church" appealed to for Consecration. Accordingly he was raised to the Episcopate on *August 19th* by Bishops Keith, White, Raitt, and W. Falconer.

(3).—While we are dealing with the strictly Episcopal aspect of our local affairs, it will not be out of place to conclude the chapter with the account of a Perth Ordination of this period. It will introduce us to our new Bishop.

There was a young man, Mr. Donald Robertson, belonging to the Perth congregation, whom Primus Keith wished to be ordained for a vacant charge in the Diocese of Glasgow, and in whom Lady Stormont took a great interest. Mr. Lyon, indeed, in his ardent zeal, felt a little uncomfortable about the candidate's Orthodoxy. Bishop W. Falconer writes to Bishop Alexander :—" I am informed that Mr. Robertson has some singularities about him: that he is a great disciple of Mr. Wesley's* in England. I hope the lad's

* Of course, Mr. Wesley was in full Communion with the Church.

piety will be no bar against his promotion, but we should be well assured of his Orthodoxy. My Lady Stormont is much his friend. I wish Mr. Lyon may not disoblige her Ladyship by opposing her views for Mr. Robertson." On this occasion, at least, Mr. Drummond's young colleague seems to have tempered his conduct with discretion, for the course of affairs was allowed to run smoothly as follows :—*April 10th, 1744.*—" At the Synodical Meeting of the Clergy of this District, held in presence and under the direction of the Right Rev. Mr. John Alexander, Bishop of Dunkeld, Perth, etc. (the Meeting being opened by prayer), appeared Mr. Donald Robertson, Student of Divinity in this town, and gave in to the Bishop and Clergy a Testificat written and signed by our Reverend Brother, Mr. Laurence Drummond, Presbyter in Perth, recommending him to them as a person in his judgement fit to be admitted to tryal, in order to his advancement into Holy Orders; which petition the Bishop and his Clergy having taken into their consideration, readily complied therewith, and appointed the said Mr. Donald Robertson to attend the next meeting of Clergy of this District, to be held in the house of the Rev. Mr. James Hill at Blairgowrie, on the 12th of June next, and there to give in a written Discourse in the Latin tongue upon the Christian doctrine of Justification by way of Exegesis: also a written discourse in the method of a Sermon on S. John III., 5 (*' Except a man be born of water,' etc.),* both of his own composition, and to apply himself with diligence, in the meantime, to the reading of the Antiquities of the Christian Church, particularly those of the second and third centuries, that he may be the better prepared to answer such questions as shall be put to him relating to the History, Heresies, and Schisms of that period. Likewise that he shall have his thoughts much employed upon the Canon of Holy Scripture and its Divine Authority, that he may be able to answer such questions as may be put to him relative thereto. That upon a fair and impartial tryal of his qualifications and abilities for the Holy Ministry, he may (if found qualified) be recommended to our Bishop for Ordination."

When we think of the Deism and Rationalism and ignorance of Catholic Antiquity, which characterized the religion of the 18th century, it is indeed refreshing to read such an extract as the above. Here in the bosom of the Church, cast out and despised by the world, we have a Bishop, who had been elected by his Clergy as "eminent for Piety, Learning, and Catholic principles," sitting in Synod surrounded by his Presbyters. There is no sign of the prevailing Scepticism amongst them: the Nicene Faith evidently supplies the spiritual breath they breathe, and the course of study, which they prescribe to the devoutly-disposed aspirant to the Diaconate, is not even an *Apology* against Deism, but simply Holy Scripture and Christian Antiquity, together with a sacramental text and a discourse on Justification. In the middle of that century such a sight is especially welcome!

June 12th, 1744.—A Testamur signed by Mr. Lyon, Mr. Innes, and six other Clergy, runs as follows:—
"Right Rev. Sir,—According to your appointment at our last meeting we have taken Mr. Donald Robertson to tryals, and he has acquitted himself upon the several subjects, which were presented to him, very much to our satisfaction, and we therefore think ourselves at full freedom to recommend him to you for

Ordination." On *June 18th* Mr. Erskine of Muthill writes to the Bishop:—"Mr. Innes at Balgowan is to present Mr. Donald Robertson to you for Ordination, and I take it for granted that it will be obliging to Lord and Lady Stormont that you do it soon." And soon it was done. On *S. Peter's Day (June 29th)* we read:—"At Alloa, in Bishop Alexander's Chapel, Mr. Donald Robertson in Perth, after tryals of his sufficiency as above, was ordained a Deacon in the said Chapel:* present, Mr. George Innes at Balgowan; Mr. William Erskine at Muthill, Priests; Mr. William Abernethy,† Deacon, and sundrie Laicks."

Nor was Mr. Robertson the only fruit in this way of the work done at the Chapel in Perth, as the following entry in the Dunkeld Register shews:— "*May 17th, 1744.*—At Bishop Alexander's Chapel in Alloa, Mr. Charles Rose‡ in Perth, was ordained Deacon: then present, Mr. Wm. Erskine in Muthill, and Mr. Robert Lyon in Perth, Priests, and sundrie Laicks."

* On January 14th, 1745, "Donald Robertson, Presbyter at Ecclefechan in Annandale, adheres" to a declaration of Bishop Alexander.

† Afterwards Dr. Abernethy Drummond, Bishop of Edinburgh, 1787.

‡ Afterwards Bishop of Dunblane, 1774, and Bishop Alexander's successor in Dunkeld.

CHAPTER XVI.

HOW CONGREGATIONAL MATTERS WENT IN PERTH BETWEEN 1740 AND 1745.

IN order to give a consecutive account of the affairs of our Bishopric, we were led in the last chapter to advance to the year 1744. We must now return to the year 1741, and gather together what is known to us concerning the two Congregations themselves between that date and the year 1745.

As for the irregular Congregation, all that is left to us is contained in two notices, which are as follows. There is a passing sentence in the *Presbytery Record* a good many years later (1748), which assumes it as matter of common notoriety that Mr. George Sempill went on officiating after his deposition. And the Rev. Robert Lyon in a letter dated *July 14th, 1740*, says :—" He most presumptuously takes upon him to administer in Holy Offices and did officiate on Sunday last in our Meeting-House, but, blessed be God, to as thin a congregation as before, and I have no reason to doubt but that he will continue so to do." We shall hear of him still being in Perth some years hence.

With regard to the regular Congregation, the Bishop, in a letter dated *June 21st, 1740*, speaks of it as "still flourishing," and in the Managers' Minute Book (which by some strange chance, is preserved to us at Pitlochry) the following fifty names occur as signing a certain resolution. The likelihood appears to be that they represent at least the great bulk of *the Communicants* :—

Lau. Drummond ; Rob. Lyon ; Thos. Carmichael ; John

Campbell; Jas. Lindsay; Geo. Drummond; Patrick Conqueror; Wm. Lindsay; Jos. Taylor; Thos. Murray; Wm. Lindsay; L. A. Grant; Ja. Smyth; George Stirling; David Conqueror; P. Murray; John Stewart; G. Young; J. Rutherford; Jas. Stewart; Thos. Rattray; James Honey; Duncan Henderson; John Balneavis. Then on another page come the female names:—M. Stormont; A. Lovett; Jean Murray; Helena Murray; E. Gray; Euphemia Bayne; Marg. Fraser; Rebecca Grant; Anna Murray; Stewart Rose; Margaret Rose; Isabel Hunter; Cicilia Martin; Anna Murray; J. L. Young; Ma. Oliphant; Ma. Kinloch; Christina Mercer; Ann Drummond; Mary Drummond; Elizabeth Schaw; Mary Brown; Helen Brown; Barbara Smyth; Isabel Murray; Alison Ogilvy.

Being forcibly excluded from the "Meeting-House" proper, they did not, of course, renounce their claim to it. But, as the whole Episcopal Church was barely, if at all, accorded legal existence, they had little chance of making good their rights, and that all the less, inasmuch as the Civic Authorities were prepared to countenance those, who were in a state of rebellion against the Bishop. Only one course was, therefore, open to our friends,—namely, to provide themselves with another temporary *place of worship*. Accordingly, on *June 18th, 1740*, we read :—" The Meeting find it necessary in the meantime that a convenient House be looked out for accommodating the Congregation for the worship of God on the Lord's Day and other days, and do therefore appoint (a Committee) to provide a convenient House for the Congregation, and whatever they shall do therein shall be ratified by the Meeting." A suitable building was therefore rented, but all attempts to identify its site have proved unavailing.

So much, then, for the number of the congregation and their chapel. What was its *constitution?* It was administered by a committee of seven Managers. These Managers were elected every year at a general meeting in February. The two Presbyters were always chosen, and one of them took the chair at every meeting The following list of names supplied the Lay members from time to time within the years dealt with in this chapter:—Dr. Carmichael; Dr. George Stirling; Bonhard; David Conqueror; Mr. James Smyth; Patrick Murray; William Lindsay; D. Stewart; David Grant; and Joseph Taylor. At their annual meeting held in January, the "Thesaurer's" accounts were inspected and passed. The revenue appears to have been altogether derived from seat-rents. There was some difficulty in collecting these; but, as a rule, the annual income, amounting generally to about £95, was somewhat in excess of the expenditure.

With regard to their *forms of worship* we should certainly have expected, now that the "Anti-Usagers" had seceded, that our friends would have adopted the *Scottish Liturgy* in its entirety, and this all the more as its use was at this epoch all but universal. But, for some reason or another, it was a combination of the two *Offices* that was actually used. Perhaps the reason was that the "Collegians" having so long compelled the use of the English formulary, it had become endeared to the people through "Use and Wont." Perhaps (and we should like to think so) it was that the adoption of the *Scottish Office* was rejected on the ground that it would have been a hopeless barrier in the way of the return of the Corbsites; but, whatever the reason might be, the Service which they now used was that of the English *Prayer Book*, enriched by the priceless addition of the *Oblation* and *Invocation* from the Scottish form. This we learn from the following extract from a letter written by Mr. Lyon, *November 28th, 1743*:—"The majority, who use the Scotch Liturgy, is so great that they are now but very few who do otherwise, and these few in the southern parts mostly, overawed by some ignorant Laity. (Is this an oblique reference to Blair of Corbs?) All in this District are unanimous in the Scotch, save myself, who, not of inclination, but for reasons too well known, was obliged to comply with borrowing only the *Invocation* and *Oblation* from the Scotch. . . . I am persuaded the most of the Clergy of my acquaintance, and with great sincerity I can say it of myself, would much sooner *resign* our several charges than *give up* the *Scotch* to use the *English Office*. Yea, the greater number of our Laity would desert us should we attempt it." That the sacramental ordinance of *Confirmation* was duly practised is proved by the following extracts from contemporary correspondence:—On *May 4th, 1741*, the Bishop writes, "I go for Balgowan to-morrow, and from thence to Perth, in order to confirm some persons there before Whitsunday." Again on *March 18th, 1744*, Mr. Lyon writes to the Bishop:—"It is generally desired that you should be with us a Sunday, and you'll find it necessary, because they expect a visit from you at Balgowan and Nairne. What number we'll have here to confirm I cannot say, because our examination is not yet over, but I presume they will not be many." It appears to be the case that this proposed arrangement was carried out, because there is a letter from Mr. Erskine at Muthill, dated *July 21st, 1744*, and addressed to the Bishop, "care of Rev. R. Lyon at Perth."

It is to be presumed that, as the *Eucharistic Office* of the English Book was made the basis of the Altar Service, the same volume was used for the lesser Services of *Morning and Evening Prayer*. But here again it is evident that at least one significant modification was introduced, "for," says Mr. Lyon, "I never prayed in express terms for any King, because for many years it has not been the practice of our Church: and to mark such in her offices I thought inconsistent for me, without the appointment or at least permission of my Superiors."

We sometimes think that Harvest Festivals are peculiar to the Nineteenth Century. But it is not so. On *November 15th, 1743*, there was a *Harvest Festival* held in Perth and the District in general, with proper Collect, Epistle, Gospel, and Psalms, sanctioned by the Bishop.

We have Mr. Lyon's own account of his *Sermons*. There were those, indeed, who on this head affirmed that "the Meeting-House was a nursery of Jacobitism and rebellion," but we know that the members of the irregular congregation were prejudiced. What our Priest says is:—"I preached the plain truth of the Gospel without touching on political matters." What he understood by this may be gathered from the following exhortation, which he addressed to certain of his friends:—"Strenuously adhere, in spite of all opposition, to those doctrines and principles which, through the grace of God and my weak ability, I have endeavoured to teach publicly and to inculcate on you in my private conversation. I mean the doctrines of the *Holy Scriptures, with their only genuine and authentic comment, the universal doctrines and practices of Christ's Church in her purest ages, even the first three centuries*,* before the manifold errors of Popery on the one hand, or Presbyterianism on the other," had been developed. Using this canon, Mr. Lyon convinced himself of (and doubtless impressed upon his hearers), the necessity of "the Apostolic government of the Bishops," and, as will appear from the following description of his domestic worship, of the customs known as the Usages. "Man," he says, "cannot be perfectly happy without the reunion of soul and body. In consequence of this principle it was my practice in my family devotions to commemorate the souls of my deceased friends who died in the Lord, . . . that they might obtain rest, peace, light, and refreshment, that they might find mercy in the Day of the Lord, and be partakers of perfect consummation and bliss, both in body and soul, in God's eternal and everlasting glory." And then, remembering the other primitive customs, which were being restored, he exclaims, "May our good and wise ecclesiastical governors with the Divine assistance contribute their endeavours to restore this (*i.e.*, prayer for the faithful departed) and other primitive Apostolical practices in due form to the public offices of our Church, which would be a means to contribute comfort and great consolation to many a pious and devout soul !" Lest any should say that because Mr. Lyon felt a peculiar interest in those truths of Christianity, which were especially forgotten by his fellow-countrymen, and that he ignored the ground of piety, which he held in common with all Christians, let the general tone of the following paragraph serve as a witness:—"Pray,

* Our readers will notice that the doctrines of the Oxford Movement prevailed amongst us all through the dark Eighteenth Century—substantially, at least.

Mr. Lyon's Sentiments.   159

then, consider," he pleads, "that God is perfect love and goodness ; that we are not only His creatures but His children, and as dear to Him as to ourselves ; that He does not afflict willingly nor grieve the children of men, and that all evils of affliction which befall us are intended for the cure and prevention of greater evils of sin and punishment ; and, therefore, we ought not only to submit to them with patience, as being deserved by us, but to receive them with thankfulness, as being designed by Him to do us that good and to bring us to that sense of Him and ourselves which perhaps nothing else would have done ; that the sufferings of this present life are but short and slight compared with those extreme and endless miseries which we have deserved, and with that exceeding weight of glory which we hope for in the other world. If we be careful to make the best preparations for death and eternity, whatsoever hardships or afflictions we suffer for our attachment to truth and righteousness, bring us nearer to our everlasting happiness : and how rugged soever the way may be, the comfort is that it leads to our Father's house."

The man, in whose mouth these words were the sincere utterance of his heart and a practical rule of life, as they certainly were in the case of Mr. Lyon, deserves in the fullest degree the title of Christian, as the former quotations entitle him to that of Churchman. But our friend, in the exercise of his Ministry, did not attempt "to wind himself too high, for sinful man beneath the sky." This his *domestic arrangements* will show. The following remark of his leads us to suppose that his dear sister Cicely "kept house for him." "It gives me no small uneasiness," he says, "that I have made some encroachments upon poor Cicely's stock: but then, I might say in my own vindication, this was not by any luxury or riot, but rather owing to a small yearly income, an expensive place for living, and being too liberally disposed on certain occasions." Moreover, he formed a still warmer attachment in another quarter. "Before I end this letter," he writes to his mother and sisters, "I might take this opportunity to acquaint you of one thing that none on earth knows, but the person immediately concerned. The matter is this: . . . I designed and proposed to make Stewart Rose, whom I know to be a virtuous, wise, good, and religious young woman, partner of my life and fortune." This lady was the daughter of the Right Rev. James Rose, Bishop of Fife (*1726-1733*), and sister of the Rev. Charles Rose, whose Ordination was related in the last chapter (afterwards Bishop of Dunblane, *1774-1791*). Her own name appears in the list of the Perth Congregation.

We may fitly conclude the chapter with one or two extracts. From Primus Keith's letters we learn that this Prelate, after the death of Bishop Rattray, regarded Lord Stormont as one of his most trusted advisers. On *April 15th, 1745*, there was a general meeting of the Congregation for the purpose of devizing steps for recovering the "Meeting-House" from the dissenters. But that there was a dark fate impending, which prevented anything coming of these plans, is hinted in the following words of the Rev. W. Erskine to Bishop Alexander, in a letter dated *September 25th, 1744*:—"If there is any new thing going on in Perth, you shall have it. In the meantime, what I hear from thence bodes little good to Robert Lyon."

CHAPTER XVII.

HOW ROBERT LYON FOLLOWED PRINCE CHARLIE, 1745.

COMPARED with what might have been, the state of the Scottish Church in the period succeeding the Concordate of 1731 was, indeed, one of depression. The number of its Clergy was now reduced to 125. But, if we compare the condition of things in this interval with that, in which they were to be placed after 1745, when the number of Clergy gradually fell to 40, we must pronounce the years 1731-1745 to be comparatively prosperous. For now the greatest disaster, which the Church had ever experienced, was to fall upon it. We are not, indeed, concerned to trace its general course in the country at large; but, though we are to confine ourselves to ecclesiastical affairs in Perth, we shall learn most of its leading features. The manner of this calamity was as follows:—In 1745, Prince Charles Edward, son of Prince James of the 1715, determined to strike a last blow for the recovery of his grand father's Crown. Accordingly, he made the voyage from France to the west coast of Scotland in the *Doutelle*, a Nantes brig of 18 tons. His personal following numbered only seven adherents, the most important of whom was the Marquis of Tullibardine. But he chivalrously hoped that those he conscientiously believed (with considerable reason) to be his own people, would rally to the standard of right, as soon as he unfolded it. Nor was he altogether mistaken. Erelong he had gathered a very respectable following, whom he inspired with the most generous enthusiasm.

How was his appeal received by Churchmen in Perth? We, taught by the event, may indeed wish that they had allowed prudence as well as ardour to guide their choice; we may wish that they had reflected how sufficient sacrifices had already been made in the cause of fidelity; we may wish that they had recognised in the failure of previous attempts, and in the 57 years' unbroken success of the new *régime*, practical indications of the decrees of Providence. But the historian's part is not to describe what might have been, but simply to record what actually happened. As a matter of fact, then, the Episcopalians of our City were, like their brethren elsewhere, and like others of different religious persuasions, inspired by the Stuart enthusiasm. As for Robert Lyon we can set forth his state of mind pretty exactly, for he has described it for us himself. First, without going into the abstract question of the divine right of Kings, he could not believe that James VII. (II. of England) had been duly deposed, even on the principles of the popular party. For the Edinburgh Convention, which, in 1689, had declared the Throne vacant, had been elected in such an irregular and masterful way, and so dominated by bodies of armed Presbyterians and Orange troops, that it was not fairly representative of the Scottish people. This was the belief of our Presbyter, shared in by many. "I never could view that convention," he says, "which pretended to depose King James VII., and dispose of his crown: I never could view that unlawful and packed assembly in any other light but as traitors to their country and as rebels to their King." Secondly, he goes on, "I was soon determined from rational and solid arguments to embrace the doctrine of passive obedience,* the divine right of Kings, and in particular the indefeasible and hereditary right of our own gracious sovereign, King James VIII. and III." And thirdly, he proceeds, "As our then injured king and his undoubted heirs have from time to time uninterruptedly claimed their right and asserted their dominion, I am so far from thinking that the royal misfortunes loose the subjects from their obedience, that I rather apprehend that they loudly call for a steadier allegience and more faithful duty." And fourthly, "In these sentiments I have been still more and more confirmed by the lamentable consequences of the opposite opinion." These are all political views. That they are not necessarily connected with Church principles† is evident, inasmuch as—Lyon himself being witness—he had not been in the habit of praying for King James in public worship, and this by the directions of the Bishop. Moreover, the English Prelates did actually so pray for King George, and, on the other hand, there were Presbyterians and Roman Catholics who took up arms for Prince Charlie.

Had these been all the motives, therefore, that guided Robert Lyon and his brethren in this town at the present crisis, we could omit all mention of his adherence to the romantic attempt to recover the British Crown for the Stuarts. This is not a secular history. Perhaps his political opinions would have induced him to act as he did, even though they had not been reinforced by other considerations, and perhaps they would not.

* This phrase is often misinterpreted. It does not mean *un-questioning subservience* to the Monarch in everything; but, while contrasted with *positive rebellion* on one side, is on the other intended to distinguish from *active obedience*.

† Liddon's *Life of Pusey*, vol. ii., p. 27.

But he distinctly assures us that his prevailing motives on the present critical occasion were religious. His most cogent reason for sympathizing with the enterprise was that the hostile legislation and administration, which had for so long depressed the Church, might be brought to an end. After finishing with his political reasons, he concludes thus: *"But what more naturally falls to my share to consider,* and what, I fear, has been still less regarded, is the long persecuted state of my dear Mother, the Church of Scotland—that Church of which it is my greatest honour to be a member and a Priest, though very undeserving of either."

Such, then, was the state of mind at which our Perth Presbyter arrived when he heard that Prince Charlie had come to win his own again. He resolved accordingly, to throw in his lot with him partly for political reasons, but still more because he thought that so he might justly render a service to the Church. He had argued the matter out to the best of his ability, and though some may think that he ought to have come to opposite conclusions, yet it must be admitted that here was a man determined conscientiously to adhere to his principles, and prepared to risk something for them.

Although, therefore, it is not actually recorded that he was present on the occasion, we feel morally certain that he mingled with the crowd, when his hero entered Perth. "The[*] Prince came in by the North Port and Skinnergate (the then usual mode of entry) to the High Street. His leading adherents surrounded him, several of whom had joined him when approaching Perth, such as the head of Drummonds, styled Duke

[*] Fittis's *Gleanings*, p. 175, which also supplies other particulars in this Chapter.

of Perth, Hon. R. Mercer of Aldie, and Laurence Oliphant, Esq. of Gask. On reaching the Cross, while shouts rent the sky, and countless handkerchiefs were waved from the windows, the happy Prince was conducted to the lodging provided for him, being the house of Viscount Stormont, an old-fashioned wooden tenement, occupying the site near the foot of the High Street now occupied by the National Bank. Lord Stormont was suspected of Jacobite tendencies, but had withdrawn to the south. Two of his sisters, however, remained in the Perth mansion. These ladies rendered sumptuous hospitality to their Royal guest." The Prince remained a week in the City, and during that time endeavoured to get his recruits well drilled on the North Inch, and was joined by Lord Strathallan and Lord George Murray. Sir David Threipland of Fingask, then in his 79th year, was making ready to come in also, but died suddenly while pulling on his boots with the intention of riding to Perth. Two of his sons, however, immediately joined the Prince. One secret of the latter's popularity was undoubtedly to be found in the fact that, at least in these years of hope, he was, as Robert Lyon says, "a stranger to every vice that high life is most subject to." This would be a pleasant change after the Courts of the Revolution Monarchs, George I. and George II.*

As before, in 1715, so now the great bulk of the Scottish people regarded the Stuart cause as identical with that of Popery, which they detested. But with the view of allaying the feeling on this important point, as had also been attempted by his father thirty years previously, Prince Charles resolved, while at Perth, that he would publicly attend Scottish worship at S. John's Church.

* See Thackeray's *Four Georges*.

He therefore appeared in the Middle Kirk on *Sunday, September 8th,* and, sitting in the King's seat, became the cynosure of all eyes. It was not to be expected that the Presbyterian Minister, Mr. Black, would be allowed to fill the Pulpit on this occasion. Neither did the duty fall to Mr. Lyon. The preacher was the Rev. Mr. Armstrong of the Episcopal Church. He chose as his text *Isaiah xiv., 1-2 :* "*For the Lord will have mercy on Jacob, and will yet choose Israel, and will set them in their own land . . and the people shall take them and bring them to their place . . . and they shall rule over their oppressors.*"

Shortly afterwards, the Prince's army crossed the Forth, and advancing upon Edinburgh, seized the city without a blow. General Cope landed at Dunbar to oppose the Highland host, but was ignominously defeated at Prestonpans. When the news of the victory reached Perth, there were great rejoicings amongst the Jacobites in the city, and the windows of Mr. Lyon's house were illuminated, and the letters "C., P. R." (Charles, Prince Regent) in large characters with the lights shining through them.

"*Ast illi interea meritis pro talibus, atras
Insidias, clademque parant!*" *

That is, George Miller, the Town Clerk, an energetic partizan of the Hanoverian dynasty, was watching and waiting an opportunity against Mr. Lyon. Meanwhile, however, the latter's star was in its brief ascendant.

†"It's informed," writes one of his opponents, "that Mr. Lyon is with the rebel army in England : he is in Highland cloaths and bearing arms." This was an adversary's account of his proceedings subsequent to the Battle of Prestonpans, and, of course, there was

* Bishop Charles Wordsworth's *Mexico.* † Fittis's *Gleanings,* p. 200.

some truth in it. But what is his own version of the matter? "Every patriot," he writes, "who had courage to resolve to conquer and suffer in the way of duty according to the will of God, joined the Royal standard. Thither many did come to whom I was attached by relation, friendship, and several other ties, dutifully exhorted, kindly invited, and earnestly requested me to attend them *as their Priest*, while they were laudably engaged in King and Country's cause. To this— agreeable as it was to my own professed principles—I readily assented. I plainly foresaw that I could not discharge my (clerical) functions with more safety in that congregation (*i.e.*, Perth) to which I have peculiar and spiritual relation, where part of the Prince's forces already lay, therein going along with my friends in their glorious expedition." The post, to which he was appointed in the Jacobite Army, was the Chaplaincy of Lord Ogilvie's Regiment. "And here I must declare, he goes on, "that, while I accompanied my countrymen in this noble expedition, I saw a decency and discipline maintained amongst them equal, if not superior to, that of any regular disciplined force; and if any hardships or severities were committed, I am fully persuaded it was unknown and very cross to the inclinations of their merciful and Royal leader. And for my own particular, I do solemnly affirm that, during this expedition, *I never bore arms, for this I thought inconsistent with my sacred character.*"

CHAPTER XVIII.

HOW THE CHURCH IN PERTH WAS OVERWHELMED IN A FOURTH GREAT DISASTER, 1746.

As if the Disestablishment of 1689, the failure of Prince James's enterprise in 1715, and the schism of 1740 did not constitute sufficient affliction for the Churchmen of Perth to pass through, another blow, more crushing than any of the former, was now to fall on them. For, between the end of the last chapter and the beginning of this, we must imagine that "bonnie Prince Charlie" has retreated from Derby to Inverness, and been overthrown on the bloody field of Culloden. Under what heads, therefore, shall we divide our description of the overwhelming disasters that now descended upon our friends.

(I.) First, let us bring the victorious general to the Fair City. His Royal Highness the Duke of Cumberland, who now triumphed, was "a clumsy German, with obese figure, puffed visage, and coarse address." The present Lord Rosebery describes* him as "the slave of violent passions," and says that "success in battle was destined to develop the worst phase of his character, i.e., a brutal disregard of all the dictates of justice and common humanity when dealing with a brave but vanquished enemy. No blacker, no bloodier page will be found in the history of any country than that, which records the atrocities perpetrated at Culloden at the command and under the eye of a British Monarch's son."

* Preface to *List of Persons concerned in the Rebellion.*

We may, however, pass over most of the sickening cruelties of the Hanoverian Prince as not connected, except indirectly, with the history of the Church in Perth. But we note that the line of his approach was marked by the destruction of Episcopal Chapels in the counties of Moray, Banff, Kincardine, and Forfar. His Royal Highness entered Perth on *Wednesday, February 5th, 1746*, to the boundless joy of the Whig inhabitants. The North Inch was no longer encumbered with the presence of the Scottish Prince's native troops, but was now honoured by the encampment of a host of 5000 Germans. Detachments of these were sent out to plunder and lay waste the lands of all the Jacobite families in the neighbourhood. "The Butcher's" orders were obeyed with merciless severity, and the spoil was brought in to Perth. Part of it was sold at the Cross, but at last His Royal Highness was compelled by the general outcry which his doings had raised to check such ruthlessness.

As the Episcopal Chapels were everywhere destroyed, it seems reasonable to suppose that both Mr. Drummond's and Mr. Sempill's places of worship shared the general fate. If we are right in this supposition, additional pathos is added to the following words of Mr. Lyon:—
"The Church of Scotland is now, alas! devoted in the intention of her adversaries to utter destruction, which I fervently pray God to prevent. Her oratories have been profaned and burnt; her holy altars desecrated; her priests outrageously plundered, deprived, and some of them imprisoned and treated with uncommon cruelty; her faithful members almost deprived of the means of salvation, and this mostly done without a form of law by a hostile force especially appointed by him who calls himself the Duke of Cumberland, and who (God

grant him a timely repentance and forgive him!) has occasioned the painful and untimely death of many innocent and inoffensive persons, and by wilful fire and sword, and by every means of torment, distress, and barbarity, exceeding Glencoe's massacre itself, has brought a dreadful desolation on my dear country."

(II.) Secondly, leaving the bloodstained proceedings of Cumberland, let us consider the penal legislation, to which our friends were now made subject. "It was enacted that from and after *September 1, 1746*, every person exercising the function of a Pastor or Minister in any Episcopal Meeting-House in Scotland without registering his letters of Orders, and taking all the oaths required by law, and praying for King George and the Royal Family by name, shall for the first offence suffer six months' imprisonment, and for the second or any subsequent offence, being convicted thereof before the Justiciary or any of the Circuit Courts, shall be transported for life to some of His Majesty's plantations in America, and in case of his return to Great Britain, shall suffer imprisonment for life." An Episcopal Meeting-House was defined to be a place "where five persons over and above the household are assembled" for purposes of worship. Sheriffs, etc., were "to shut up or otherwise suppress such Meeting-Houses." Worshippers who were present were to report under severe penalties. All Laity resorting to Episcopal assemblies were to be punished.

Now, though these were excessively severe measures against a Church which, in its corporate capacity, had not required her sons to join in the rising, yet the Government might at first plead that all the Episcopal Clergy, who would take the oaths of allegiance, were free to exercise their calling without let or hindrance. We do not see what civil rulers, be they Stuarts or be they Hanoverians, can do, except require a recognition of their civil authority.

But on the present occasion the "Powers that were" advanced further than this. The boundary, which divides secular from religious affairs, was now clearly overstepped. For, after first enacting, legitimately enough, that those of our Clergy, who refused to take the oaths of obedience, must come under legal penalties, they went on to enact that *no Scottish Priest, whether he took the oaths or not, was to be allowed to officiate.* This amazing enactment ran as follows :—" All letters of Orders would be deemed void in the registration, except those granted by a Bishop of the Church of England or of the Church of Ireland." Nor was this allowed to remain a dead letter. The Rev. John Skinner of Linshart ("Tullochgorum") took all the oaths required by Government, and was, in fact, a thoroughly loyal Hanoverian, but was thrown into prison for the purely religious act of ministering in spiritual things as a Scottish ordained Priest. The intention evidently was to destroy the Church, not merely in its supposed capacity as a dangerous political organization, but as a religious society. Even those, therefore, who sympathise with the Government against the Jacobites, have strong grounds for sympathising with the disestablished Churchmen against rulers, who were either tyrannical or else criminally ignorant of ecclesiastical affairs.

(III.) Thirdly, having seen his victorious Royal Highness arrived in Perth, and having given a general view of the legislation by which his action was fortified about this period, let us return and see how the army and the law combined completed the work of repression in our City.

Cumberland had now fairly settled down to his work. He appointed a junto under the name of "The Town of Perth Committee" to manage the civic affairs, and especially "to denounce all those who had been concerned in the Rebellion."* Let us see how they acted. They met at Perth *February 9th, 1746*. The Preses reported to the members that by order of His Royal Highness he had caused the underwritten advertisement to be published by tuck of drum round the town on the 7th and 8th current, viz. :—

BY ORDER OF H.R.H. THE DUKE OF CUMBERLAND.

"Any person who, within the Town or Liberty of this place, shall conceal any Rebell or arms, ammunition, or anything else belonging to the Rebels, and shall not immediately bring in the said Rebel or stores or goods to Provost James Crie shall, upon proof of disobedience to this order, be hanged."

In a list of persons reported to the Duke by General Hawley, the following names of undoubted Churchmen occur :—

"That the said Robert Lyon, non-jurant Clergyman, a noted Jacobite and suspected to be Popish, went from Perth with the Pretender and his Rebel Army, September, 1745." The witnesses are the same that witness against John Rutherford and the rest of Lyon's congregation. "And that, when the news of the battle of Preston reached Perth, Mr. Lyon's windows were illuminated, and the letters C., P. R. in large characters and the lights shining through them; and it's informed that, when the Rebel Army were in England, the said Lyon was in Highland cloaths, bearing arms." We have seen that this last particular is directly contradicted in Lyon's own narrative.

* Fittis's *Gleanings*, pp. 194 to 202.

"John Rutherford, Writer, habit and repute a Jacobite in so far as he has always attended public worship in Robert Lyon's non-juring Episcopal Meeting-House, where the King and Royal Family were never prayed for, and which was a noted nursery of Jacobitism and Rebellion, although the said John has sworn the oaths to Government as a Public Notary, Sheriff Clerk Substitute, and as Procurator before the inferior Courts of Perth, and that the said Rutherford did, on *September 11th* last, openly insult and throw off the hats of some of the inhabitants on the street for not bowing to the Pretender when he was passing out of Perth." Other Churchmen on this list are:—James Lindsay; Duncan Henderson; ———— Stewart: shoemaker, merchant, and journeyman glover respectively.

George Drummond is accused of "aiding in the assault upon the loyal inhabitants, who were ringing the bells on *October 30th, 1745*, being the King's birthday," and of "being otherwise a tool of the two Rebell Governors of Perth."

Mr. James Smyth, Surgeon; Mr. George Stirling, Surgeon; and Mr. James Oliphant, Merchant, brother of Gask, "did introduce several ladies to the Pretender, both in his bedroom and also in the Town House." They are also accused of taking part in the affair of the bell-ringing on George II.'s birthday.

Mr. William Hall is a "noted Jacobite, and alwise attended Mr. Lyon's Meeting-House," and is accused "of furnishing carriages for cannon to, and otherwise serving, the Rebells."

William Lindsay, Wright, is "a noted Jacobite, and a disciple of Mr. Lyon's," and is accused of "felling and cutting down the Town of Perth's planting, and fitting the wood for pallisades to the Rebels."

The following names of Churchmen occur in the Town Council's report:—"Thomas Powrie, son to Wm. Powrie, Bedall to a Non-Juring Meeting-House."

Some reputed Jacobites and constant hearers in the Non-Juring Meeting-House, namely, Dr. Thomas Carmichael, Physician; Patrick Blair and Walter Keir, Merchants, are reported as not being known to have taken part in the Rebellion.

The only Episcopalian, who appears actively on the Hanoverian side, is Patrick Conqueror, who bears witness against John Rutherford. The probability is that he did not stand altogether alone, but it is uncertain whether he was Orthodox or Corbsite.

The full list of names is a very much longer one, but the rest are omitted as they cannot be shewn to have been Churchmen.

The wretched prisoners could look for no pity nor mercy from "Butcher" Cumberland. They were, in fact, crammed into the Tolbooth to the number of 79. Let us describe this miserable place. "It* was close to S. John's Church, and had formerly been part of a religious house. On the ground floor there was one cell 12 ft. square and arched above. The window was raised 8 ft. from the floor, and so thoroughly set with a triple grating that very little light entered the place. The inner door was composed of thick oak planks: there was also an outer one of iron. This was what was generally termed the 'Condemned Cell,' or 'Laigh Iron House.' Here the criminal was fastened to a chain in the floor; his bed, a little straw on the damp stones, and a single blanket for a covering. Above stairs there was only another small cell for criminals, and a small dark room for debtors. To these were

* Penny's *Traditions of Perth;* pp. 10-11.

added other two garret rooms for the latter class. The upper cells were about 16 ft. by 12 ft. In the lower one there were three cages, each about 6 ft. long and 4 ft. wide, built up to the roof and of double plank. The door into them was about 4 ft. high and 18 inches wide, with a hole (for handing in prisoners' bread) about 12 in. by 9 in. with iron gratings. Within were chains for locking the prisoners to the floor, a bundle of straw, and a blanket. Beside them was placed a wooden stoup, which was filled with water twice a week, and the place was only cleaned once a week. In the upper cell, which was usually allotted for women, there was only one cage situated in the centre of the room. In these wretched places, with only a scanty allowance of bread and water, the poor unfortunates used to be confined for months and some of them for years without seeing the light of day or breathing a mouthful of fresh air." It was into this veritable "Black Hole of Calcutta," evidently small enough to be crowded by a quarter of their number, that the 79 Jacobite prisoners were crammed by the ruthless Cumberland.

Possibly Mr. Lyon was amongst them; but, as he had been away acting as Chaplain in Prince Charlie's army, it is likely that it was not in Perth Tolbooth that he was confined. He certainly was for a time prisoner at Montrose.

However that might be, these fourscore friends and fellow-churchmen of his were in a deplorable condition in Perth. No adequate provision existed for their daily maintenance: they were in danger of absolute starvation. Even the Committee felt ashamed of a state of affairs more "wicked and unnatural" than the Rebellion itself. At least they did not want the prisoners to become a burden on the town, and accordingly we have the following Minute :—" The Committee* of the Town of Perth recommend it to Provost Crie, their Preses, to represent to H.R.H. the Duke of Cumberland that there are many prisoners taken by the army and committed to the Tolbooth of Perth, who are referred by His Royal Highness's order to be examined by the Deputy Sheriffs of the Shire of Perth : that these prisoners will starve for want of food, or be a burden on the inhabitants of the Town, unless His Royal Highness will be pleased to appoint some proper fund for their maintenance, and the Preses having made the above representation to His Royal Highness, he received for answer *(February 11th, 1746)* that *application must be made through the Lord Justice-Clerk to the Commissioners at London for the sick and wounded* (!) " If the prisoners had been Covenanters and the Duke a Stuart Prince, there would have been tolerable unanimity in favour of viewing this answer as sufficient cause to justify forfeiture of its author's Royalty.†

In May two batches of the unfortunates were removed from Perth : one sent to Inverness on *May 10th*, and thence transported to London by sea, and the other carried to Stirling on the 12th. It was probably about the same time that Mr. Lyon was removed from Montrose to York. It is difficult to see why Scotchmen, arrested in Scotland for offences committed there, should not have had the right allowed them of being tried by their own law and their own countrymen, but should have been transported across the Border. If a Stuart Prince had

* Fittis's *Gleanings*, p. 205.
† The frontispiece of the *Gentleman's Magazine* for 1746 was a portrait of the Duke with the words " ECCE HOMO " beneath !

carried Covenanting prisoners to their certain doom in England after some such battle as Bothwell Bridge, it would have been universally considered as a proof that he was unfit to reign.

CHAPTER XIX.

HOW THE REV. ROBERT LYON SUFFERED DEATH AT PENRITH, 1746.

IT is not known what eventually became of the generality of the Perth prisoners. We must therefore leave them. But we can fully describe the fate of Robert Lyon.

In October he is in captivity at York.* After seeing what the prison arrangements in Perth were, we are not surprised to find him complaining of the hardships of his close confinement. "It has pleased Almighty God," he goes on, "in His unsearchable Providence, for some time past to afflict me with grievous and sore troubles: everything that could be looked upon as comfortable in this world has been denied me." One painful trial he had to suffer over and above the rigours of confinement. "Hereby," he says, "the unmerciful disposition of the Hanoverian family appears the more evident, and the injustice and cruelty of the Elector's Council-at-Law in this, that they indicted, arraigned, and condemned William Baird, a person whom I had forced up by a sub-pœna to attend my trial at Carlisle as an exculpatory witness, notwithstanding he had long before delivered himself up in consequence of the pretended Duke of Cumberland's proclamation, and had obtained a protection and had got a pass. This the more deeply concerns me in case any of his friends should imagine I had any design against him by forcing him to run such a hazard. But I here call God to witness I esteemed the man,

* Lord Rosebery's *List of Persons*, p. 371.

Mr. Lyon in Prison.

and, as I thought him perfectly safe, I had no other view in bringing him this length than to do myself justice." Then he adds :—"I have reason to believe that George Miller, Town Clerk of Perth, was prosecuting me to the death, whom to my knowledge I never injured in thought, word, or deed."

Nevertheless, he had one consolation. " I acknowledge, with all the tender-heartedness of a brother, the grievous troubles and afflictions, both of mind and body, my dear sister Cicely has undergone, in order to be of use and comfort to me under my severe trials. Her firm love to me has made her follow me too far, and be a witness of more of my troubles than I could have wished. But, whatever she has suffered on my account (which, indeed, cannot be expressed), she has been of unspeakable service to me. May Almighty God reward her, and whatever love all of you bore to her formerly, I hope it will be enlarged to her on this very account." One good result of these truly romantic efforts of his sorrowing sister was that, at her instance, the Primus of the Scottish Church (Keith) and Mr. Lyon's own Bishop (Alexander) ran the risk of writing the prisoner a sympathetic letter of consolation.* This could not fail to greatly cheer a Priest of Mr. Lyon's principles.

When the trial came on at Carlisle, he "was forced by surprise and the advice of his counsel to confess that, though he had never carried arms, he had followed the Prince's army in a purely pastoral capacity." "Upon which," he goes on, "my pretended judges declared and the jury found me guilty of high treason and levying war, for barely accompanying the Royal army, as before mentioned. This their rigorous procedure they founded on a pretended Act of Parliament,

* Episcopal Chest MS.

made since I was personally engaged in the Royal cause, and, for what I know, since I was prisoner: which plainly shows that, whatever my private sentiments might have been, my life has been greedily sought after and unjustly taken away, inasmuch as they passed their sentence without any other act of high treason (even in their own sense) proved against me."

The sentence was that he was to be executed at Penrith on *October 28th*. Against this sentence he was persuaded to appeal, and indeed, to the ordinary mind, it appears that, if justice had been the point aimed at, the ingenuity of the legal mind might have been successful in detecting flaws in the proceedings. But the appeal failed. Whereupon Mr. Lyon writes:—"I do hereby acknowledge publicly, and with a strong and inward sense of guilt, that through fear, human frailty, persuasion of lawyers, and the promise and assurance of life, I was prevailed upon . . . to address the Elector of Hanover for mercy and my life. Which address, petition, or anything of that kind I have signed derogatory to the Royal cause . . . I hereby retract, and with sorrow and contrition of a dying penitent most humbly beg forgiveness of my Heavenly Father for this my great offence."

Probably the Eucharistic Office of the Scottish Prayer Book of 1637 has been used only a very limited number of times. If Mr. Chambers* is making no mistake concerning the edition of the northern Office, we may at least say that never has it been recited under such memorable circumstances as it was now. He informs us that fifty of the condemned followers of the last Stuart Prince assembled together in Carlisle

* *History of the 1745*, p. 464.

Castle, and there, in the form of the Royal Martyr's Liturgy, the Rev. Robert Lyon offered the Memorial of Christ's Sacrifice and administered the Holy Communion of His Body and Blood. Long afterwards, Bishop R. Forbes treasured the copy of the Office, which was used on this occasion, as a sacred relic.

While lying captive under these circumstances, Mr. Lyon composed two documents,* which have already been largely quoted in these pages, *i.e.*, a long letter of farewell to his mother and sisters, and a speech to be delivered on the scaffold. From these let us now draw a picture of his state of mind in view of immediate death.

(1).—First, what were his sentiments towards those who stood in the position of *enemies* towards him? He tells us:—" In obedience to the precept, and after the Divine example, of my Blessed Master, Jesus Christ, I heartily and cheerfully forgive them, as I do all my adversaries of whatsoever kind : particularly George Miller, Town Clerk of Perth, Lord ! grant him repentance that he may obtain forgiveness of God! And more especially I forgive the Elector of Hanover, by virtue of whose unlawful commission I am brought to a public and violent death, and whom I consider as my greatest enemy, because the mortal enemy of Holy Mother Church, of my King, and of my country !"

(2).—And did his afflictions make him forget his *Congregation* in Perth? Far from it. "I cannot conclude," he says, "without offering my best wishes (as they have always had my prayers) to Mr. Drummond, my colleague, and every individual person a member of our congregation. May Almighty God bless all of

* See Bishop R. Forbes's *Lyon in Mourning* and Stephen's *Episcopal Magazine*, 1836, pp. 10, 111.

them, both in temporal and spiritual concerns, and of His infinite goodness reward them for their love and kindness, their attachment and concern for me in the several difficulties I have undergone. May the same God in His due time afford them authorized guides to perform Divine offices amongst them, to administer to them the means of grace and bread of life that they may be no longer as sheep without a shepherd. . . . You will be pleased to offer my hearty and sincere wishes to Balgowan and to all that worthy family : I gratefully acknowledge their remarkable and undeserved favours. May Almighty God return them sevenfold into their bosom! I sincerely pray that Almighty God may reward the family of Moncrieff, Mr. Smith's, Mr. Stirling's, Dr. Carmichael's, Mr. Green's, the Ladies of Stormont, Lady Tindals, and all other of my kind benefactors and well-wishers with you (who have so bountifully ministered to my necessities) with His eternal and everlasting good things!"

(3).—If he remembered these friends so affectionately, the last sentence will remind us that he was not cold at this dreadful crisis towards his *Mother and Sisters*. "Before this reaches you," he writes to them, "the last fatal scene of my sufferings will be over, and I set at liberty (even by my enemies themselves) from the heavy load of irons and chains I have so long dragged. . . . You labour under affliction for the death and loss of your only son, and you of your only brother, and all of you of your dearest earthly friend. . . . I find in myself a great tenderness in parting with you, my dearest relations, which, I must confess, doth very sensibly touch me. My dear mother and sisters, I commend you all to the Father of mercies and God of all consolation and comfort, beseeching

Mr. Lyon's Last Words.

Him to increase your faith, patience, and resignation, and to stand by you in all your conflicts and difficulties and troubles, that when you walk through the valley of the shadow of death you may fear no evil, and when your heart fails, and when your strength fails, you may find Him the strength of your heart and your portion for ever! Farewell, my dear mother! Farewell, my loving sisters! Farewell, every one of you, for ever, and let us fervently pray for one another that we may have a happy meeting in another world!"

(4).—Nor, we may be sure, was his *Betrothed* forgotten in her grief and sorrow. "May Almighty God support and comfort her!" he cries, and then continues, "I commend her to you, my dear mother, always to look upon her as your daughter, and do you, my dear sisters, so treat her always as your own sister, she being really so in my most serious intention and fixed resolution. I am sensible that all of you esteemed her before on your acquaintance with her and on her own proper merit, and am convinced that my discovering my mind thus far will more and more increase, and not lessen, your love and regard to her!"

(5).—And what thought he of the poor, despised, *Scottish Church*, now that devotion to her had brought him to this terrible pass? "Continue," he pleads, "steadfastly and constantly in the faith of our holy persecuted Mother, the Church of Scotland (in the which I have the honour to die a very unworthy Priest), whatever temporal inconveniences and hardships you may wrestle with in so doing. . . . It is a Church national and independent of any other, and every, power on earth, happily governed by her own truly primitive Bishops, as so many spiritual princes presiding in their different Districts, and in them accountable to none but God for the administration of her discipline: a Church whose Creeds demonstrate her soundness in the Faith, and blest with a Liturgy (I mean the Scots Liturgy) compiled by her own Bishops, nigher to the primitive model than any other Church this day can boast of. . . In a word a Church very near resembling the purest ages, and which, after more than half-a-century groaning under persecution and mourning in her own ashes, but all the while distinguishing herself not less by forbearance and charity to her bitterest enemies than by standing to principles and Catholic Unity, is now at last (alas!) devoted in the intention of her adversaries to utter destruction, which I fervently pray God to prevent. May the gracious hand of Heaven interpose and stop this wide destruction! May our Church once more resume her ancient lustre! Her Presbyters be clothed with righteousness, and her Saints sing with joyfulness! May her members yet be multiplied, blest with grace and felicity in this world, and crowned with immortality in that which is to come!"

(6).—There is yet one more subject, on which he discourses, ere the fearful moment, and that is his *Personal Religion*. "I heartily thank God's holy providence," he says, "for vouchsafing me the honour and felicity of dying for the sake of conscience, and of sealing with my blood those heavenly truths I have mentioned, particularly that of loyalty to my King and Prince. And I do declare upon this awful and solemn occasion, I feel no sting of conscience for the part I have acted in our civil discord, and do sincerely profess before God and the world that, had He of His infinite wisdom thought proper to prolong my life, I should ever, by His all-powerful aid and grace, steadily have persisted in the same faith and principles in the hearty and zealous belief and open profession of which I now die, and with fervent charity to all men, imploring the pardon and forgiveness of all my sins through the merits and mediation of my Crucified Saviour, our Lord Jesus Christ. . . Lord! loose me from the burden of my sins, assist me in my last and greatest trial, receive my soul, and bring me into the way of eternal happiness and joy." Mr. Lyon then repeated the Collect for the day (S. Simon and S. Jude, *October 28th*), then that for S. Stephen's day that he "might steadfastly look up to Heaven and behold by faith the glory that shall be revealed, and being filled with the Holy Ghost might learn to love and bless his persecutors." He then added, "Good Lord! lay not innocent blood to the charge of this people and nation! Lord Jesus receive my spirit."

And so, after having discoursed for about 20 minutes in a spirit of charity towards men, and with a deep and chastened sense of fear towards God, he resigned himself into the executioner's hands. The method in which the prisoners, in various batches, and to the number of 77, were put to death was this:—They were first hanged for three minutes, and then disembowelled. It is much to be feared[*] that life was not in all instances extinct before the second process was proceeded with. Let us hope that it was, in the case of Mr. Lyon. It is difficult again on the present occasion, as in the matter of the barbarities on the field of Culloden and the imprisonments at Perth, not to feel that, if the victims had been Covenanters, and the reigning monarch a Stuart, these wholesale and dreadful executions would have covered the perpetrators with lasting

* *Gentleman's Magazine* for November, 1746.

obloquy. Surely, if it is fair to remember from generation to generation the sufferings of the Covenanters, it is fair to do likewise with those of the Jacobites. "And yet, shew I unto you a more excellent way," *viz.*: that the sufferings of the Jacobites should be at last allowed to cancel out those of the Covenanters, and that, while Episcopalians cease to cast the one in the teeth of Presbyterians, Presbyterians should cease to cast the other in the teeth of Episcopalians.

A sorrow-stricken friend of Mr. Lyon must have been present on the scaffold with him, for some of his blood was preserved and set within the glass jewel of a ring. This ring is now in possession of Miss Christian Bruce of Dunimarle, and bears the following inscription on the outside of the circle:—"Mr. Robert Lyon, E.S.P. (*Ecclesiæ Scoticanæ Presbyter*), 28th October, 1746, ætat 36;" and in the inside the legend runs:—"*Pro rege et patria trucidato.*" Some of the sawdust also from the scaffold was collected and formed into a pincushion. This is now in possession of the same lady, who owns the ring; and on the silk of the pincushion is printed in the centre a white rose, round which appear the names of the 77 martyrs.

CHAPTER XX.

HOW THE PERSECUTION RAGED FROM 1746 TO 1756.

CONSIDERING the Duke of Cumberland's achievements, the Town Council of Perth thought that His Royal Highness ought to receive some tangible mark of their gratitude. Accordingly they presented him with that interesting relic of Scottish antiquity, the Gowrie House.* His Royal Highness was graciously pleased to accept the gift, sell it, and take himself off for good.

This, however, did not mean that the shattered fragments of the Church were to be allowed to reorganize themselves. On the contrary, everything was done which ingenuity could devise to stamp Episcopacy thoroughly out, and it took about two years to bring those penal laws to perfection, a general view of which was given in the central part of the chapter before last.

Our present object is to shew how our local Church history fared during the ten years or so, during which the repressive legislation was actively enforced.

(I).—The Rev. L. Drummond's signature is appended to a document dated *January 14th, 1745*,† but nothing more is heard of him afterwards. Doubtless the awful experiences, through which he had been compelled to come, proved too much for one in so frail a state of health. But whatever Mr. Drummond's fate was, it is certain that a new name now occupies his place. The Rev. George Innes‡ appears prominently upon the scene.

* Town Council MS.   † Dr. Gordon's *Scotichronicon*, vol. v.
‡ Not to be confused with his contemporary the Rev. George Innes of Forres, afterwards Bishop of Aberdeen.

We have already been introduced to this Priest. He was present on *S. Peter's Day, 1744*, at the Ordination of Mr. Donald Robertson by Bishop Alexander at Alloa. He is described on that occasion as "at Balgowan." In the same year he is also spoken of as "at Perth." The fact seems, therefore, to have been that he was the Chaplain, whom Bishop Rattray had procured for the Balgowan family, and also that he used to render assistance in some manner to the Congregation in Perth.

Of course, for some time after the disasters just related it would be necessary for Mr. Innes to do whatever pastoral work he did do as secretly as possible. We need not, therefore, be surprised that for the four years following Mr. Lyon's death we hear nothing either of Mr. Innes or of his flock. But at the beginning of 1750 our Presbyter is still "at Perth," and from this time onwards his letters to Bishop Alexander, which are still extant,* give us a pretty full account of the affairs of the Congregation. On *February 5th* he writes, "The story, which you would see in the newspapers, of Highlandmen being in arms is absolutely false. It had its rise from a party's going up from hence (Perth) to assist a factor in taking a rental of Strowan's estate." Four months later, however, he thinks that, though the feelings of the populace are as bitter as ever, the Government are inclined to be less severe. "I learn," he says, "that those in power are become a little more favourable. You are happy; everybody, *I believe*, is happy except myself. I am hunted and watched every day, and yet I make a shift to do what some would not have done (*i.e.*, celebrate Divine Service?)." The truth was that neither

* Theological College MSS.

himself nor his brethren were "happy." On *July 6th, 1752*, he writes:—"As for Perth, the military have orders to take up all strangers who come there, and have them examined before the Sheriff and Magistrates. They have accordingly taken up severals: some are detained in prison: some sent to Edinburgh under a guard: others are dismissed as soon as examined, if their papers, etc., are found unexceptionable. Even Lord Lyon did not escape their examination." On *July 20th*, he continues:—"My* alarms grow upon me. I have had no peace since S——t came here, which is now some more than four weeks ago. In order to frighten my people he gives out that he will have every one of them sworn, whether they have seen me transgress the law, and too many are weak enough to believe he can and will do so. He has, I am told, joined with some of—(?)—to surprise me, and yesterday was the time appointed for the revengeful malice. But, thanks to God, He has hitherto protected me, and, I trust, will do it. The design of these mine enemies is to terrify my people so as to make them leave me, or to make my life so uneasy as to make me leave this place, either of which they think will answer their design of increasing their own numbers, and truly they have reduced me to a very disagreeable situation. The generality of my people are giddy, and so thoughtless as to tell me that if I do not give them preaching and singing they must go elsewhere. In the end I generally humour them, which gives me no small fatigue, as it obliges me to run such risks, as I am at present really unwilling to do." On *August 11th* he hears that the Sheriff has been informed that he "is a transgressor in point of numbers, and warrants are being prepared

* MS. lent by the Rev. W. Hawdon.

for the breaking open of doors, etc. This," he goes on, " I at first fancied to be only a design to intimidate, but found afterwards that the thing was well designed, and that I was really in danger." A little later he adds :—" My situation deserves to be pitied. This last alarm frightens many who slighted the former. I have great reason to fear that precognitions will be taken here, and then I know my fate. What shall I do? How shall I behave? If I keep to the legal number I am sure more of my people will leave me. If I exceed I must go to prison : hard dilemma : both horns wound! I pray that God, who alone can do it, would speedily deliver me out of these straits, and in the meantime direct me to do that which is right and proper."

Thus was our Presbyter himself afflicted by the persecution, and his brethren were harassed in a similar way. On *November 19th, 1753*, the Bishop writes* to inform him that "three of Mr. Jaffray's hearers have been summoned anew and fined £5 sterling each, and were obliged to pay, only the Clerk passed from his third part. The two brethren in Enzie have been obliged to abscond, their hearers also have been summoned, and upon their appearance threatened with the penalty if ever they hear such pastors. And this is the method which it is said the persecutors do hereafter intend to take, as being more effectual and less invidious."

Again, on *January 30th, 1755*, Mr. Connachar, a fellow Clergyman near Stirling, was arrested for celebrating marriages. It was proved, indeed, that, on those occasions, every circumstance legally necessary was attended to, the only offence being that the

* College MS.

ceremony was performed by a person, who was not a minister of the Established Church. One of the laws, which were so wicked when used by a Stuart Prince against the Covenanters, was revived and brought into play against him.* The Lord of Justiciary, before whom he was tried at Inverary, said that non-juring Episcopal Clergymen of the prisoner's activity were dangerous to the present happy Establishment. The jury found him guilty, recommending him to mercy. He was sentenced to *perpetual banishment* from Scotland, and forbidden to return *under pain of death.* His fellow Churchmen seem to have done what they could for the unfortunate Priest, for on *October 8th* we find Mr. Innes sending £6 3s. 0d. to the Bishop, which he had collected for Mr. Connachar.

But the whole incident brought home vividly to the Perth flock how utterly they lay at the mercy of their enemies. This comes out pathetically in the following extract, written by our Incumbent to the Bishop while the last case was proceeding:—"Though my folk promised to you to take a House (*i.e.*, for Worship), or at least to assist me in taking one, yet, now when it's come to the push, they will do nothing: *a shadow frights them at any time,* and now this story is turned into a bugbear and makes them tremble, though, if there be danger, it's only I must suffer. But I trust to the same Providence as has hitherto protected me, and am resolved to go on, though with caution, in the duties of my office."

(II).—The Corbsites too had their troubles. As we have seen one of the differences between the "Collegians" and the "Diocesans" had been that, while the former advocated subservience to the (exiled) Civil Power, the

* Grub, vol. iv., p. 42.

latter insisted on a substantial amount of ecclesiastical independence on the part of the Church. Now, Mr. George Sempill and his party being "Collegians," we must not be surprised to learn that they got into difficulties with their Jacobitism as well as the Orthodox. It came about in this way.

In *December, 1747,** "four soldiers rushed suddenly into a room in Perth [this certainly favours the theory that Cumberland had destroyed the Meeting-House] in which the Rev. George Sempill was performing Divine Service, and, finding his audience more numerous than the law allowed, they secured him. He was carried before the Magistrate on the following day, and committed to prison for six months in terms of the *Act*. The persons present were also cited to appear, and to pay their fine of £5 each; but they proved that they had given information within the proper time and were assoilzied."

We are fortunately able to follow Mr. Sempill's case up, after he was committed to prison. The following extracts (very characteristic of the times) from the *Presbytery Record* continue the story for us:—

January 27th, 1748.—"The Moderator produced a letter from the Rev. Mr. Cumming, Minister at Edinburgh, in answer to one write to him by some members of the Presbytery, desiring him to deliver a letter to my Lord Justice Clerk, begging that he would cause the imprisonment of Mr. Sempill, a non-jurant Episcopal Minister, to be rendered more safe for his weakly constitution by changing his prison, which is bad. Which letter the Moderator begged leave to inform the Presbytery, though signed in the name and by authority of the Presbytery, they had not adverted,

* Lawson's *History*, vol. ii., p. 294.

when it was wrote, that the Presbytery was not actually constituted. The Presbytery, after some reasoning, came to a question :—Whether it was proper to make an application to the Duke of Newcastle, in favour of the said Mr. Sempill, in a Presbyterial capacity or not? and, rolls being called and votes marked, it was carried :—Apply in a Presbyterial capacity. Against which sentence the Revs. Messrs. Lindsay and Stevenson protested and dissented for reasons to be given in, and thereupon asked and took instruments in the Clerk's hand. Then it was agreed that a letter should be write in name of the Presbytery to His Grace the Duke of Newcastle, enclosed in another letter to the Earl of Leven."

February 24th, 1748.—" Mr. Warden, the Moderator, represented that, in consequence of the Presbytery's orders laid on him on *January 27th*, he had signed and transmitted the letters from the Presbytery to the Duke of Newcastle and the Earl of Leven soliciting an easier and less hurtful imprisonment for the Rev. G. Sempill, and that the Moderator had got a return from the Earl of Leven signifying that there will very soon be orders given to remove the poor old man to a more wholesome place of confinement, and that more could not reasonably be expected. Which being considered by the Presbytery, they appoint the Moderator and Messrs. Bannerman and Black to return their most hearty thanks to the Earl of Leven for his trouble in this affair. The Clerk represented that Mr. Stevenson had transmitted to him his reasons of dissent from the resolve of the Presbytery of *January 27th*. Of which reasons the tenor follows :—

1mo—" I judge it extremely unsuitable to the character of any Presbytery of the Church of Scotland to interpose in favour of a non-jurant Episcopal Minister convicted of transgressing a statute framed for the support of the Government and Constitution, to which all such persons are known to be enemies, and upon the preservation of which the very being of this Church does, under God, depend. 2*do*—Because I apprehend that such a recommendation or petition coming from a Presbytery of this Church may bring such Presbytery under suspicion of disaffection to the Government. 3*tio*—Because I conceive the arguments used for the recommendation, drawn from Mr. Sempell's pretended moderation in his principles and his great age and infirmity, and the dampness of the prison in which he is confined, are extremely weak. That Mr. Sempell was deposed by his pretended Bishop is allowed, but it is not aleaged that his loyalty to King George was the cause of · his deposition, but his not complying with the imposing spirit of his party in the matter of the Usages : nor is it aleaged that he in the least degree differs from the other non-jurant Episcopal Ministers in Scotland in his sentiments and principles with regard to the Government, which he is known to regard as a usurpation. And, though Mr. Sempell might have preached against Popery during the rebellion as he did formerly after his deposition, yet this will never be allowed to be a proof of his loyalty." (Mr. Stevenson then argues against old age as a reason for mitigating the sentence).

April 20th, 1748.—The Presbytery answer Mr. Stevenson's reasons of dissent. The following are the heads of their reply :—1*mo*, They did not vote for suspension of the law, but only that a sentence of imprisonment might not inadvertently be turned into one of death. 2*do*, They do not want the Government to think them narrow and vindictive. *3tio*, Mr. Sempell is a man of great moderation, charity, and benevolence.

No doubt it is pleasant to read of the Presbytery taking this line with regard to an Episcopal Clergyman, but too much must not be made of it. In benefiting this particular Presbyter, who was openly rebellious to his Bishop, and a fatal cause of weakness to his Church, they were, in fact, aiming a blow at Episcopacy. We shall soon see that they did nothing to help another aged Presbyter, who was obedient to his Bishop, in precisely similar circumstances.

(III).—The following incident, though not strictly belonging to the Churchmanship of our City, yet happened at so little a distance from it, and is so illustrative of the times, that it is well to insert it. Under the date *March 20th, 1750*, the Rev. W. Erskine of Muthill writes in his Baptismal *Register*:—"*N.B.*—With such excessive severity were the penal laws executed at this time that Andrew Moir, having neglected to keep his appointment with me at my own house this morning, and following me to Lord Rollo's house at Duncrub, we could not take the child into a house, but I was obliged to go under the cover of trees in one of Lord Rollo's parks, to prevent our being discovered, and baptize the child there."

(IV).—The last case of suffering even to bonds on behalf of the Church, which we shall have to chronicle, occurred eleven years after the "Forty-Five,"—namely, in *October, 1756*. It was that of an old friend of the reader. The Rev. Walter Stewart, who was ordained Deacon in 1711 and Priest in 1712, and who had contributed his share to the forces, which passed the Toleration Act of the latter year, was, as we saw, obliged to leave Perth, along with the Rev. Henry

Murray, in 1716. After that he served in Doune, and then removed* to Blair-Athol (Kilmavœnig) in 1728. And there he had been ever since. He now reappears in that Perth gaol, into which 79 prisoners had been thrust in 1746, and confinement in which in 1748 appeared to the Presbytery to be equivalent to a sentence of death to an old man. He† was apprehended in Athol and brought to Perth by the Sheriff-Depute, but was released on bail. His trial before the same Magistrate took place on *December 28th*, and he was *charged with having performed Divine Service in his own house every Sunday* from Christmas, 1755, to October last, or at least on one or another of those Sundays, when more than four persons were present besides his own family, and craving that the penalties of the *Act 19, George II.*, should be inflicted. Mr. Stewart confessed the charge, and was *sentenced to six months' imprisonment*, during which his Meeting-House was to be shut up. He was accordingly committed to the gaol of Perth, and, as he was in his seventieth year, his friends very naturally dreaded the consequences of such a punishment. Four of Mr. Stewart's hearers were also indicted for being present, and not giving information. They confessed, and were fined £5 sterling each, which they paid at the bar,—the one half adjudged to the King, the other to the prosecutor. One of the gentlemen fined was a notary-public, and he was declared to have forfeited his office, and to be incapable of bearing any office, civil or military, for twelve months.

When, as often happens, it is said that the Scotch people have in the past shown no liking for Episcopacy,

---

* See Appendix to this Chapter.
† Lawson's *History*, vol. ii., p. 309.

it is only fair to remember what Episcopacy meant, at least from 1689 to 1756, and that was loss of established position; loss of endowments; legal proceedings; fines; loss of position; banishment; imprisonment and death. Doubtless their own want of worldly wisdom was partly to blame for bringing these things upon our friends, but the fact remains that during the sixty-seven years, with which this "History" has hitherto been dealing, it was only Episcopacy *plus* all these afflictions, and not Episcopacy pure and simple, that was before the Scottish people. We are at least entitled to our opinion that the discomforts engendered during so long a period by these penal proceedings had a good deal to do with opening the eyes of our shrewd countrymen to the undesirability of our Church principles. To these sixty-seven years, moreover, we must add the next thirty-six, during which the penal laws, though no longer actively enforced, still remained on the Statute Book.

APPENDIX TO CHAPTER XX.

The following letter of invitation addressed by the Blair-Athol people to the Rev. Walter Stewart, while he was at Doune, is too amusing to withhold :—

*" REV. SIR.—After several meetings of gentlemen concerned in
" our Meeting-House, we have all unanimously made choice of you
" as the properest and most acceptable to be our Pastor, and
" therefore now, for ourselves and in the name of the gentlemen
" and commons of our Meeting-House in the Parish of Blair-Athol
" (Kilmavœnig), do hereby most heartily call and invite you to
" be our Minister, and for your encouragement we promise you
" £25 stg. yearly, to be paid out of our hand, which is as much
" as you get where you are : we expect your satisfactory answer
" by the bearer. Our congregation is very much to be sympathized
" with by all good men, and we are hopeful the good gentlemen
" you live amongst (tho' they may be sorry to part with you)

* Kilmavœnig MS.

" will not only part with you willingly but press your coming to
" such a congregation as we have, which may, by the blessing of
" God, be for the good of the Church and State. We know no
" scruples you may have against coming, if it is not being out of
" the use of the Irish (Gaelic) tongue. But you'll soon overcome
" that difficulty by a little practice, and in the meantime your
" English discourse will atone sufficiently for that little defect,
" and your countrymen hope, now that we unanimously make
" choice of you, that you'll frankly embrace this our cordial
" invitation home to your native country, and prevent our asking
" the interposition of the Bishop's authority, which we are
" determined to have, if you refuse our kindly call.—We are, Sir,
" your humble servants : J. ROBERTSON of Lude ; A. ROBERTSON
" of Faskally ; J. STEWART of Kynachan."

CHAPTER XXI.

HOW THE TWO CONGREGATIONS FARED BETWEEN 1750 AND 1776.

HAVING in the last chapter seen the Orthodox Congregation "frighted at a shadow" during the time when the penal laws were being actively enforced, and the Revs. G. Sempill and W. Stewart imprisoned, let us now pursue our history further through that epoch, when the Scottish Church had neither the freedom of legal toleration to enjoy, nor yet the excitement of persecution to animate her zeal.

(I).—And first, for the irregular or Anti-Usage Congregation. But before coming directly to it, a few general remarks will be necessary. After the failure of the first Jacobite enterprise of 1715 a new danger had begun to threaten the Scottish Church. As we have already seen, the differences, which prevailed amongst the Scottish Bishops concerning the lines of organization and worship on which the shattered Church ought to be re-organized, and which generated the "*Diocesan-Usage*" and "*Anti-Usage College*" parties, never produced an actual schism, at least amongst the Prelates themselves. But nevertheless schismatical action was taken by a body external to their Communion. Congregations began to spring up which, though professing and calling themselves "Episcopal," repudiated the Episcopal authority of the national Prelates. They professed to place themselves under the jurisdiction of English or Irish Bishops, although these could neither have such jurisdiction in the Dioceses of their Scottish brethren on any ecclesiastical principle, nor yet, for fear of political consequences, practically affect to exercise it. The position, therefore, of the congregations in question was in itself utterly anomalous. One excuse, indeed, they had during the eighteenth century, and that was that the Scottish Church had gone too far in the direction of erecting a non-essential (*i.e.*, the political principle of loyalty to a hereditary monarchy) into a term of Communion. But even so their conduct was schismatical, for instead of proclaiming their adherence to the national Episcopate in matters religious, and leaving the burden of rejecting them for purely political reasons on the Prelates themselves, they professed to repudiate the latter as Bishops, and to intrude their English and Irish brethren into their Sees.

In any case these anomalous "English" congregations, independent of all Episcopal jurisdiction, sprang up after 1715, and increased after 1745. And this fact enables us to understand the step, which Mr. Sempill's congregation now seems to have taken. As they had schismatically separated from the Usager Bishop, and had not been taken up even by Bishop Ochterlony, they were plainly severed from the Scottish Church. At the same time they had hitherto professed to be "Scottish" and not "English" Episcopalians. They were, in fact, altogether *sui generis*. Now, therefore, that their old Clergyman was in prison, and they were compelled to reconsider their position for the future, we are not surprised to learn that they determined henceforth to pose as an "English" congregation. The proof that they did so is simply this, that the Anti-Usage Congregation is never more heard of as such after this date; that they did not re-unite with the regular Congregation, and that the *Register* of S. John's

S. JOHN THE BAPTIST EPISCOPAL CHURCH, PERTH.

Church, Princes Street, contains an MS. note to the effect that itself (which used to be "English") was founded about the year 1750. That the Rev. A. Wood of the "English" Episcopal Congregation was simply the successor of the Rev. G. Sempill of the Anti-Usagers is beyond reasonable doubt.

We have several references to him in Mr. Innes's correspondence.* On *November 9th, 1750*, the latter writes to the Bishop:—"We have got a *qualified* man here," and the Rev. W. Abernethy (Drummond) remarks on *December 29th*:—"I am sorry to hear your accounts about Perth. Pray, who are to be the supports of a Complier there? I know of none but M———, and I should not think he would care to launch out for Religion's sake." Mr. Innes again writes to the Bishop:—"When I have learned something of my neighbour's character and conduct, you may expect to hear it; he has been here a fortnight, but I have been much out of town." On *November 27th* he has learned a little more, for he adds:—"I can as yet give you no satisfactory character of my neighbour. So far as I know he is discreet enough himself, tho' I cannot say so much for some of those he is concerned with. But you know the men, *they bred a schism in the Church before.*" This last observation proves that Mr. Wood's and Mr. Sempell's congregations were the same.

Of course the new position which they had taken up involved the desertion of a principle, to which hitherto they had been no less loyal than their brethren, namely, their Jacobitism. And this was not the only link binding the two congregations somewhat together that was now broken. For the following extracts from

* Theological College MSS.

Mr. Innes's correspondence with the Bishop shew that some financial bond had lingered on for a few years. On *February 5th, 1750*, he writes :—" Mr. Rutherford has got nothing done at Corbs, but is going to summond and pursue him in a legal way." Three weeks later he adds :—" Corbs has at last paid your £10; it's in J. Rutherford's hands, and will be given to any person you order to receive it." Again, on *May 7th*, he says :— " Corb refuses to pay any interest, and I think you you would as good have no more dealings with such a man."

It will be as well, before passing on to the regular Congregation, to say what little can be said concerning the other, so as to bring it to the end of the period embraced in this chapter (*i.e.*, 1776). All that is known is that Mr. Wood stayed in Perth but a few years, and the note in the S. John's *Register* records that he was succeeded by the Rev. John Cameron, whose ministry lasted till 1770, when he left for America. The Rev. Adam Peebles then followed, and remained on long after 1776.

(II).—Let us now turn back to the regular Congregation, and allow Mr. Innes to speak of himself at some length, and so paint for us the picture of a Scottish Presbyter, faithfully serving the Church during that trying and depressing period in which his lot was cast.

(*a*) And first with regard to the *place in which Public Worship was conducted*. We have already seen that in 1755 the Congregation were in such fear that they could not pluck up courage to provide themselves with a Meeting-House. Previous to that time, therefore, we must conclude that they had more or less recourse to the same expedients, which the historian tells us were adopted in the district at large. "In some cases," says Lawson,* "the people were congregated at the mansions of noblemen and gentlemen. In order to evade the law against more than four persons being present, the Service was performed in a large room on the ground floor, in which were the Clergyman, the family, and four persons. Two window-frames, however, were removed, and as many as could look in or hear from the outside, listened and responded. If the apartment was so constructed that it communicated by folding doors with another room, the doors were removed for the time, and the room was filled with people, who could hear and see with the greatest ease. If the apartment were not so constructed, the passages and staircases were crowded with worshippers, and every spot in the vicinity of the room where the pastor's voice could be heard. Amongst other districts, we are told, *this practice was very common in Perthshire*. In towns it is evident that the same thing could be done by the Priest standing with four persons in a passage, and the rooms opening off the passage being filled with people."

(b) As for the *Services*, which were thus conducted, it is to be presumed that the *English Book* was in the main followed by Mr. Innes. With regard, however, to the Celebration of the Eucharist, there is an interesting notice. On *September 15th, 1755*, he writes to his Diocesan:—" The 50 copies of the *Scots Liturgy* came to my hand this day. What is their price, or are they to be given *gratis?* It is the *Scots Liturgy* that I use, but have been in great want of copies." This was an advance on the Rev. Robert Lyon's usage. Probably, as we saw, with a view to leaving a door of

* *History*, vol. ii., pp. 301-2.

return open for the dissentients, that Priest had been obliged to content himself with grafting the Scottish *Invocation* and *Oblation* upon the *Office* in the *Book of Common Prayer*. Now, however, that the transformation of the dissentients into an "English" or "Qualified" congregation had put the hope of reconcilement out of the way, Mr. Innes evidently felt that there was no call for his people to deny themselves any longer the privilege of the nobler Liturgy. That he was able to understand the question is to be inferred from the fact that there is still extant a copy of Brett's *Antient Liturgies*, with Mr. Innes's MS. signature on the title page.

(c) On *May 21st, 1750*, he lets in an amusing light upon his *Sermons*. "My people," he writes, "are continually teizing me for preachings. I have just now little time to write any. It will be a great favour done me if you will send me, or bring with you when you come, 40 or 50, with some *occasional* ones. I promise to be very careful of and punctually return. I am sure you (the Bishop) have numbers to spare." Twelve years later there is a similar request:— "I would fain beg the favour of some good discourses, such as you have last used or judge most proper; and particularly if you can spare them for the holy days in the enclosed list, which I much want, being very ill provided on the 5 first, having but one Sett on the next 3, and on the rest none at all, except an old one on S. Thomas, and some few for Lent." It is unlikely that in those days, when books were dear and incomes slender, Mr. Innes had much of a library, and it is only those, who feel equal to producing a constant supply of sermons to the same people without the assistance of study, who will consider his requests as

ought but reasonable. Surely he did far better to let his flock have the benefit of their Bishop's well-written discourses (as no doubt they would be), than to palm off his own rambling rhetoric upon them, on occasions when his heart and mind refused to produce a satisfactory original sermon.

(*d*) And here we have a glimpse of Mr. Innes's *Church principles*. It is gratifying to find that he carries on through his section of the eighteenth century that tradition of deference to the Primitive Church, to which the Revs. William Smyth, H. Murray, and others appealed in 1711; which Bishop Falconer kept alive till 1723; which Bishop Rattray vigorously defended against much opposition till 1743; and to which the Rev. Robert Lyon bore such sincere witness till 1746. On *May 21st, 1750*, Mr. Innes informs the Bishop that he is "reading Dr. Middleton's *Enquiry into Miraculous Powers*. But," he goes on, "I am not pleased with him; he horridly abuses the Fathers, and treats them with the outmost contempt; he endeavours to overthrow the credit of all Church history."

(*e*) That our Priest was also attentive to his *parochial visitations*, and "bore his people in his heart," we gather from the following "*Vignettes from a Parson's Album.*" On *February 5th, 1750*, he writes :—"My poor congregation has been much distressed of late, which was the cause of my being so long in acknowledging the receipt of yours. Miss Græme has been ill of a fever and the nerves, and I'm afraid she's not yet quite out of danger. Mrs. Smyth has likewise had a feaver, but it is better, and like to do well: some others also have been sick that you are not so well acquainted with. I am just come in from attending M. Belby Blair in her last moments. Poor Mr.

Stirling died on Wednesday last, and has left behind him a very disconsolate widow. These were all sick together, so that you may believe I had little idle time on my hands for some weeks bye-gone." The report on *May 28th* is in a more cheerful vein :— " Mr. D. Young has held out this winter exceeding well ; better than ever I have seen him ; but about fourteen days ago he got some disorder in his stomach which kept him some days, but he has now got the better of it and is quite well, and is gallanting the ladies as much as he did fifty years ago !" On *October 3rd*, however, there is more sorrow :—"I doubt not but you have heard the news of George Stirling's death. He sickened on *August 16th* at Paris, and died of a feaver. I need not say what a heavy stroke this was to his poor disconsolate mother. He was always a ground of comfort to her, but now nothing here can comfort her, and, till reason resume its authority, motives of comfort drawn from religion have no weight. Indeed, his death is not only a loss to his friends, but to the place in general, being one of the most hopeful, promising young men of my acquaintance." In the same letter he mentions that he was pressed by the generality of the Dunkeld people to remove thither, but he says :—" I was determined not to give up (Perth) as long as my people stuck by me." On *October 8th, 1755*, we have another vivid character sketch :—" Yesterday Mrs. Murray dyed here in the same way the rest of the family did, keeping the world as long as she could, and then leaving her share of it to such as had no need of it." On *May 20th, 1762*, he presents us with a not unfamiliar little drama :— " You would hear that I have lost Miss Murray as a parishioner, the most considerable one I had to lose,

Mr. Innes in the Country.

and, if my information be good, she is lost to us all. The laird, they say, being positive not to let her hear a non-juror. Be that as it may, he has attended the kirk ever since his marriage, which he did not use to do before." Can we not see it all?

(f) Mr. Innes's attentions were not confined to the City itself. He did his best to keep the Church alive in *the neighbourhood*. On *February 26th, 1750,* he writes:—" I am heartily sorry there is no likelihood of getting (a Clergyman) for the poor folks at Nairn. I am very willing to do all the good I can; but, unless they come to me, there is but little in my power." On *May 7th* he continues the subject:—" I was at Stanley last week. My Lady Nairne and people thereabouts are very pressing to have somebody amongst them, and I must own they deserve a supply, if it was possible to procure one for them. Logie has reflected very severely upon me for saying that, if he had given what he had first promised, a man had been settled in these parts. I forgive him." On *May 28th* we read :—" How D. Lyon would please the N. people I cannot well tell, but my opinion is that, if another could be got, it would be better." On *November 9th* he says:—" If they find themselves neglected, I will not answer for the consequence. I am afraid some of them are wavering already, and have the more need of a proper person to keep them steady. It is not in my power to do them any service in my present situation. I have enough to do at home to take care of my own people." On *November 27th* :—" I am still of opinion that there is danger of the Dunkeld people particularly (*i.e.*, getting a 'Qualified' man). I am nearer those of Nairn, and shall not fail to do all in my power to keep them steady." On

December 12th he thinks David Lyon might be acceptable to the Nairn people, but not to Logie and Dunkeld. On the last day of the year he " would be glad his friend's settlement in the district would take place, but is afraid the encouragement (*i.e.*, income) here will not answer expectation." On *September 15th, 1755*, we find the following :—" One of the gentlemen of the Glenisla congregation came to me a few days ago and desired me, in the name of that Society, to thank you for the supply you have sent them. He promises that they will make good the £6, and begs of you to advance the other £6 to such of the Clergy as supply them." Mr. Abernethy (afterwards Bishop of Edinburgh) was also considered by Mr. Innes in connection with Logie, Dunkeld, and Nairn; but he says :— " Though the people of Nairn know him,* and he might do very well with them, with the others, if I understand them and him aright, he will not." Altogether it is to be feared from the foregoing that our good Bishop and his faithful Priest could not make bricks without straw, and supply all their outlying people, when they had neither men, money, nor legal toleration.

(*g*) Meantime the worthy man's *private finances* were on a very humble scale. Yet, though this fact is sure to have contributed towards rendering him insignificant in the eyes of the world, it must have had a very different result in the sight of Heaven. For thus does he allude to his circumstances. " You see," he says on *February 5th, 1750*, "my people are mouldering away (*i.e.*, through the many recent deaths), and my

* On January 14th, 1745, "Wm. Abernethie, Deacon at Nairn and Logie," had signed a document still extant (Dr. Gordon's *Scotichronicon*, vol. v.).

finances every day growing lower, and, indeed, in a little time they are like to be scarce worth notticing. Yet, I am better content than I thought I could have been on so considerable a reduction. Providence, I hope, will provide." This account of his affairs seems to have moved the Bishop, for on *February 26th* we find him again writing to the latter:—"I think you have a little mistaken my last, for, though I told you my finances were still decreasing, I did not, if I remember right, say I was uneasie or disconcerted. I have no cause to be so. I have hitherto had food and raiment, and the same good Providence that has formerly provided for me is able, and, if I deserve it, will be willing to take care of me in time coming. Nay, I verily believe I am still better than some of my brethren. . . . Balgowan has, without my asking it, given me £15 for (*i.e.*, instead of) my £20, and, as I was resolved not to quarrel with him, I thankfully accepted."

(h) Meantime his *health* was none of the best, as we learn from the following:—"*September 15th, 1755.*—I have been in the country several times, but my cough still continues." On *December 15th* he is worse:—"I had yours of *October 13th*, to which I ought to have returned answer long ago. But I have been so distressed that it has made me forget everything of the kind. My cough still continues. I have gone through all the jargon of the shops. Last time Dr. Bayne and Mr. Wood saw me I asked what I was to take next: they answered '*Nothing.* You must go to the country for some weeks, if that does not answer you must go to Aberdeen, perhaps the journey will do you good, your native air may recover your health.' I understand this language pretty well, and yet,

perhaps they are mistaken, for I still flatter myself with hopes that (through the mercy of God) I may recover. But this town is certainly unwholesome. I begin to wish I was out of it, and yet some have lived in it to a good old age."

(i) A glance at the *postal arrangements*, though not an ecclesiastical subject, may be allowed here. On *November 27th, 1750*, Mr. Innes writes:—" I had yours of the 24th from Edinburgh, with one enclosed for Mr. Cameron, which I shall convey to him on the first opportunity. If there be nothing in the letters, which you have occasion to enclose to me that you would not have me know, I would be glad if you left them open. I would thereby make a better judgement of what haste was required in conveying them to those, for whom they are directed, besides, a double seal is almost always a double postage." On *April 11th, 1755*, we read:—"I have now written you twice without any return. Whether my letters have reached you I know not; but they are sent in the ordinary way." On *April 16th*:—"I had yours of the 14th, wherein you blame me for not writing, and yet this is now the fourth time I have done it without return. What has become of my letters I know not. I put them into the Post Office myself; three enclosed to Mr. Mitchell, and the last directed to yourself without any cover and franked by our post-master, which favour I asked of him, as I suspected my letters had been neglected at Edinburgh." On *September 15th*:—"I had yours of *August 25th*, which had been perused before I saw it; but no great matter, it contained no secret."

(j) Perhaps those who employ themselves upon the subject of the *general finances* of the Church, may not be uninterested by such glimpses as Mr. Innes gives

Church Finance.

us into the arrangements of those days. It appears, then, that the custom was for collections to be made in the Congregations for, and donations given by individuals to, the Bishop. Some of these were intended for himself, and others to be distributed by him, at his discretion, amongst his Clergy. We have the following notices on this head from Mr. Innes's letters :—[The first has already been quoted to illustrate a different point.] " Corbs has at last paid your £10 ; it's in J. Rutherford's hands, and will be given to any person you order to receive it." On *November 19th, 1753*, Bishop Alexander writes :—" Mr. Innes at Perth had not then got my letter ordering him to send in the £16, but it will surely come. He says Mr. David Young's verbal legacy of £10 stg. to the poor Clergy in the District is confirmed by the Executor, and will be paid up in the beginning of the year." On *September 15th, 1755*, Mr. Innes writes :—" My folks have made their collection, and I have got Balgowan's and Lady Balgowan's, so that I have now in my hand of yours something more than £20, which I shall remit to Edinburgh, as soon as I hear from you how much I am to retain in my hand, as you formerly told me to keep something in case of your having to send any money this way." On *October 8th* :—"I had yours of *September 17th*, and in answer to it sent to Mr. Calendar on the 19th a bill on Mansfield & Hunter for £20 17s., desiring him on receipt to write either to you or to me." And again, " Balgowan bids me tell you he has left money to pay your bill in the hands of James Græme of Damside, Writer, at Edinburgh." On *August 12th, 1755*, the Rev. Robert Lyon (formerly of Crail in Fife, now of Stretton in Bedfordshire) writes to Bishop Alexander, and introduces us to one, who conferred invaluable benefits on the Scottish Church in the days of her poverty:—" That worthy friend, Thomas Bowdler, Esq., ordered £15 15s. into my hand, to be applied to the relief of the most needy brethren, provided only they be not Seceders, nor stand in opposition to their Bishops. I have sent £7 7s. to Grd. [Gerard, Bishop of Aberdeen ?], and you have here a remainder. Ye have no occasion to mention this even to any of your own Order, but just to send me a receipt of so much money, and to fulfil the good man's intentions so far as ye can."

(k) We may now say what little is possible about our *Bishop* himself. Doubtless, if his letters to Mr. Innes had been found, they would have thrown a flood of light upon things, but not more than one or two unimportant specimens have come to light. We must be content, therefore, with Mr. Innes's allusions to him. Under this head we notice that the latter always addresses his communications thus on the outside:— " To the Right Reverend Mr. John Alexander at his house in Alloa." In the inside they begin with " Right Rev. Sir," or " R. R. S.," and end with " I recommend myself and all under my charge to your benediction, and am, with the most sincere esteem, your most affectionate son and most humble servant, George Innes." On *May 28th, 1750*, our Presbyter " would be glade the Bishop would fix a day for coming to Perth that he may not miss him: he much wishes it had been convenient for him to come sooner: he believes he'll miss several of his friends: he is almost tempted to advise him to put off his journey till the beginning of August, when he hopes he'll find all or most of his friends at home; but the Bishop can best judge what it is convenient for himself to do." On

June 11th, 1750:—" I am heartily glade to find that the affair of the Confirmation is quite over; there has, I find, been more noise than danger; your account of it gives me a great deal of satisfaction." On *October 30th* he is sorry he missed seeing the Bishop at Balgowan. On *May 10th, 1762*:—" As I expect to have the pleasure of seeing you here soon after Trinity, I beg you'll be so good, whenever you have fixed your time, to let me know as near as may be the day on which you intend to be in Perth, that I may not be absent when you come." Mr. Innes's tone to the Bishop is always very respectful, notwithstanding his evident intimacy with him. Thus he writes:—" But I hope you will not so understand me as if I meant either to dictate or even to advize, but only to inform you (which I look upon as my duty), since by my nearness to and place of conversation with the people, I may possibly know more of their inclinations than you at such a distance can be supposed to know."

(III.)—So much for the two congregations during this period. We shall conclude the chapter with notices of four visits paid to Perth by two Bishops not connected with the Diocese, and not appearing in their Episcopal capacity.

In 1760 Dr. Pococke, Bishop of Down and Connor, passed through the Fair City on his tour through Scotland, but did not here concern himself with any ecclesiastical matter.*

Two years later, "Mr. Robert Forbes," Bishop of Ross and Caithness, also passed through the town. The following is the account, which he himself gives of his visit:—†"*July 12th, 1762*—At Bridge of Earn of several

---

* Bishop Pococke's *Diary*.
† Craven's *Bishop Forbes' Journals*, pp. 140, 241-2.

arches at a half after seven, where a toll is paid for all machines and four-footed beasts. At Perth by 8 p.m. : a Royal Burgh, pleasantly situated on the west bank of the Tay, between two beautiful natural greens called the South Inch and the North Inch. *Tuesday, July 13th*—Set out from Perth half after six in the morning, and had a most charming road to Dunkeld, where we arrived 10 minutes before 10." So far, indeed, it looks as if he did not meet Mr. Innes on this occasion, but that this is a false conclusion to draw from his silence appears from the entry under date *September 1st*:—" Set off from Inver of Dunkeld 20 minutes before 10 o'clock. . . We arrived at Perth 24 minutes before 1 o'clock. As the Rev. George Innes spent the evening here going northward, I now sent for him to dine with me, but he was gone a-visiting into the country."

Eight years later this same enthusiastically Jacobite Prelate again passed through the Fair City on the way from his Incumbency at Leith to his northern Diocese of Ross, Argyle, and Caithness. Although no mention is made in his "Journal" of Mr. Innes, the entry is too characteristic of the times to be omitted :—"*June 4th, 1770*—Set out from Kinross at 27 minutes after 9, and at Perth 10 minutes after 1, where we dined at Stewart's. We made all the haste we could out of Perth, as the town was in an uproar with a birthday, and therefore we left at 2.35 p.m." The characteristic point in this entry lies in the fact, which the Bishop disdains to mention,—namely, that *June 4th* was George III.'s birthday! A smile, not unmingled with sadness, passes over the countenance, as we leave the faithful-hearted Prelate wrathfully shaking the dust of our City off his feet, and urging on his swift steeds towards Dunkeld·

CHAPTER XXII.

HOW THE ECCLESIASTICAL SUCCESSION WAS CONTINUED IN PERTH, 1776-1791.

BISHOP ALEXANDER died in Alloa on *July 17th, 1776*. Though he was not a man of the same power or position as his predecessor, yet he seems to have been a most worthy Prelate. That he continued Bishop Rattray's policy appears evident from those of his letters, which are published in Dr. Gordon's *Scotichronicon, Vol. V.* No doubt he was a Jacobite, politically, but on the other hand he energetically withstood Primus White's proposal, in 1759, to consecrate Henry Edgar as Coadjutor for Fife, on the nomination of the Prince, and boasts of the fact that not one of the Scottish Prelates owed his promotion to the (exiled) Secular Authority. He also advocated keeping the See of Edinburgh still vacant, though it had been in that condition since the death of Bishop Freebairn in 1739. His reason for this advice is instructive. It appears that, though Bishop Rattray had been able to establish freedom of election in every other Diocese, yet the Prince had issued an *Inhibition** against filling that of Edinburgh without his sanction. This was well known. Therefore (Bishop Alexander argued), it would be better to continue making no appointment to the Metropolitan See, because, if they filled it up, it must either be by obtaining the Prince's leave, which would be suicidal; or, if they did so without such permission, yet the Government would

* *Scotichronicon*, v., p. 296.

assume that they had obtained a suspension of the Inhibition from the exiled Court, and trouble would be the consequence all the same. But, perhaps, the saying of our Prelate's, which will longest dwell in the memory, is that sentence addressed to Bishop W. Falconer, in which he alludes to the difficulty of preserving even the existence of the Episcopal Order in those dangerous times. "*The Succession,*" he writes, "*lyes as near my heart as it can do yours—many an anxious thought and waking hour it gives me.*"

At a meeting held in Coupar-Angus, after Bishop Alexander's death, the Dean produced a Mandate, signed by all the members of the Scottish Episcopate,*" empowering the Presbyters of the District of Dunkeld to meet and elect a successor to our late worthy Bishop." Their choice fell upon Charles Rose, Bishop of Dunblane and Incumbent of Doune, who, as we have formerly seen, was the son of the late Bishop James Rose of Fife, and brother of the Rev. R. Lyon's betrothed. He acquiesced in his election, remarking, "I am fully determined with myself that I will never proceed to do anything of moment, without first advizing and consulting with you." The new Bishop was an enthusiastic Jacobite, and therefore on very intimate terms with his neighbour, Laurence Oliphant, Esq. of Gask. Little has been recorded of him, but there is still a path at Doune called in his memory, "The Bishop's Walk," because he used frequently to take exercise there. Unfortunately, by the year 1786 he had fallen into his dotage. While retaining Dunblane, therefore (now but "the shadow of a shade" as a Diocese, and consisting of only one Presbyter†), he was induced to resign Dunkeld.

* Dunkeld MS. *Register.*
† Dr. Walker's *Gleig,* p. 200.

*Accordingly on *October 5th* there was a meeting of the Clergy of our Diocese held at Shielhill, Kirriemuir, for the purpose of electing a successor. As there were now but 40 Clergy remaining in the whole of Scotland, the range of choice was limited, and was taxed to the uttermost in vain. The electors' first choice fell on Dr. Abernethy-Drummond (afterwards Bishop of Edinburgh), but he refused, as also did the Rev. James Lyall, the next selection. On *November 9th* there was another Synodical Meeting, at which that powerful ecclesiastic, Dr. Gleig of Pittenweem, editor of the *Encyclopædia Britannica*, was chosen. But he was too powerful. As leader of the Southern party he had become obnoxious to Bishop John Skinner of Aberdeen, the leader of the Northern, and the latter, owing to the vigour of his own character and the absence of all canonical restraint on the Bishops of those days, was practically sole Ruler of the Church. He therefore vetoed Dr. Gleig's election. The Diocese then remained vacant for six years, during which time Bishops Skinner, Abernethy-Drummond, and Strachan (Brechin) performed the necessary Episcopal offices. At last, on *July 4th, 1792*, a meeting of Clergy, held at Forfar, applied for another Mandate. The result was (as Dr. Walker has shewn) that Dr. Gleig (now of Stirling), was again elected. But Bishop Skinner, who two years previously had become Primus, again vetoed his Consecration. The Clergy then "transferred their votes to Mr. Jonathan Watson, a young man of 31," who had been Presbyter at Laurencekirk since *August, 1791*. He, "seriously considering the situation

* For this paragraph see: Grub, iv., pp. 91, 99, 111 ; Walker's *Gleig*, pp. 198, 222-3 ; Brechin *Register* ; Dunkeld *Register* ; T. Stephen, iv., p. 481.

of our Church, and trusting on the gracious support of her Almighty Head, if the Bishops shall be pleased to confirm the election, humbly acquiesced." Accordingly he was consecrated at Stonehaven, on *September 20th*, by Bishops Skinner, Macfarlane, Abernethy-Drummond, and Strachan. "Bishop Watson was a native of Banffshire, and, like most of his contemporaries in the Diocese of Aberdeen, he had been trained for the Ministry by Mr. Skinner of Linshart. He was a diligent and successful student, and his classical and theological acquirements did credit to his venerable instructor."

And now, having taken the Bishops to the end of the period included in this chapter, let us return by way of *the Deans* (who, it may be of interest to note, are always described as "*The Very Rev.*" in the *Diocesan Register*) to Perth itself. We have seen that at the meeting convened to elect a successor to Bishop Alexander on *July 17th, 1776*, the Dean presided. That official was none other than our friend, the Rev. George Innes, who had been unanimously elected to the dignity on the same day. His predecessors in the Decanal office had been as follows. At the date of the Revolution Alexander Balneaves, Parish Minister of Tibbermuir, was Dean of Dunkeld. After his death* there can be little doubt that the confusion of the times prevented his place being filled. But the appointment of Diocesan Deans followed the Concordate of 1731. It is uncertain what steps were taken in consequence of this in our Diocese immediately after that agreement; but, in 1743,† the Rev. W. Seton of

* The date of which I have not been able to ascertain. He was alive in 1699 (Scott's "*Fasti*").

† Dunkeld MS. *Register*.

Forfar is found presiding as Dean over the Synod at which Bishop Rattray's successor was elected. In 1754 he was succeeded by the Rev. David Guthrie of Restennet and Carsebank, near Forfar, who held the appointment till 1764. The next who enjoyed the dignity was the Rev. James Hill of Wester Gourdie (1764-1776). After his election in 1776 we hear nothing of Dean Innes for two years. On *January 26th, 1778*, however, he receives a solitary vote as successor to Bishop Rait of Brechin. Again on *May 16th, 1781*, the Rev. J. Allan writes thus to Bishop Petrie:—
*" Mr. Innes in Perth is struck with a palsie, and as he was anxious when in health to have a Clergyman settled in his place, to whom he professed himself willing to resign the Congregation, there is an absolute necessity of having it done immediately, otherwise, as there is a *qualified* man there, the people will be lost. Simon Reid is willing to take his chance there in case Bishop Kilgour consents, and a decent provision can be made for him." There is nothing, however, to shew that Mr. Reid was actually enabled to come to the old man's assistance. And there is something significant in the circumstance that, on *May 11th, 1784*,† Lord Stormont contributes £5 5s. towards the fund for the relief of indigent Clergy. On *October 12th, 1785*, Bishop Petrie writes a letter to our aged Priest, who, in 1786, rendered unfit by age and infirmity to perform his duties,‡ resigns the office of Dean, and is succeeded by "Father Skene" of Forfar.

At last, in *June, 1789*, he died. There is something

* Canon Archibald's *Historic Episcopate*, p. 380.

† This was the notable year in which the Scottish Bishops, out of their poverty, gave the Episcopate to America.

‡ MS. in Episcopal Chest.

very admirable, as we conclude from his letters, in the patient diligence, with which he fulfilled his pastoral duties during nearly 50 years in Perth, amid every incentive to discouragement. The cause, which lay so near his heart, was slowly but surely declining throughout his life.* But he lived to add his signature to a document, which was to prove the dawn of better things. The year before he died Prince Charlie passed away, and it was resolved by the Bishops that Churchmen were now free to transfer their allegiance to King George. Old Bishop Rose of Dunblane, indeed, and the Laird of Gask utterly refused to take the step, and others manifested their disapproval by blowing of noses and shuffling of feet, when the State prayers were first read in their altered form; but Mr. Innes was sensible enough to concur in the Episcopal resolution.

During the last three years of his life he was assisted successively by *two young colleagues.* We learn from the *Diocesan Register* that, in 1786, "Mr. William Jolly at Gask, having been ordained Deacon on S. Peter's day at Down (Doune), was then sent by the Bishop to be assistant to the Very Rev. Dean Innes at Perth, who, by age and infirmity, was several months before rendered incapable of officiating." On *December 6th* of the same year, and *June 20th* of the following, the Rev. Wm. Jolly is entered in the account book as receiving two successive grants of £2 10s. each, from the relief of indigent Clergy Fund. On *October 5th, 1786,* we find him acting as Proxy for his Senior Colleague at a Synodical meeting held at Shielhill, Kirriemuir. In fact he is appointed clerk of

* In 1756 there were 88 Clergy in Scotland; in 1786, 40.— Dean Nicolson's MSS., p. 150.

the meeting. On *November 9th* he is present at a precisely similar assembly in the same capacity. On *May 10th, 1787*, Mr. William Jolly is removed from Perth and ordained Priest at Forfar.*

As we learn from the *Register*, he was succeeded by the Rev. David Low. This Clergyman, says Mr. Conolly,† had little more than completed his nineteenth year, when he was appointed to take charge of the remnant of the old non-juring congregation at Perth, and was ordained Deacon *December 5th, 1787*, by Bishop Strachan of Brechin. The place of his ministrations at Perth seems to have been a very humble one, *i.e.*, the Wrights' Hall in the Watergate, and the congregation proportionately small. Like his predecessor, he, in 1788, receives a grant of £2 10s. from the Indigent Fund. After fifteen months' service in the Diaconate, the Congregation presented a request for the advancement of their Pastor to full Orders, and accordingly, on *February 4th, 1789*, he was ordained Priest by Bishop Strachan, the assisting Presbyters being the Revs. W. Nicoll and W. Jolly.

Of course, these Ordinations were conferred on one who had not yet attained the canonical age, but they were amply justified, both by the present distress, and also by the exceptionally faithful subsequent career of the youthful cleric. To the thoughtful mind, nothing can well be more pathetic than the indomitable faith of these good men, who, amid the ruins of their Church, the pressure of an unjust law, and the contempt and dislike of the public, clung with unconquerable tenacity to " Evangelical Truth and Apostolic Order."

* Bishop Watson mentions meeting Mr. Jolly at Forfar in *December, 1792* (see MS. letter, c/o Miss Torry).

† *Life of Bishop Low*, p. 29.

That Mr. Low did not stay long in Perth appears from the following entry in the *Dunkeld Register*:— "The Rev. Alexander Walker, Presbyter at Luthermuir in Mearns, having been invited to take charge of the Congregation in Perth, now vacant by the translation of Mr. Low to Pittenweem in Fife, was translated thither." He seems to have been a man of about the same age as Mr. Low, having been ordained Deacon and Priest in 1787-8 by Bishops Abernethy-Drummond and Strachan (*Brechin MS. Register*).

On *December 16th, 1784*, we have a glimpse of the Rev. Adam Peebles of the "Qualified" Chapel. He is then present at a meeting held "in a room adjoining the Perth Academy," at which the *Literary and Antiquarian Society of Perth* was founded, and his name subsequently appears as one of those, who used to read papers before its meetings.

During this period there seems, at least for a time, to have been a third congregation in our neighbourhood. In the *Brechin Diocesan Register*, the name of the "Rev. Thomas Beat at Inchyra" appears from *January 29th, 1777*, till *August 2nd, 1787*. It was this Presbyter, who recorded his vote for his neighbour Dean Innes as successor to Bishop Rait in the Diocese of Brechin.

BOOK III.
Repeal and Exhaustion.

CHAPTER XXIII.

HOW PERTH CHURCHMEN CONTRIBUTED TO THE
REPEAL OF THE PENAL LAWS, 1789-1792.

AT last, in 1789, after a century of almost unparalleled misfortunes, a happier period was about to dawn upon the well-nigh exhausted Church. Taking advantage of the fact that the death of Prince Charlie in 1788 had set Churchmen free to acknowledge the reigning family, it occurred amongst others to "Tullochgorum's" son, Primus John Skinner, Bishop of Aberdeen, that the time had come, when application might be made for the repeal of the Penal Laws. Accordingly, accompanied by Bishops Strachan and Abernethy-Drummond, he went up to London. The Perth family of the Lords Stormont had honoured themselves, as we have seen, on many former occasions, by aiding the cause of the Church in her afflictions. A Lord Stormont had sheltered Dundee before Killiecrankie, and had maintained the Episcopal Clergyman of Scone in his place for years after the Disestablishment: a Lord Stormont had taken part with Prince James in the 1715, and may therefore be presumed to have been friendly to the Church: Lady Stormont helped Bishop Rattray in 1740: in 1745, the Lord Stormont of the day was the trusted friend of Primus Keith, and his sisters entertained Prince Charlie: in 1784, Lord Stormont had subscribed for the relief of Dean Innes, and now once more a Lord Stormont is found strengthening the

O

hand of the Scottish Prelates. For Bishops Skinner and Abernethy-Drummond carried with them to London the following letter addressed to Lord Stormont from Lord Henderland :—*"Edinburgh, *April 2nd, 1789*—The gentlemen, who will wait upon your Lordship with this, are Mr. Abernethy and Mr. Skinner, Bishops of the Ancient Episcopal Church of Scotland. They go to London to obtain a repeal of the disqualifications imposed by Act of Parliament upon persons of that persuasion under certain circumstances, and will, with your Lordship's permission, explain more fully to you the nature of the business. They, as well as all of their Order that I know of in Scotland, are men of irreproachable character and exemplary conduct, and, as they desired a letter of introduction to your Lordship, who receives with so much politeness every person engaged in public concerns, I thought you would excuse my presumption in giving it. I have stated what I believe to be a fair testimony in their favour. As to the propriety of the measure, I leave others to decide upon it."

The recipient of this letter, along with another Perthshire nobleman and others not connected with the shire, evidently decided in favour of the "propriety of the measure," for, in a letter to the Archbishop of Canterbury, dated *May 1st*, Bishop Skinner says: "The Earl of Breadalbane, Lord Stormont (and others), did us the honour to call for us and proffer us their services." With this support, the *Relief Bill* prospered excellently at first. It actually passed through the House of Commons; but on reaching the House of Lords, it encountered the opposition of the all-powerful Chancellor, Lord Thurlow. He had no sufficient reason

* Dean Skinner's *Annals*, pp. 92-93, 99, etc.

for his conduct.* He did not even understand the matter, and Bishops Horsley and Warren, who laboured to enlighten him, "found him so uninformed upon the business that it would take them too much time to make him understand it, to give any reasonable hope of success." The *Bill* was therefore lost. The Scottish Bishops at once returned home, and the Primus summoned a Convention of the Church to meet at Laurencekirk. It was here determined to continue the fight, and a Committee of three Bishops, three Priests, and three Laymen were appointed to deal with the matter. One of the three Laymen was from Perth, *i.e.*, John Pattullo of Balhousie.

On *February 24th, 1790*, the Committee met in the Fair City. The Members present were Bishop Skinner, Revs. Allan, Gleig, and Aitken; John Stirling, Esq. of Kippendavie; and John Niven, Esq., of Peebles. Bishop Strachan and Mr. Pattullo sent valid excuses, but cordially approved of the resolutions formed, of which the following statement is extracted from the Minutes:—"The Preses gave the Committee a detail of our extensive correspondence, which he had held on the subject of the proposed *Act of Repeal*, particularly with Dr. G. Gaskin, James Allan Park and William Stevens, Esqs., all of the City of London. The

* Probably the motive, which influenced him, was a suspicion (to which the preliminary hesitation of the Bishops to agree to the introduction of Prayers for King George by name lent a faint semblance of excuse) that the Episcopal Church was still disloyal to the German dynasty. But this was not a sufficient excuse for his conduct, for the Bishops were ready to take the oaths of loyalty, and for Parliament to dictate to them, over and above that, what prayers were to be addressed to Almighty God, was a tyrannical act. For a fuller treatment of the incident, see Dr. Walker's *Life of Bishop Gleig* (pp. 201-204).

Committee, having considered that correspondence, and heard each other's sentiments on the present state of affairs of this Church, were unanimously of opinion that an application should be made in the present Session of Parliament for obtaining redress of the grievances complained of." It was further resolved to enlist the sympathies of the Universities of Oxford and Cambridge, and of all Members of Parliament, and a circular was drawn up for this purpose. The London Committee was thanked, and Bishop Skinner empowered to act on behalf of the Scottish Committee.

After this our City does not come into connection with the Repeal Movement again until 1792. Suffice it to say that the Lord Chancellor's surly hostility was sufficient to defeat the measure in three successive Sessions. In 1792, however, the result was at last different, and there can be little doubt that, along with Bishop Horsley's successful oration, the following speeches* of our two Perth laymen largely contributed to the happy result:—"*Lord Stormont* then (*i.e.*, after Lord Thurlow) rose and began with assuring their Lordships that, as there was no question before them, he was conscious it would ill become him to detain the House long. Whatever fell from the mouth of the noble and learned Lord (Thurlow) had so much weight on the minds of noble Lords in that House, and with so much justice, that he begged to speak a few words *in reply to some parts of the speech of the noble and learned Lord*, and also shortly and simply to explain the principle on which he thought it his duty to support the *Bill*.

"His Lordship then proceeded to detail the grounds, on which the penalties had been imposed, which the

* From a contemporary pamphlet.

present Bill went to repeal. When the *Statute of Queen Anne* passed, their Lordships, he said, would recollect that the circumstances of the times were peculiar. Those of the Episcopal Communion in Scotland were then known to be disaffected to the Government of the country from motives of conscience, not thinking themselves at liberty to withdraw their allegiance from the heir of the abdicated Sovereign. On those persons, therefore, and on those only, it was that the *Statute* was intended to attach.

"The case, however, at present was totally different. There now existed no such description of persons as those who were the objects of that *Act*. The Scottish Episcopalians of the present day were well affected to the Government of their country, and prayed for His Majesty and the Royal Family, as formally and sincerely as those in England did.

"With respect to what the noble and learned Lord had said concerning Toleration, Lord Stormont declared that he did not think it necessary to discuss that point, or to state his opinion on the subject. The noble and learned Lord, he observed, had said that Toleration ought to be extended to those persons only, who were known to profess some principles of religion consonant to the doctrines of Christianity.

"It was, however, a circumstance rather strongly in favour of the objects of the present *Bill*, that the members of the Established Church of Scotland wished them to be relieved from the penalties in question, which, although certainly sharper than necessary under the present circumstances of the times, were perhaps justifiable at that period of our history when they were first imposed. In Scotland, his Lordship said, he should no doubt be deemed a dissenter, yet he could not but feel some degree of national pride on observing the liberal sentiments, which the Established Church of Scotland had manifested of this occasion.

"With regard to what the noble and learned Lord had said respecting the necessity of every Episcopalian Pastor being able to prove that he had been regularly ordained by a Protestant Bishop of England or Ireland, Lord Stormont said he must beg leave to differ entirely from his Lordship. If their Lordships would but attend for a moment, they would see that in many cases it was from its nature utterly impossible. If Episcopalian Pastors were men of conscience, as he hoped they were, they could not submit to receive a *second* Ordination; and, if they did, he would only ask how the case would stand in the eyes of their congregations. Their hearers might justly tell them, 'You have passed upon us those 20 or 30 years for what you are not; you have preached to us and we have listened to you; but we now at last find that, before this time, you were never duly qualified.' Besides, if these Episcopalian Pastors were to apply to a Bishop of England or Ireland, where would they get a title? If an Episcopalian candidate for orders were to say, 'My friends in Scotland will procure a Meeting-House for me and provide for my support,' would any of the learned prelates opposite to me (said Lord Stormont, pointing to the bench) deem that a competant title? Most certainly not!

"With regard to what the noble and learned Lord had said respecting marriage, it was well known that in Scotland marriage was considered merely as a *civil contract*, as appeared from the frequent reports of what was transacted at Gretna Green, a place where he had some concern; and, if a counsel were at their Lordships' bar, and attempted to bring a witness to prove that marriage was anything else than what he had now stated it, he was persuaded that the noble and learned Lord on the Woolsack would immediately think it his duty to stop him.

"The validity of an Episcopalian Pastor's ordination, his Lordship contended, was totally out of the question. In considering the principle of the present bill, the house had nothing to do with it; and, if he held in his hand the book written by Father Courayer, some few pages of which he had once read, he declared he would not resort to the volume for a single argument in support of the doctrine he was then maintaining.

"The sole and, as he had before stated it, the simple point, on which rested the claim of the Episcopalians in Scotland to the relief which the *Bill* would give, was that, when the penalties complained of were imposed, they were clearly meant to attach on persons, who were disaffected to the existing government of the country and to the Prince upon the throne; whereas, the present Episcopalians, both Pastors and Laymen, were persons of a wholly different description. There was no occasion, his Lordship said, for him to go back to the reign of Constantine to prove what Episcopacy was; and, therefore, after apologizing to their Lordships for having detained them so long, he would conclude with declaring that it appeared to him an irrefragable argument in favour of the present Bill, that the Episcopalians of Scotland had exactly and precisely the same claims on the indulgence of the Legislature as those of the Dissenters in this part of the Kingdom from the Established Church of England."

After Bishop Horsley had lifted the debate into a somewhat more ecclesiastical atmosphere, "the Earl of Kinnoull (Lord Hay) made a short speech in favour of the Bill, and delivered his sentiments with much emphasis and energy. He described the members of the Scottish Episcopal Church as a decent, quiet, respectable body of people, who, in the most trying time, had always behaved in a very becoming and quiet manner, and were therefore well entitled to every indulgence which the Legislature could show them. Whatever amendments might be proposed, he could see no good ground for any objection to the principle of the present *Bill*, and declared himself to be thoroughly convinced that a marked distinction of legislative liberality ought ever to attach to the Established Church of either part of the Kingdom."

Thereafter the *Bill* successfully passed its second and third readings, and the Disestablished Church entered an important new phase of its history.

CHAPTER XXIV.

HOW THE REPEAL OF THE PENAL LAWS WAS FOLLOWED BY THE EXTINCTION OF THE CHURCH IN PERTH, 1792-1810.

(1). AFTER the happy result of their efforts the Primus wrote formal letters of thanks, both to others, and also to Lords Stormont and Kinnoull.*

It was, indeed, a time for congratulation to all members of the Church. But a good many years were to elapse before the benefits of the Repeal could be actually enjoyed. For, although Lord Chancellor Thurlow, on the very eve of his fall, had at last allowed the *Bill* to pass, he had hampered it with certain conditions, in which the promoters of the measure had found themselves forced to acquiesce. The *first* of these was, that the Clergy should be bound to take the oaths of Allegiance and Abjuration, and, although all were ready enough to take the former, which was a reasonable and practical stipulation, yet many scrupled at the latter, which was a requirement that, after all, was not absolutely needed. The *second* of Lord Thurlow's conditions was a surprising one: it obliged the Scottish Clergy to sign the *Thirty-nine Articles* of the Church of England before Toleration could be extended to them. Now, many of the Clergy scrupled at this theological formula, erroneously supposing that it could only be interpreted in a Calvinistic sense. But, even if they had been satisfied with its subject matter, they might well have

* Lawson, ii., p. 392.

asked by what authority a secular Assembly was dictating a theological formula to them. For twelve years, therefore, the Church did not avail herself of the benefits of the *Repeal Bill*. Her state was like that of a convalescent during the earliest stage of recovery from a severe illness. Primus John Skinner, indeed, was all energy; Bishop Jolly all learning and goodness; and Dr. Gleig all intellect; but (if we may change the metaphor), there was a prolonged twilight before sunrise.

How were the local affairs of Perth progressing during this transitional period?

With regard to the regular congregation, very little is known. It certainly, indeed, continued to exist. If we cannot be sure that, of the 18 Episcopalians, who at this time *(1795) "lived peaceably with their neighbours in Kinnoull," any owed allegiance to their true Bishop, it is at least probable that some did; for the Rev. A. Walker, whom we have mentioned as succeeding Mr. Low in 1789, was still to the fore. This is evidenced by two circumstances. *First*, because Miss Helen Laidlaw, who died somewhere about the year 1870 at a very advanced age (*circa* 86), used to tell trustworthy witnesses, still alive (1894), that, while her father occupied Balhousie Castle, the Episcopal Service was held under his roof, and that the circumstance was amongst her own earliest recollections; and this would carry us back to the times, with which we are now dealing. And, *secondly*, Mr. Walker's name appears in the year 1802 as Secretary in the Records of the *Perth Literary and Antiquarian Society*, and the titles of some of the papers, which he read before that body, are still preserved. But

* *Statistical Account of Perth*, pp. 84-90.

there can be little doubt that, although existing, our congregation was in a declining state. The very fact that they had left off worshipping in the Wright's Hall, and had migrated to a gentleman's private residence, seems to imply that both their means and numbers had fallen off. And in 1802 it must have been recognised that the end was not distant, for in that year Lords Mansfield (Stormont) and Kinnoull renounced their allegiance to the Scottish Bishops.

*While this was the state of affairs in Perth, the Dean of the Diocese (Skene of Forfar) died, after a ministry of 43 years, on *April 19th, 1797*. He was certainly succeeded in his Decanal capacity at some time, and probably at once, by the Rev. John Robertson of Strathtay.

With regard to the irregular Congregation, it has to be recorded both that its affairs were more prosperous, and also that it has left fuller memorials behind it. That they still had the Rev. Adam Peebles in their employment as minister (he had succeeded Mr. Cameron in 1770) is evident, because his name occurs as one of the Vice-Presidents of the same society as that of which Mr. Walker was secretary. Under his *régime* an important step was resolved upon. Owing to the increase of the Congregation and the growing dilapidation of the Parliament House, where they had assembled since 1750, it was resolved to build a new Chapel.† With this end in view a subscription was started about the year 1793. Two years later a site was acquired in what is now Princes Street, and five years later still, it was formally made over to the Congregation for a sum of £70, by Col. Mark Wood of Potterhill. A condition (shewing a somewhat irreconcilable spirit)

* Dunkeld MS. *Register*.   † S. John's MSS. *Minute Books*.

was made to the effect that a place of worship, in which only the Services of the Church of England should be performed, must be built upon the spot. The erection of the Chapel was, of course, the next thing proceeded with. This was completed in the year 1800, and the Congregation moved into it. The chief contributor to the building fund was Sir William Nairne, Lord Dunsinane, who paid off a debt of about £550 after the completion of the edifice. In 1802 the Earls of Kinnoull and Mansfield joined the Congregation; but one is compelled to believe that there can have been no great fervour of true Church life there, when we learn that, while the upper flat of their new building was the Chapel proper, the lower (*horresco referens!*) was let out for wine and porter stores! In 1804 Mr. Peebles died.

(2). The same year was also noteworthy in the history of the Church at large. For on *October 24th* at a Convocation held in Laurencekirk,* the Church, by the free exercise of her own will, determined to accept the *XXXIX Articles*. And this had two happy effects: *first*, that now the provisions of the *Bill* for the repeal of the Penal Statutes were formally complied with; and *secondly*, that the various irregular and (so-called) "English" Congregations at the same time resolved to return to the unity of the Church, and so brought its numbers up to about 25,000,† or double of what it was before. On the one side Primus Skinner and the rest of the Bishops did all they could to smooth the way, and on the other Dr. Sandford, the leading "English Episcopalian," set his brethren a noble example of dutifulness by coming over, and was, to the satisfaction of all, consecrated

* Dean Skinner's *Annals*, pp. 345-351.   † Dr. Walker's *Gleig*, p. 213.

Prospects of Union. 237

Bishop of Edinburgh—Bishop Abernethy-Drummond having resigned on purpose to make way for him.

While union was thus the characteristic of the age at large, in what way was it forwarded in Perth? Surely the Scottish Congregation in the City, now that it has weathered so many violent storms, has at last sailed into a haven of peace! Surely the "English" Congregation will at length repay the wrong it did the Church, through its indefensible schism in Bishop Rattray's time, by returning and imparting to its decaying Scottish sister a share in its worldly prosperity! But no! Not yet was this happy consummation to be reached.

> "*Facilis descensus Averni,*
> *Sed revocare gradum superasque evadere ad auras,*
> *Hic labor, hoc opus est!*"

The narrative of the failure is this:—*On the death of the Rev. A. Peebles, it was resolved to hold a general meeting of the Congregation for the purpose of electing a Vestry; and elected a Vestry was, with powers such as are calculated to make

> "*each particular hair to stand on end,*
> *Like quills upon the fretful porcupine,*"

of any Churchman, who is made acquainted with their tenor. For they ran as follows, leaving no possible opening for a Bishop in a professedly Episcopal Congregation :—The newly-appointed body is "to have powers to elect new members as vacancies might happen: *to appoint and remove Clergymen, and to do everything for the complete management of the temporal and spiritual affairs in every particular, without control.*"

Clothed though they were with these truly Papal prerogatives, they nevertheless judged it expedient to

* S. John's MSS. *Minute Books* supply the main outline.

delegate some of their spiritual authority to a humbler individual, who should be responsible for the actual reading of Prayers and delivery of Sermons; or, in other words, they proceeded to institute a Clergyman. And, in the carrying out of this project, we are thankful to say that they began to act on better principles than they formally professed. For it so happened that Mr. Walker left Perth at this conjuncture and settled at Monymusk,* in Aberdeenshire, and thus both our Incumbencies were vacant at the same time. It is certain that the opportunity was therefore taken of trying to unite the two Congregations. On the one hand, Bishop Gleig, acting for the Bishop of the Diocese, advised Mr. Walker's people to attend the "English" Chapel;† and, on the other, when the election came on there, they were made welcome to join in it.

There can be no doubt that the popular understanding was that, what was going on everywhere else, was about to take place in Perth also, and that a Presbyter in communion with the Bishop was to be chosen. Even the Vestry, who appear to have been somewhat reticent on the point, gave considerable support to this view by writing the following letter to the Primus:—"*March 12th, 1805.*—The Vestry, considering that there is a difference of opinion among the members of the Congregation whether the Clergyman should be a member of the Scots Episcopal Church, and with a view to conciliate that difference as much possible, agree to write Bishop Skinner at Aberdeen to enquire if one of his sons, who was educated in England, and ordained by an English Bishop, would undertake the Charge." To this the Primus replied

* Aberdeen MS. *Diocesan Register.*   † Dr. Walker's *Gleig*, p. 390.

cautiously: he evidently endeavoured to encourage the unmistakeable movement towards union, but yet was unwilling altogether to commit himself till the Vestry were more definite. On *March 16th* he wrote :—" I am just now favoured with your letter containing a proposal from the Vestry of the English Episcopal Chapel in Perth that my son, who was ordained in England, should offer himself a candidate for the present vacancy in that Chapel. Both he and I consider ourselves as much obliged to the gentlemen of the Vestry for this mark of their respect and good opinion of my son's qualification, and I think it my duty to lose no time in informing you that my son is settled here in the character of my Assistant. With that view he received his Ordination from an English Bishop, to shew that there is no inconsistency in persons so ordained uniting themselves to the Scottish Episcopal Church. Such a union, therefore, I would beg leave to recommend as highly worthy of the attention of so respectable a body as the Vestry and Congregation of the now vacant English Episcopal Chapel, Perth; a measure, which has met with the warmest approbation of some of the most distinguished Prelates of the Church of England as the best means of promoting the truest interests of Episcopacy in this part of the Kingdom."

The result of this correspondence was that the Vestry had done nothing formally to commit themselves to the union project, and, at the same time, the members of the two Congregations, knowing that the Primus was being taken into counsel, must have concluded that there was a serious intention of doing what so many Congregations in like circumstances were doing, *i.e.*, coming to an agreement with the

Bishops. This impression could not fail to be much strengthened by that, which followed the failure to obtain the Rev. W. Skinner's services. For the Vestry, continuing their enquiries, fixed upon the Rev. Mr. Fenwick, who was recommended by the Congregation of Leith. Now this Congregation had joined in the union, having before been in the same position as our irregular Chapel. Hereupon, when the election took place, twenty-one "members of the late Scots Episcopal Congregation" joined in the vote in favour of Mr. Fenwick. And he, on his arrival, came to an understanding with the Bishop of the Diocese (Watson).* Thus the members of the two Congregations were amalgamated, on terms that were, ecclesiastically speaking, satisfactory enough.

But, alas! Mr. Walker's people should have made certain that the terms were not only satisfactory, but also rendered formally binding on both parties. There was a want of business exactness about the whole transaction. The mass of the Congregation is shewn by their election of Mr. Fenwick to have been quite glad to have a Clergyman, who submitted to the Bishop. But the Vestry had never cancelled their own episcopal powers, and seem never to have intended to allow the Chapel to pass under the Bishop's hands, whatever the people and the Clergyman might choose to do. And so, when it was found that Mr. Fenwick did not give satisfaction, and went to England in 1808, they secured the appointment of the Rev. H. Skete, Curate of Wooler, in the Diocese of Durham. And he, notwithstanding the fact that, †"when passing through Edinburgh on his way north, he had waited on Bishop Sandford and promised to maintain the union, renounced

* Neale's *Torry*, p. 303.   † Neale's *Torry*, p. 335.

his allegiance in a letter to his own bishop under the pretence that he was connected with the Church of England." This was in 1810. He was probably inspired in his action by one or two of the very influential personages on the Vestry. The Constitution clothed them, as we have seen, with autocratic powers, and these they were determined to preserve by thwarting the union.

It is not to be expected that the Bishop of the Diocese would allow a flock, which had practically come under his jurisdiction, and which in any case had absorbed a congregation that wholly belonged to him, to drift back to schism without at least a fatherly attempt to stop the relapse. And, in fact, such an attempt was made. If there was to be a renewal of the division, the blame was not to lie at his door.

But, before we describe the Bishop's conduct in this matter, we have to relate a change with regard to the occupant of the Episcopal Throne. Bishop Watson had fallen *" into a complete prostration of strength and as much bodily imbecility" as if he had reached the three score and ten years of the Psalmist, although in fact he was only forty-seven. And this circumstance may explain how it was that the movement for union in Perth was carried through on such unsatisfactory lines. In 1808 he died. There was again some difficulty in the choice of a successor. For the third time Dr. Gleig was pitched upon by the Clergy; but, owing to the continued opposition of Primus Skinner, the confirmation of the election fell through.† Accordingly

* T. Stephen, iv., p. 181.
† This same year, however, Dr. Gleig was unanimously elected to Brechin, and the Primus was obliged to consecrate him. The two Bishops worked, after all, harmoniously together (Walker's *Gleig*, 259).

another meeting was held under the presidency of Dean Robertson, at which Patrick Torry, Incumbent of Peterhead, was chosen.* The Bishops having ratified the vote, the Prelate-elect was consecrated at Aberdeen, and continued, according to the custom and necessities of the time, to live at Peterhead. He was, indeed, a thorough Scotchman of the old-fashioned school; but this description must be understood as comprising a cultivated mind, dignified manners, and a decided will. Theologically also he was thoroughly Scotch, inheriting all the old traditions of the school of Bishop Rattray and Bishop Alexander. "He often," said his son, the Dean, "refreshed his memory with the works of (the old non-juring Divines) Kenn, Hickes, Collier, Brett, and others." And the maintenance of the *Scottish Eucharistic Office* was the passion of his life.

Such was the Prelate whose lot it became to make the last paternal effort for restraining the Perth Congregation from Schism. What he did was to write in the following entirely friendly way to the Vestry:—
"*June 30th, 1809.*—As I have been called by the good Providence of God to discharge the duties of the Episcopal Office in the Diocese of Dunkeld;† and, as I intend by the Divine permission to hold my primary visitation of the Diocese in the month of August next, I have deemed it incumbent on me to notify this intention to you and to the Clergyman officiating in

* Neale's *Torry*, pp. 68, 299.

† The late Bishop Wordsworth once suggested to me that Bishop Torry made a mistake in claiming Perth as being in the Diocese of Dunkeld. And, of course, it is originally part of the Diocese of S. Andrews. Over this Bishop Torry did not preside when he wrote the above letter. But surely the *Concordate* of 1731 must be looked upon as an act of the Scottish Church. Even the dissentient Perth Managers acquiesced in it till 1740.

End of the Orthodox.

your Chapel, and to say that, if you are desirous of having the sacred and Apostolic Rite of Confirmation administered to the young people of the Congregation, with which you are connected, I will most gladly come forward to Perth for that purpose." And the good Bishop added a few kindly words about "there being such a beauty in the entire harmony and unity of those who are distinguished by the same name and profession." But it was all in vain. In reply "the Clergyman and Vestry of the Qualified Chapel *declined* his services on the *pretence* that they belonged to the Church of England: a pretence so groundless that Bishop Horsley, when pleading the cause of the Scottish Church in the House of Peers, . . . declared, in reference to those gentlemen called the 'Qualified Clergymen,' that they had no more connection with the Church of England than they had with the Church of Mesopotamia."

And so our Congregation, the history of which we have been relating, and which 120 years of trouble had not sufficed to destroy, came to an end at last by yielding a too ready compliance to the suggestions of seeming friends. In any case, the termination of so long and so brave a struggle for existence against overwhelming odds would move our sympathy. But it is all the sadder because, while our flock was dying, the

And by the *Concordate* Perth, if not actually transferred to the *Diocese* of Dunkeld, was placed under the jurisdiction of the *Bishop who presided over that See*, and from that time till 1837, while the two Dioceses were separate, the Perth Clergy took part in all elections to the Bishopric of Dunkeld, and were subject to the occupant of that See. Until, therefore, our City is as formally restored to the Diocese of S. Andrews as it was transferred to the Bishop of Dunkeld in 1731, it must be looked upon as under the jurisdiction of the latter.

first pulse of renewed life was beating in the veins of our northern Zion. *The Dissentients elsewhere were being reconciled. £12,000 was being collected for the hitherto unpaid Bishops and the more necessitous of the Clergy. The Government was being persuaded to grant the *Regium Donum*. The Friendly Society was beginning its beneficent career for the widows and orphans of the Clergy, and a fund was being raised in England for the building and repair of our Churches. God only, who chastiseth every son whom He receiveth, knows why our flock should have been at length starved to death in sight of food. But, whatever the reason, so it was.

(3).—But, in fact, these first signs of new life did not prevent our country districts too from suffering much the same fate as Perth itself. In them also the Church was dying from the exhaustion engendered by her prolonged distress. It is related,† for instance, that about this time, "in a certain glen in *Perthshire*," the inhabitants were lost to our Communion from the want of means to maintain a Clergyman. At first the Church portion of the community, whilst they frequented the Established worship on Sundays, continued for a long time to resort to the nearest Episcopal Church on the high festivals. At last even this practice fell into disuse. Here and there, however, a few stood firm in the faith of their fathers, and these were frequently subjected to a good deal of ridicule on account of their alleged bigotry. The following tale of this period still survives :—"On the day before a certain Good Friday, a Highlander, clad in his best, was seen wending his way southward through his

---

* Dr. Walker's *Last Hundred Years*.
† *Scottish Ecclesiastical Journal*, 1862, p. 23.

native glen. Passing a group of his acquaintances, he was saluted with the question, evidently meant as the introduction to a little bantering: "*Ou, Alister, far will ye be gaen this fine day?*" "To ———," was the reply, mentioning a town 25 miles distant. "*An' fat may be tackin' ye awa' sic a distance at this time o' year?*" —was the next enquiry. The questioner had himself once been a Churchman, and drew down upon himself the quick retort: "*Just to get the Bishop's blessing, a thing that was ill waured (bestowed) on you.*"

No longer need the Perth Presbytery be "in a very sad taking, and needing our sympathy very much." The district, where they had struggled in vain between 1690 and 1712 to abolish Episcopacy, was now almost completely reduced to the state at which they aimed to bring it. But, indeed, even they had probably by this time come to understand that it was their former adversaries, who really "needed sympathy very much."

Nevertheless, thus saith the Lord:—"*Yet will I leave a remnant, that ye may have some that shall escape, . . . when ye shall be scattered*" (*Ez.* vi., 8).

CHAPTER XXV.

HOW THE LAND LAY DESOLATE, 1810-1846.

The *Scottish Magazine**informs us that "the Orthodox Party in Perth contented themselves with abstaining from participating in the Sacraments of their Minister." Notwithstanding this last effort to retain their individuality, however, it is likely to have been made on a small scale and for a limited period. Like the Highlanders in the glen, described at the close of the last chapter, the discouraged remnant probably began to force themselves to make the best of inevitable circumstances, which they disliked, but for which they could hardly be blamed. And so, with the exception of whatever protests it was in their power to record, the history of the Church in our City is a mournful blank for the next thirty-six years.

Bishop Torry was grieved at the result, but what step could he take to help it? "Something, indeed," he says,† " must be done, and done soon, or the few faithful people will be for ever lost to us." And he welcomed the suggestion of Mr. Low (who had left Perth in 1789) to the effect that the best thing to do was " to get a young man of decent manners and respectable talents to open a Chapel. But unluckily," he adds, " what was Mr. Walker's Chapel *has fallen down*, and I know not where the rent could be found for some time for another house sufficiently large." Doubtless it was the lack of funds which hampered the Bishop. It was out of the question to suppose that the 21 voters of the old Congregation,

* 1850, p. 18.   † Dr. Walker's *Gleig*, p. 290.

Stagnation. 247

who had been enticed over to Princes Street, could both pay for a Clergyman's salary and the expense of procuring and maintaining a Chapel. None of them could have been wealthy. And it must be remembered that, while there was a lack of local resources, a Bishop in those days had no "Representative Church Council," or anything of a general kind answering to it, to fall back upon. The fact is, that after Primus Skinner had gathered together the fragments of the Church that remained after the Repeal of the *Penal Laws*, these remnants were found to be afflicted with extreme poverty and lack of corporate organization. Each congregation aimed at simply struggling along for itself. They hailed the permission to exist, which they had now gained, as a great gift, and an aggressive Mission policy did not come within the range of their practical politics. And it is a curious fact that not the Scottish Church alone was invaded at this epoch by this passive spirit. The Church of England, too, shared in it, and had to be roused by the Oxford Movement of 1833; the Scottish Establishment shared in it until it was roused by the Secession of the Free Kirk in 1843; and the State itself shared in it, and had to be roused by the Reform Bill of 1832. Things, therefore, being in this state, Bishop Torry found it impossible to make an energetic forward movement in Perth. And, even if he had attempted it, he would have been met by the opposition of all the titled and landed gentry, who, professing to be Churchmen in the neighbourhood of the Fair City, constituted the Vestry of the Princes Street congregation.

And so the land lay desolate. The history, therefore, of the Church in Perth between the years 1810-

1846 can only consist of three, and these hardly genuine, kinds. *First*, we may look for some account of our quasi-episcopal Chapel; *secondly*, we may wander from Perth and take a glimpse of Bishop Torry in the other parts of his Diocese; and, *thirdly*, we may chronicle the passing visits of outside Churchmen to our City. We shall take these three in their order:—

(I.)—First, therefore, with regard to the quasi-Episcopal Chapel in Princes Street.*

Since in them was lodged the power "to appoint and remove clergymen and to do everything for the complete management of the temporal and spiritual affairs (of the Congregation) in every particular without control," we must, of course, begin with the Vestry. After the general meeting of 1805, which had conferred on them such plenitude of spiritual authority as no Bishop in the Church would dare to claim for himself (for *he* would admit some "control" in the shape of the Canon Law of Synods and Councils), there was no subsequent election, and the Earl of Kinnoull, the Earl of Mansfield, Lord Dunsinnane, Lord Gray, Sir David Moncrieffe, Sir J. Richardson, and John Grant, Esq. of Kilgraston, continued at their posts.

From this right reverend body we descend to their Minister. He, good man, was bound by the *Prayer Book* (which was supposed to be accepted in the Chapel) " to instruct the people committed to his charge "; " to minister the discipline of Christ " to the same; " to use both publick and private monitions and exhortations as well to the sick as the whole "; and " reverently to obey his Ordinary." But, considering the powers claimed by the Vestry, the social position of

* S. John's *Minute Books*.

the gentlemen composing it, and the fact that he was absolutely dependent on them for his £100 a year (or £150 in good years), we are not surprised to learn that the requirements of the *Prayer Book* were exactly reversed, and the unfortunate Minister of Christ "*was in all things subject to the Vestry.*"

The income of the Chapel was derived from a collection taken at the door and from seat rents. The letting of the latter occupies a great space in the *Minute books*. Of course this source of revenue forms matter for discussion even to the present day. We are, therefore, not surprised to find that it was found to have its drawbacks under the circumstances, which we are considering. The following notices in connection with this point afford food for reflection. We find one noble Lord (forgetting, it would seem, that he was referring to the House of God) " conceiving that the seat he occupied was *his absolute property*, and protesting against any alteration which might in the smallest degree encroach upon or tend to diminish the comfort and convenience of it." And then he and his colleagues meet together in obedience to a Christian instinct, which was better than the principles, which they formally professed, to lament the fact that the attendance of the poorer members was falling off. Might it not have occurred to them that the cause of this was possibly to be found in the fact that self-respecting working men must have had some delicacy in intruding into a building, over which a Committee of Grandees claimed such absolute powers of ownership and control? A Labourer might be excused for a suspicion that perhaps his presence or that of his family next a seat, in which a noble Lord claimed an absolute property, might be held " to

interfere with the comfort and convenience of it."
Of course the Vestry would have been distressed to
think that such ideas got about, and they very
properly endeavoured to remove all ground for them by
agreeing to set apart a few seats as free; but the
diminution of the attendance of the humbler classes
was doubtless caused, unknown even to themselves, by
that absence of the Catholic conception of the Church,
which characterized the administration of the Chapel.

The military also attended, and were a slight
additional source of income.

In 1809 a subscription for an Organ was opened,
and estimates invited both "for finger and barrel."
An instrument of the required kind was therefore
procured. It is probably the earliest instance of "a
kist of whustles" in a Perth Church since the
Reformation. At first all seems to have gone well
with its management: the only change necessary was
that Worship should begin a little earlier than had
been usual; and on *October 22nd, 1810*, the Vestry
resolve that, "considering that the time of service is
lengthened by the Organ, it will be necessary for to
go in at 11 o'clock." Afterwards, however, it is
evident that effects not aimed at by the best com-
posers must have been persistently produced on that
instrument; for on *November 9th, 1832*, "the
meeting direct Mr. Moncrieff to desire that the Clerk
occupy the lower desk when reading the Service, and
make arrangements for the Organ being grinded in
place of being played." On *February 9th, 1844*, "Mr.
Watson, one of the Choir, is appointed along with
four or five boys to make the responses, which can be
accomplished at the expense of £5 or £6."

As the old Scotch Episcopalians did not wear the

surplice either before or after their Disestablishment in 1689 (in the former period owing to the excessive moderation, which they practised from prudential reasons towards those without, and in the latter owing to the succession of storms, through which they had to pass, and which rendered it advisable to make themselves as little conspicuous as possible), Mr. Skete was probably the first to use that vestment in Perth. We presume that he did so at the ordinary Services; and we are informed* that he attempted to do so at a funeral, but that in the latter case he was compelled to desist, as it elicited a volley of stones from the crowd which had assembled.

Considering the theological bent of the congregation, we are as much surprised as delighted to find them speaking of the "Holy Table" as the "Altar." Since, however, this was in 1809, shortly after the Bishop's congregation was absorbed, and as the old Scotch Episcopalians were very "high" in doctrine, however "low" they were in Ritual, we may presume that the use of the word was due to the influence of the "Catholic remnant."

When things were in their most flourishing condition during this period, Mr. Skete had about 120 communicants; but, as a rule, in these pre-railroad days the ecclesiastical vigour displayed seems to have been very moderate in volume.

(II.)—But to proceed now to our second point—*viz.*, a glance at the Bishop in the other parts of his Diocese. Such a glimpse as we desire is provided by the following reminiscences of his father's Episcopal tours by the Rev. J. Torry (afterwards Dean):—†"The

* *Scottish Magazine*, 1849, p. 251.
† *Scottish Ecclesiastical Journal*, 1862, p. 57.

late Bishop Torry," he says, "lived at a remote extremity of Aberdeenshire, and his Diocese of Dunkeld and Dunblane (he was not yet Bishop of Fife or S. Andrews) extended over a large portion of the counties of Forfar and Perth, the nearest part of it being about 100 miles from his place of abode. Every third year he went forth, according to the regulation of the Church, for the purpose of confirming and discharging other Episcopal duties. It was not then the days of "Defiance" coaches or railway speed. The Bishop's practice, therefore, was to hire a horse and gig at Peterhead, and in that conveyance to continue his journey from day to day during the three or four weeks his peregrinations lasted. The gig of those days was a vehicle of very humble description, and furnished with a steed which, generally speaking, would go about five miles an hour. In the summer of 1816, I accompanied my Father through his Diocese, and as his charioteer acquired my first lessons in driving. The Bishop's territory and professional labours began at Forfar, and after they were over for the day, we enjoyed at the pleasant villa of Inchgarth the hospitality of the Incumbent, the Rev. John Skinner. The next morning took us to the neighbouring town of Kirriemuir, five miles off. On our way to Alyth on the following day, the unskilfulness of the driver caused the gig to be upset, with, however, no serious results. A few days after the accident found us at the residence of the Dean (Robertson), Incumbent of Strathtay-cum-Blair-Athole-et-Tummel-Bridge (for in those days our Clergy were few, though their charges were many and far between). This gentleman lived in a house overlooking the pleasant valley of Strathtay; but O! how unlike the

Decanal Palaces of merry England! It could not even be said of it in Goldsmith's words—

> '*Near yonder copse, where once a garden smiled,*
> *The village preacher's modest mansion rose.*'

No flowers grew there, and the semblance of a garden contained only some Scotch kale and leeks and a few other useful herbs. It was a small, rude cottage, with a solitary ash tree or two growing near it, which bore the Celtic name of *Tillypourie*, and stood on the face of a bare hill at an elevation of not less than 500 feet or 600 feet above the Tay. There was a small farm attached, by means of which the old Dean (otherwise 'passing rich with forty pounds a year') contrived to treat his visitors hospitably. On the first day of our arrival we had service in the little Church below, and there occurred one of those scenes of the Bishop imparting his Blessing to large numbers —a thing which I witnessed for the first time, and which is fixed indelibly on my mind." The form which he used was as follows:—*" The Blessing of Almighty God and the Comfort of His Holy Spirit be upon you and abide with you for ever!" From Strathtay the Bishop and his son travelled first to Pitlochrie, then to Blair-Athole and Tummel Bridge, where "the Services being over, both the ladies and the gentlemen repaired to the Inn to entertain the Bishop to lunch. The latter had now reached the most distant part of his Diocese, and returned by a hilly but otherwise excellent road to the valley of the Tay. In proceeding down its banks from Aberfeldy to Dunkeld, we stopped about half-way at Balnaguard Inn. Such were some of the comforts incident to Episcopal journeys in bye-gone days."

* According to the memory of an aged Churchman.

Episcopal History of Perth.

And now, while the absence of local Perth history is inviting us to make this *excursus* into general Diocesan affairs, a statistical view of Bishop Torry's Diocese* will not be uninteresting, especially as it has not before appeared in print.

In 1801, there were *six* charges in Dunkeld under the Bishop of that Diocese; and *five* in Dunblane and Fife, which Sees were not then united to Dunkeld: total, 11.

No statistics till 1829, when, beginning with *Dunkeld* alone, things went thus:—

YEAR.	CONGREGA- TIONS.	BAPTISMS.	COMMUNI- CANTS.	MARRIAGES.	FUNERALS.
1829.	5	25	345^4	3	6
1830.	5	39	435^4	0	13
1831.	5	33	427^4	5	20
1832.	5	39	451^4	3	19
1833.	5	33	436^4	8	22
1834.	5	36	425^4	12	21
[1]1835.	6	40	480^4	8	22
1836.	6	56	482^4	8	29
[2]1837.	6	45	479^4	5	29
[3]1838.	—	—	—	—	—
1839.	9	57	682^5	9	25
[3]1840.	—	—	—	—	—
1841.	11	41	518^4	4	14
1842.	11	70	541^4	4	23
1843.	12	80	673^4	11	38
1844.	13	78	702^5	8	27
1845.	13	60	847^5	9	27
1846.	14	74	871^5	7	29

1 In 1835, the Diocese of Dunblane was added to that of Dunkeld.
2 In 1837, the Diocese of Fife (S. Andrews) was added to Dunkeld and Dunblane.
3 Returns very incomplete.
4 Number of Persons, who actually communicated at the chief Festivals.
5 Number of "Communicable Persons."

A consideration of the table shows, on the one hand, that in the area comprised by the three Dioceses the

* From the MS. *Diocesan Register.*

Church must have been retrograding during the first forty years of the century, since it is not till the year 1840 that the total of Incumbencies for the year 1801 is equalled. On the other hand, there is a steady increase, in a small way, over the whole district after 1840, and in Dunkeld alone there seems to have been a slight advance previous to that year.

This will be the proper place to carry on the Decanal Succession. Dean Robertson died in 1829. He was succeeded by the Rev. John Skinner of Forfar. The new Dean was the grandson of "Tullochgorum" (Skinner of Linshart); the son of Primus John Skinner; the brother of Primus William Skinner; and the father of him, who was afterwards well-known as the Rev. James Skinner of Malvern. He himself was well known as the author of *Annals of Scottish Episcopacy* which was practically a fourth volume to his grandfather's *Ecclesiastical History of Scotland*, and he was undoubtedly a man of great ability and energy. Had his ideas been carried out, the Church's period of torpor would certainly have been shortened. In 1838, ill-health compelled him to resign; and he was succeeded by the Bishop's son, the Rev. John Torry, Incumbent of Meigle, and afterwards of Coupar-Angus.

(III.)—And now, thirdly, we must chronicle the temporary visits of outside Churchmen to our City:—

(a) *In 1819, Bishop Torry was passing through Perth on his way to Stirling to assist at the Consecration of our former Incumbent, the Rev. David Low, to the Bishopric of Ross and Argyle. While tarrying here, he received the following letter from the venerable Bishop of Moray (Alexander Jolly):—" Will you then

* Archibald's *Church in Keith*, p. 152.

bespeak a snug little bedroom (single), easily warmed by a good fire, kindled some time before the arrival of the coach, that a friend of yours, valetudinary, may retire to it—making the proper acknowledgement of what he may want *there*, and not in the travellers' room?"

(*b*) *In 1824, the Bishop authorized a meeting of Clergy to be held in Perth, "as the most convenient place," and fixed the date "for the third Wednesday after Easter, because the Festival duties of even the most scattered charges will then be over." The meeting was held as appointed. Its object was the consideration of a proposal made by Mr. Skinner of Forfar to the effect that Synods ought to be more frequently held, their powers extended, and the Laity admitted to their deliberations. Mr. Skinner's zeal on the subject had been kindled by the visit of the American Bishop, Dr. Hobart, and he felt that it was necessary that his proposal should be carried out, in order that the Church should be roused from its stagnation into life and action. Whatever may be thought about his project of admitting the Laity as constituent members of the *Synods*, there can be no question that their complete exclusion from an official position in ecclesiastical work, which then obtained, was a grievous wrong inflicted on the Church, and some recognized sphere of usefulness ought at once to have been made theirs. There can also be no doubt that there was crying need for the more frequent meetings of Synods, both Diocesan and General. But Mr. Skinner's proposals came to nothing at the time: his aims were regarded with some consternation. It was held revolutionary even to ventilate suggestions on any subject before the Bishops moved.

* Neale's *Torry*, p. 116.

(c) In 1835, we have the following characteristic but pathetic peep into the ecclesiastical affairs of our City:—" 'Twas on a fine morning about the beginning of November," says an anonymous writer in *Stephen's Magazine*, "that I found myself pretty comfortably seated on the top of the *Defiance* coach. Nothing worthy of notice occurred during our journey to Perth. But here my musing began. What a pity, said I to myself, to see so many fine houses inhabited by intelligent people, without a single one, that I am aware of, being occupied by a member of the Scottish Episcopal Church! That all, who attend what is anomalously called 'The English Chapel,' are ignorant of Episcopacy I cannot allow myself to suppose; nay, in the spirit of charity, which ought always to pervade our minds, I can even imagine that some of the best informed amongst them would not be hostile to an indigenous Bishop, were their present state fairly and fully brought before them. . . . Just as I was about to contemplate in imagination the pleasing spectacle of a Confirmation in Perth, the guard of the coach desired the passengers to replace themselves. Of course, I obeyed the summons, and after proceeding a few miles sleep seized me with such a firm grasp, as I reclined on a pedlar's pack, that nothing but the dirl of the coach on the streets of Forfar had the effect of awakening me."

(IV.)—We shall conclude this chapter by returning to the first of our three heads, and adding something more on the subject of the quasi-Episcopal Chapel. And fortunately it is matter, which both completely justified the charitable meditations of the traveller on the *Defiance* coach, and also conducts us to the comforting conclusion that the schismatical position of the Congregation was not due to the Congregation itself, but to the determination of some powerful individual or individuals, who loved to wield the Episcopal authority in their own influential but unordained persons. The circumstance, to which we allude, consisted of an outburst of genuine Church principle from within the Congregation itself. This was probably created, *first*, by some remnants of the old Scottish flock still existing in the shape both of people and of tradition; and *secondly*, by the contact of this element with the great Movement, headed by Keble, Newman, Pusey, and others, which was now quickening the life of the Church of England.

The form which this local revival of true ecclesiastical principles took is recorded in a Minute of *December 4th, 1840*, which also throws some light upon the question of who was, and who was not, responsible for the schism. Mr. Grant of Kilgraston "proposed that measures should be taken for a union of the Chapel with the Episcopal Church of Scotland, assigning his reasons for the proposition, which was seconded by Mr. Ross. Lord Mansfield objected to the proposition. Mr. Lorimer, Lord Kinnoull's factor, stated that he had reason to believe that Lord Kinnoull concurred with Lord Mansfield. It was, therefore, agreed to postpone further consideration of the subject."

The Earls had been powerful enough to put down this first attempt to question their spiritual authority. But they had by no means heard the last of it. Catholic principle is a very real thing, and it had now fairly taken hold on the minds of the party, which was growing in favour of reconciliation with the Church. The result was that they returned to the

Address on Union. 259

charge on *May 3rd, 1842*, with the following pointed and admirable "Address":—

"We, the undersigned members of the Congregation, beg humbly to bring under the serious consideration of the Vestry the necessity there exists of the Chapel being placed under the jurisdiction of the Scottish Episcopal Church. And in support thereof will observe that, as now constituted, we do not recognize the Episcopal Church in Scotland tolerated and allowed by *Act 10th of Queen Anne* and subsequent Statutes; in particular by a Statute introduced by the Archbishop of Canterbury and passed in the year 1840. That, except one other Chapel, we form the sole and only congregation in this country, which does not belong to the Scottish Episcopal Church. It is further to be observed that, though the Service of the Church of England is performed and the Clergyman is of English Ordination, yet the Chapel being situated in a country not included in the *Colonial Act*, but even where the jurisdiction of English Bishops is excluded by Act of Parliament, and therefore that spiritual Jurisdiction, Confirmation, and Control, which as an Episcopal Church we are entitled to enjoy, cannot be procured.

"This glaring defect in a Congregation professing Episcopacy is attempted to be got over, as will be seen from the Minute constituting the Vestry, which gives power 'in doing everything for the complete management of the temporal *and spiritual concerns* (see *XXXIX. Articles, No. 20*) in every particular without control' to that body. The Vestry, as thereby constituted, assume a power which can only be exercised by the Church, if we are Episcopalians. Besides, the exercise of the above spiritual power by a

Vestry we humbly consider not to be recognized by the Catholic Church, but is a Presbyterian invention.

"The attention of the Vestry is next directed to the Scottish Episcopal Church, which has been recognized by the Church of England. Although not the Established Church by *Act of Parliament*, and therefore enjoying no pecuniary emoluments from the State, yet it exists as a pure, spiritual Episcopacy. Having been cast off at the Revolution by the State, it then reverted to that, which had been the condition of every Church in Christendom before the Establishment of Christianity in the Roman Empire by the Emperor Constantine. The Scottish Episcopal Church, in that discarded condition, has regularly kept up the succession of its Bishops amidst all the privations and persecutions, to which it has been subjected. Moreover, the Bishops form examples of piety and learning, and it is our earnest desire that we be placed under their spiritual guidance and control, so as not to remain a body of Schismatics, which accusation, we are afraid, is only too truly and correctly applicable to our present condition.

"We will now, in conclusion, briefly call the attention of the Vestry to the opinion of that learned Divine, Bishop Horsley, the first Theologian, and Sir W. Scott (Lord Stowell), the greatest ecclesiastical Lawyer, of their day. Also to the speech of the Bishop of S. David's in the House of Lords, *May 2nd, 1792*, and to that of Lord Stormont (afterwards Earl of Mansfield) and that of the Earl of Kinnoull. To these opinions the attention of the Vestry is directed, in the earnest hope that they will adopt such steps as are desirable, and in accordance with the government of the Episcopal Church."

Union Frustrated.

This excellent Memorial was signed by no less than sixty prominent members of the Congregation, and it seemed as if it were going to be successful; for the Vestry, having considered it, were decidedly of opinion (with the exception of Messrs. Geekie & Lorimer, factors, who appeared on behalf of Lords Kinnoull and Mansfield) that the union should take place, but adjourned the meeting with a view to secure unanimity.

But, alas! this was not to be obtained. The influence of the two Earls, alienated from the principles of their ancestors, again prevailed against the general sentiment of the Congregation. The Chapel was doomed to remain in its anomalous position for some years longer.

BOOK IV.

Revival.

CHAPTER XXVI.

HOW THE SCOTTISH CONGREGATION WAS REVIVED IN PERTH, 1846.

BUT, though our local affairs seemed at the end of 1842 to be more hopeless than ever, the period of lethargy in the Church at large had given place to a time of energy and action. "For some time," says Dr. Walker,* "every year witnessed the adoption of a fresh measure of Church progress. 1838 had its General Synod, which revised the Canons, enacting one which formed the first step towards a sound system of Church finance. 1839 saw the Church Society in full operation; 1840 the repeal of the most humiliating restriction of the Relief Act of 1792—that, namely, which prohibited a Clergyman of Scottish Ordination from even officiating in an English Church. 1841 witnessed the effective launching of the project, which resulted in Trinity College, Glenalmond. . . . All was life and motion, and those, who lived through that stirring period, will remember the glow of enthusiasm that animated the breasts of the zealous northern Churchmen in the first stage of the Oxford Movement."

And the new life reached Perth. It was already (1846) thirty-six years since the Rulers of the Princes Street Congregation had defied Bishop Torry. Since then, for one reason or another, as we have seen—partly owing to the weakness of the Church after its disasters in the 18th century; partly owing to the great local influence of the Dissentient Vestry; and

* *Last Hundred Years*, p. 10.

partly because he hoped they might yet return to the fold—our Prelate had done nothing in the matter. But, now that the movement towards union, so long hoped for, had (as related in the last chapter) been made and ended in failure, things assumed a different aspect. The Bishop aroused himself. Animated by the signs of progress visible on all sides, he resolved to do something for Perth. He determined to act on what was a principle unknown during the first half of the Century. He made up his mind that a Mission must be set on foot in the City as a rallying point for the faithful in Princes Street and as the germ of new spiritual life.

But, granted that means for carrying on the work were to come from the recently-established " Church Society," where was the Priest to be found ? And here we touch upon a new phenomenon, as characteristic of the new epoch as the Missionary idea itself. Since our "*History*" began, everything connected with the Church in Perth, and the Diocese at large, has been thoroughly Scotch. The Bishop, both by blood and sympathies, was so. He represented, as it were, the vessel of our old non-juring divines, which had sailed through so many storms, arrived in new seas. Warmer breezes from the south had begun to salute it. Mr. Wordsworth, an Englishman, was presiding over Trinity College ; the members of the Episcopate were no longer of the old-fashioned Aberdeen School, but men influenced by England ; congregations of a similar tone were springing up, not now among the farmers of the north, but amongst the well-to-do inhabitants of Edinburgh and Glasgow. And Bishop Torry himself acknowledged the affinity between his old-fashioned Scottish School and the new light that

had arisen at Oxford. *" The theologians there started from the point where his predecessors had held their ground so long through evil report and good report!" And it shall be by an alliance with these powerful restorers of the old ways in the South that our northern Prelate must rekindle the life of the Church in Perth. Accordingly he †" authorizes the Rev. A. Lendrum to endeavour, while engaged in raising subscriptions in England for building a Church in Crieff, to obtain the services of a Missionary Priest" for our City. The Rev. J. C. Chambers, a stout upholder of the Tractarian views, offers himself for the work; and on S. Andrew's day, being also Advent Sunday (1846), a start is made. Mr. Chambers thus describes it :‡—
"The notices of services having been published in the Journals and posted in the Town, I commenced the exercise of my functions, without having any hope of more than six persons as members."

And so we must now record a few particulars concerning the Bishop's revived congregation in our midst. The place of worship where Mr. Chambers officiated, was a hall in Athole Street, situated on the traveller's left hand as he walks from the North Inch towards Methven Street. It stood in that block of buildings, which occupies the space between Kinnoull Street and North William Street, almost facing Stormont Street, and was fitted up in as ecclesiastical a manner as the nature of the case admitted, with Altar and other necessaries of Christian devotion.

With regard to the Worship itself we are assured that "daily Prayers, frequent Communions, and Choral Services were introduced;" and, as might have been

* *Last Hundred Years*, p. 10. † Neale's *Torry*, p. 298.
‡ Cathedral MS.

foretold, the Bishop insisted as a *sine quâ non* that the *Scottish Eucharistic Office* should alone be used. A volume of the *Sermons*, which Mr. Chambers preached, still stands on the shelves of the library. They are characterised by an earnest pastoral desire for the good of souls, and an outspoken assertion of Church principles. In connection with the choral part of the services, it may be remarked that there is still living a poor woman in South Street, who remembers it as the proudest (but most anxious) moment of her life, when she saw her son enter the Chapel as probably the first surpliced chorister in Perth since the Reformation. In *September, 1847*, the Bishop confirmed 18 candidates.

Day and Sunday Schools were also begun. There was, however, little nucleus for this in the town, as there were scarcely any poor, who had remained faithful to the Church. But gradually the attendance increased until Mr. Chambers was obliged to obtain the assistance of a student in the teaching of the children. And thus, amid the often wearisome routine of a Parish Schoolmaster's work, our Priest bore patient testimony to the fact that (despite all School Board theories of a later day) it is the Church's duty to feed Christ's Lambs by providing them with a *sufficient and systematic religious education.*

Having thus seen the ecclesiastical machinery, which was brought into play with a view to restoring a Congregation to the Church in the most central town in the Diocese, we may ask how the effort was responded to by the people. And we are assured that, though the Mission was only opened on the first Sunday in Advent, about 30 communicants had enrolled themselves by Christmas.* These, of course, must have

* Neale's *Torry*, p. 300.

The Revived Flock.

been Episcopalians previously. With regard to those outside, progress was necessarily slow, since there was an invincible prejudice, at that time universal in Scotland, against the Church, and also the grandees of Princes Street would thoroughly confuse the minds of the people with regard to Church principles by their schismatical position. Nevertheless, stranger to pliability and compromise as Mr. Chambers personally was, he gathered a congregation about him, which, though small in number, was strong in principle.

And now, having got a congregation once more together in the Fair City, let us examine it with a view to discovering whether it is the introduction of something absolutely new, as the inhabitants of the town took for granted that it was, or whether it was merely the revival of the old Scottish Congregation, which had been betrayed by Mr. Skete's secession in 1810. In support of the former contention it may, of course, be said that the whole of the machinery of the Athole Street Mission was different from that of the late Mr. Walker's, and the English element and way of looking at things, which Mr. Chambers inevitably brought with him, was also quite new. But, in favour of viewing the Mission as the restoration of the old Scottish Congregation, there are certain important circumstances to be considered, viz. :—Notwithstanding the introduction of the Surplice, Choral Services, and the unquestioning acceptance of the whole of the English *Prayer Book* in all its parts, which distinguished the later from the earlier Congregation, the theological principles represented by the two were identical : the great truths of the Apostolical Succession, the Grace of the Sacraments, the Oblation in the Eucharist, and the repudiation of Calvinism as well as Papalism, were common alike to the Tractarians of Oxford, whom Mr. Chambers represented, and the Scottish non-jurors, who had been presided over by such men as Bishops Rattray and Alexander. And the Mission was not only a revival of the principles of the older Congregation, but the two were also bound together by as many personal ties as the lapse of 36 years admitted of. Bishop Torry himself was an important link binding the two together. And then, concerning those 30 communicants, who joined Mr. Chambers as soon as he was settled in Perth, they must (as there had been no Confirmation) have come from Princes Street. And is it unreasonable to suppose that at least some of them had either themselves been members of the submerged Congregation in 1810, or else the inheritors of the orthodox traditions of those who had been? But we are not left altogether to conjecture on this point. For it is within the memory of old members of the Congregation still living that the two Misses Laidlaw, who used to worship in Balhousie Castle in the days of the Rev. A. Walker, together with a Mr. Robertson, who did likewise, were actually amongst that 30 who left Princes Street and came to the Mission in Athole Street. There was also a Mrs. Monk, who was either in the same position, or else had inherited the orthodox tradition from her people. Moreover, in the Cathedral Library there is an old non-juring *Prayer Book*, with an MS. inscription to the effect that it was presented to Mr. Chambers by him, who used to be the Precentor in the old Congregation. Thus there are real grounds for regarding Mr. Chambers as the successor, after a long interregnum, of Mr. Walker.

Turning now to the financial view of affairs, let us enquire how the Mission was supported. Doubtless the humble flock, which assembled in the Upper Room, contributed according to their means, but help was also looked for from the Church Society, which, as we saw, had begun seven years previously to make a system of finance possible for the Scottish Church. "It is to be remarked," says Dr. Neale, "that in most places in Scotland the Bishops usually waited till a number of persons formed themselves into a congregation, and then, after having selected a Minister, petitioned the Bishop to receive them into his flock. In such a case the Minister relied on an engagement entered into betwixt himself and the Vestry in order to his maintenance and support. In this, however, of Perth, the Missionary had no such certainty; he had to hire and fit up the temporary chamber, and support himself and keep up the school till the annual meeting of the Church Society, when the retrospective salary, both of Minister and Schoolmaster, would be submitted to a vote." Faith was evidently making a venture here.

The Bishop now thought that he saw a means of strengthening Mr. Chambers's position.* It occurred to him that the soldiers, who were still being marched to the Princes Street Chapel, were thus, whether they liked it or not, being officially forced to separate themselves from the Bishop of the Diocese, and consequently from every regular branch of the Anglican Communion. There could be no doubt that this was a grievance. He therefore made an attempt to have it redressed, but the authorities of the War Office decided that it was a less violence to the troops to compel them to worship in schism from the Anglican Church altogether, than to order them to a Chapel, where the local rulers of

* Neale's *Torry*, p. 307.

that Church had decided that one rather than another of the recognized Anglican *Communion Offices* should be used. It was a blow aimed from an unexpected quarter at the principle of discipline, but there was no remedy.

Notwithstanding all obstacles, however, Mr. Chambers persevered, and, as we gather from one of the Bishop's letters in 1849, the Mission was about to take an important step forward. "Nothing is wanting," he writes to Mr. Chambers, "to the further prosperity of your Mission than the erection of a Church, which I trust will be commenced early in spring. Preparation for it, by quarrying stones, ought to be going on at present, but I fear is not, as I hear nothing about it."

But the Church, which the Bishop thus contemplated, was destined never to be built. Late one night, Mr. Chambers ran into the house of one of his faithful working-people, full of news, which he could not withhold. We must delay the discovery of what that news was, until we relate, in the next chapter, one of very happiest incidents, which ever occurred in the History of the Church in Perth.

CHAPTER XXVII.

HOW THE SCHISM OF 1740 WAS HEALED, 1842-8.

AT no time had the prospects of the reconciliation of the Princes Street Congregation with the Church seemed darker. Not only had the attempt at union in 1842 proved abortive, but the ranks of the schismatics in the country had been trebled. In 1842, as we saw, there was only one Congregation in Scotland to bear Mr. Skete's company, *i.e.*, Montrose: these two, alone of the " Qualified " Congregations of the Eighteenth Century, had not come in. But, in 1842, a certain Mr. Drummond* had been persistently violating the Canons, and had, in consequence, been admonished by his Diocesan, the Bishop of Edinburgh. In consequence, he defied his superior, and inaugurated a new schism. His example was followed by the Rev. Sir William Dunbar, in Aberdeen. Moreover, the opening of the Mission in Athole Street was exasperating our friends in Princes Street : " the Bishop, they thought, was forcing not only a Minister but a Liturgy upon them." And, on their side, the Orthodox, who had lain quiet in an inferior position for nearly forty years, were evidently determined at last to call a spade a spade and a schism a schism. Mr. Wordsworth, the Warden of Glenalmond, refused to receive one of the Princes Street Congregation to Holy Communion,† and the Bishop wrote to his brother of

* T. Stephen's *History*, iv., ch. 83-4.
† Bishop Wordsworth's *Annals*, ii., p. 46.

Durham expostulating against two Clergy from that Diocese presuming to officiate in the separated Chapel. Union never seemed less likely.

The darkest hour, however, they say, comes before the dawn. It was so in this case. To the mere man of the world, no doubt, the differences between the two flocks only formed a subject for laughter. But the active controversies over the true principles of order in the Church could only have one result with fair-minded people. They could only end in revealing how completely untenable the position of the Princes Street Congregation had all along been, and how just were the Episcopal claims.

This was what happened in the present instance.

On *Christmas Day, 1846*, Mr. Skete,* the Minister of the Chapel, died. Then came the tug of war. The Congregation split into three parties—one, under Lord Mansfield's influence, for total independence of all Episcopal Authority; another for connecting themselves with the Drummond schism in Edinburgh; and a third, undaunted by their failure of 1842, for submission to the Bishop.

†Bishop Torry, indeed, did not know "whether the death of Mr. Skete . . . would prove obstructive or promotive of the good work of reconciliation," but he

* Mr. Skete's grave is situated in the Greyfriars Cemetery, just outside the east end of S. John's Church. The inscription on the stone is as follows:—"*Sacred to the Memory of the Reverend Henry Attwood Skete, M.A., Oxon, Incumbent of S. John's Episcopal Church, Perth, for a period of 38 years. He was an accomplished Scholar and eloquent Preacher. He died, lamented by his Congregation and Family, on December 25, 1846, aged 68 years.*" That date, "December 25th," on a Clergyman's Tombstone is eloquent!

† Neale's *Torry*, p.p. 300-333.

had far too deep a sense of responsibility to allow the present opportunity for good to pass by untried. Accordingly, he addressed a communication to the Vestry, which contained these words:—"My dear friends: The relation, which I bear to the Diocese of Dunkeld, wherein you are located, and a strong sense of my obligation to promote the interests of my Heavenly Master's Kingdom, combined with the account, which I must render of my Ministry before the Judgment Seat of Christ, have induced me to incur the hazard of perhaps offending you by this address, although my wishes are to promote your good, both for time and for eternity. My nearness also to the confines of another world (being in my 84th year) makes it at least expedient, if not absolutely necessary, that, if I can be of any service to you, I ought not to delay the attempt. I allude to your position as Episcopalians by profession, and yet living in a state of separation from the only Bishop in the world who is authorized ecclesiastically to direct and interfere with your spiritual concerns. . . . I feel myself constrained by the love of Christ, and of those for whom He died, to address you *most seriously* on the danger of your position, and to invite you to avail yourselves of the opportunity of entering into that fold, the door of which has been opened to you . . .; the opportunity now set before you of connecting yourselves with a pure portion of the Catholic Church of Christ."

Nothing could have been better from the Church's side. How was it responded to by the separatists? Almost unanimously in an equally admirable spirit.

The Rev. G. Wood, who had been appointed by the Vestry to succeed Mr. Skete, addressed a pastoral letter to his flock, strongly advocating union ; and once more a determined effort to bring about this desirable end was resolved upon. For the first time since 1805 the Congregation was assembled to elect a new Vestry.* Lords Kinnoull, Mansfield, and Gray, Sir Thomas Moncreiffe, Sir J. S. Richardson, John Grant, Esq. of Kilgraston, Major Jelph Sharpe, and Messrs. Ross, Archer, and Ransom were returned. It was significant that the new body did not assume unlimited spiritual power " without control," as their predecessors had done. This preliminary over, a general meeting of the Congregation was summoned to meet in the George Hotel to deal finally with the question of union. There was a large attendance, and Lord Mansfield occupied the chair. Lord Gray proposed the following motion, *That this Congregation should immediately take steps to place itself in communion with the Scottish Episcopal Church, reserving to itself the use of the Liturgy and Communion Service of the Church of England, exclusive of all other Services."* Major Græme of Inchbrakie moved as an amendment, " *That no steps be taken for one year.*" The Earl of Kinnoull frankly stated that having great diffidence in his own ecclesiastical knowledge, he had consulted the Bishop of Rochester, and he advised union. This short speech boded well for the good cause, as the Earl of Mansfield was now thoroughly isolated in his opposition to it. When the motion was put, 108 voted for union ; 17 against it ; and about 30 members did not declare their opinions. A motion by Mr. Grant was then carried *unanimously* that the Vestry be instructed to complete the union. Hereupon the occult influence, which had been the real cause of the schism, became defined and

* S. John's MS. *Minutes.*

evident: Lord Mansfield resigned his seat on the Vestry.

Mr. Wood at once wrote to the Bishop announcing the good news. But the latter, remembering the evil results of the rashly entered into reconciliation of 1809, assumed a cautious attitude, and replied:—"On the whole, you and I cannot, as times go, settle the matter under discussion, unless you write under a commission from the majority of your Congregation, or their Preses and Secretary acting in their name. It might otherwise all be overturned, as in the case of Bishop Watson and Mr. Fenwick." Accordingly, at a meeting of the Vestry on *December 20th, 1848*, "The Vestry, in the name of and acting for the Congregation, do hereby acknowledge the Episcopal Church of Scotland, into whose communion they are desirous of being admitted, and promise that spiritual obedience, which is due by the congregations of the said Church, this Congregation reserving the exclusive use of the Liturgy and *Communion Service of the Church of England*. . . And further, the Vestry hereby authorize and empower the Rev. George Wood to sign the Canons of the Episcopal Church of Scotland," etc., etc.

But even now the Bishop was in no hurry. He went so far to meet the returning wanderers that he reluctantly dropped his intention of inducing them to accept the *Scotch Office*, but he insisted, as it were, upon an oath of abjuration : he must have a formal expression of regret for the late long-continued schism. Since the Vestry, in the absence of Lord Mansfield, no doubt honestly felt such a regret, as the Bishop wished them to express, they, with an admirable Christian humility, "learned of Him who was meek and lowly of heart," and agreed to the Bishop's demand. The final terms of reconciliation were agreed upon as follows :—

*Whereas we, Patrick Torry, D.D., Bishop of S. Andrews, Dunkeld, and Dunblane, in answer to the application of the majority of the congregation of the so-called English Chapel in Perth, to be received into union with the Scotch Episcopal Church (which application and desire we hereby commend as good and wise); yet, whereas, from the experience of former failures and infringements of such union, when formed, to the great disturbance of the Church, and excitement of much hostile and uncharitable feeling, due precaution in this important matter becomes necessary : therefore, we, the Bishop aforesaid, deem it our duty, for the peace of our own conscience and as an evidence of our faithfulness to the Divine Head of the Church and sense of our accountability to Him, to require of the Clergyman on his part to express a faithful adherence to the union during his life or residence in Perth as pastor of said congregation, and of at least two respectable and influential lay members of the congregation in the name thereof to express a *deep regret* for having so long delayed to make the application as above stated ; while the Bishop on his part solemnly promises not to attempt to concuss the Clergyman or Congregation into compliance with the use of the Scotch Communion Office, although for their own sake he greatly deplores their opposition to it, and hopes the day is not far distant, though he may not see it, when they will of their own accord desire it. In testimony whereof, we, the Bishop, the Clergymen, and the Laymen above alluded to, adhibit our names, date, and place as follows :—Peterhead, January 8th, 1849, Patrick Torry, D.D., Bishop of S. Andrews, etc. ; Perth, January 10th, George Wood, M.A., Lincoln College, Oxford ; Edinburgh, January 11th, John Grant of Kilgraston ; Perth, January 12th, William Ross, Rose Terrace.

Immediately after this, Mr. Wood signed the Canons and Thirty-nine Articles, in the presence of and was instituted by the Dean of the Diocese, John Torry, son of the Bishop, acting for his father. The latter was prevented by the infirmities of extreme old age from officiating on the occasion.

* Neale's *Torry*, p. 318.

The Vestry, now that the Chapel was in connection with the Scottish Episcopal Church, were of opinion that it should be known by some other appellation than "The English Chapel," and they "hereby decree that its name and designation shall be from henceforth 'S. John the Baptist's Episcopal Chapel.'"

It was a bright day for the Church in Perth! Since that sad Easter (1740), when Bishop Rattray had been compelled, by their lawless conduct and partizan animosity, to debar Blair of Corbs and his faction from the Altar, the Church here had been unnaturally crippled. It seems clear indeed that, both, in the origin of the schism, the defiance of the Episcopal authority was indefensible; and, in its continuance, the assumption of the *rôle* of an English Congregation in Scotland, anomalous, and—at least since 1788, when the Bishops recognized King George—utterly inexcusable. But, on the other hand, for the last forty years the perpetuation of the split seems to have been caused by one influential individual, rather than by the wishes of the Congregation at large.

And what could be imagined more truly Christian than the ample manner in which the Vestry confessed their error to Bishop Torry? "*Blessed are the peacemakers!*" Those members of S. John's, who carried through the re-union, certainly deserve to be enrolled amongst the most faithful sons whom the Church has had in Perth!

CHAPTER XXVIII.

HOW THE IDEA OF A CATHEDRAL BEGAN TO TAKE ROOT, 1847-9.

WE must now unfold the news which had brought Mr. Chambers, at the end of Chapter XXVI., to his friend's house at an unusually late hour of the evening.

It seemed to some as if more than the reconciliation of the long-separated Congregation might be brought about, and the Warden of Glenalmond gave voice to this feeling in a pamphlet entitled *A Call to Union*. His proposal was the amalgamation of the two Congregations upon the basis of one large and handsome Church, with becoming Services, and the alternate use of the *Scotch* and *English Offices*. To this day (1894) the plans of the proposed edifice adorn the walls of S. John's Vestry. There was much indeed to be said in favour of this scheme from an abstract point of view; but, upon the whole, it was scarcely practicable under the circumstances. The Athole Street Congregation was inclined to maximize, and that of Princes Street to minimize, the Catholic element in the *Prayer Book*, and human nature being human nature, it was perhaps wisest, after all, to allow the two types of Churchmen to go their ways as friendly members of the same Communion, rather than to force on a marriage of convenience between them.

While the proposals for amalgamation were still going on, good Mr. Chambers was visited by some searchings of heart: he was afraid that the Congregation which he had called into existence, and on which he had impressed the full Catholic teaching of the *Book of Common Prayer*, was about to be swamped by the superior number and social position of those, who had for so many years been imbued with the spirit of Protestantism. But the Bishop wrote to reassure him by making known the terms of the recent reconciliation. "You," his Lordship added, "and your little flock have nothing to fear." This letter of his Diocesan would, indeed, be calculated to cheer any despondency, which our Presbyter might have begun to feel. But there was still greater cause of joy behind. And it was the intelligence of this that drove Mr. Chambers out on that evening, to which we have referred, in order to unbosom himself to a member of of his flock.

The fact was this :—The late Lord Forbes happened to be residing in Oxford, and the Hon. G. F. Boyle (afterwards Earl of Glasgow) was still (1847) an undergraduate in the same University. Now the prospects of the Scottish Church would often form the subject of their discussion, and it occurred to their ardent and patriotic hearts, stirred by the vigorous movement by which they found themselves surrounded, that they ought to inaugurate some grand attempt for the revival of the northern Zion. The proposal to begin a restoration of our Cathedral institutions was no sooner suggested than it fascinated their minds. The then practice of Bishops residing at long distances from their Dioceses in the capacity of ordinary Incumbents might be justifiable in times past on the ground of necessity, but it was not to be tolerated in this period of Church revival. At least one Prelate should be brought to reside at the centre of his Diocese ; be released from the need to act as an ordinary Parish Priest, and be enabled to celebrate the Divine mysteries with becoming dignity. Mission Clergy must likewise be attached to the proposed Cathedral, in order that its life might course through the veins of the Diocese at large.

The question was then asked whether one of the old Cathedral structures might not be restored and revived. Of course, however, that, as a practical measure, was out of the question. Nevertheless, "they considered that the present wants of the Church and their own present duty were paramount to every other consideration." If, then, the scheme was to be proceeded with apart from the old buildings of that character, what was the most suitable locality, in which to erect it? Bishop Torry seemed the Prelate most likely to welcome the proposed institution in his Diocese, and after mature consideration, Perth was selected as the actual spot for the following reasons. It was a City of considerable population; it was in the very centre of the land; there passed through it perhaps a greater number of strangers than through any other town in Scotland, except Edinburgh; Trinity College was in the neighbourhood, and in this place it might consequently be expected to exercise a powerful influence on the future destinies of the Church throughout the country.

And so, a definite outline having been formed in their minds, Lord Forbes addressed to the Bishop, then in his 84th year, a formal communication, in which it was proposed "to erect a Cathedral in Perth, together with a Collegiate Residence for the Bishop of the Diocese and a staff of four or five Clergy to conduct the daily and Sunday services of the Cathedral, and to celebrate Divine Service in surrounding localities where there are no Clergy resident, as the Bishop for the

The Bishop's Sanction. 283

time being may direct and require, and also to endow the Bishopric and the requisite staff of Clergymen." The Bishop replied as follows to this communication (*July 2nd, 1847*):—"It is in my estimation a noble scheme, and would doubtless, if carried into effect, be, through the Divine blessing, productive of great benefit to the Church. When contemplated even in prospect only, it excites joyful feelings: how much more, therefore, when it shall become a reality? Were it the will of God it would gladden my heart in the evening of my days to witness even the commencement of it, and its partial execution by the erection of the Chancel to serve as an interim Church. The entire completion of the scheme I dare not hope to see, for I am in my 84th year and the oldest Prelate in the island of Great Britain, with the exception of the Archbishop of York. It appears that your Lordship is the originator of this noble scheme, and that you have shewn your liberality by contributing a considerable sum of money towards its accomplishment. For this your Lordship deserves the hearty thanks of the Church generally, and particularly of myself for the interest you have shewn in the welfare of the Diocese, which I hereby respectfully and cordially offer to you. I may have occasion to address your Lordship again after I have seen Mr. Lendrum."

The interview with the latter resulted in the publication of a second letter recommending the scheme in a formal manner. As it was of considerable length, and of much the same tenor as that addressed to Lord Forbes, already quoted, we shall mention only that in it the Bishop constitutes a Committee to carry out the plan, and places the following names upon it: (1) The Bishop; (2) Mr. Chambers; (3) Mr. Lendrum;

(4) Mr. Macmillan; (5) Dean Torry; and of the Laity (6) Lord Forbes; (7) Viscount Campden; (8) Hon. G. F. Boyle; (9) Sir J. Ramsay; (10) Sir J. Forbes; and (11) Mr. W. E. Gladstone.

Having thus obtained the Diocesan's sanction, the persons mentioned at once set to work. They printed and circulated the Bishop's formal letter to Lord Forbes, and "repeated appeals were made to Churchmen both in Scotland and in England during the two following years," 1848 and 1849, and contributions, given for building and endowment, were advertized from numbers of subscribers. "It seems now to be quite certain," the Bishop writes, "that the building of the Chancel of a large Church at Perth will be carried into effect, as a considerable number of gentlemen of influence and fortune have undertaken to act as a committee for that purpose. The Hon. Mr. Boyle, brother of the Earl of Glasgow, and heir-presumptive to his immense property, came to (me at) Muthill to signify his concurrence with others in that business; and, as they have subscriptions amounting to £3000 and more (as I believe), there can be no doubt that the work will be commenced and carried forward with energy in the spring, unless some unseen obstacles start up."

So certain, indeed, did it now appear that a Cathedral would be erected in Perth, that the Fair City, which had for so long been one of the weakest spots in the Scottish Church, began already to be considered the proper centre of Diocesan life. "On *June 21st, 1848,* the annual Synod met in the Upper Room in Athole Street. There was a choral Service at 11 a.m. conducted by Mr. Chambers. The Dean then opened the Synod in the absence of the Bishop. There were in all 12

Clergy present." The same Assembly seems to have met here again in 1850, for on *April 6th* of that year Bishop Torry writes:—"I have received the report of the proceedings at Perth last Thursday by the Clergy of my Diocese, the general result of which, after much discussion, was a unanimous recognition of the doctrine of Baptismal Regeneration as the truth and the only truth of that Sacrament of Baptism, without the *admission* of which no person is qualified to claim institution to a benefice in the Church of England, although regularly presented to the same." Thus our Diocese tried to repay their Orthodox friends in England, as best they could, by supporting them in the gallant effort they were making in the Gorham controversy to "contend earnestly for the Faith once delivered to the Saints!"

CHAPTER XXIX.

HOW THE CHURCH OF S. JOHN, PRINCES STREET, WAS BUILT AND PROSPERED, 1849-1870.

It has become apparent that we have entered upon a new and happier era of our history. The troubles of the Eighteenth Century are things of the long past. The state of collapse that characterized, roughly speaking, the first half of the Nineteenth Century has also disappeared. We have already seen the Scottish Episcopal Congregation revived in a modest manner, the schismatic flock reconciled, and even the idea of a Cathedral broached.

There is now another advance to be chronicled. On *March 8th, 1849*, a Sub-Committee of the S. John's Vestry was appointed to enquire into the advisability of providing 150 additional sittings in the Chapel. The result was that early in 1850 the following *Appeal* was issued :—" The small Episcopal Chapel, Princes Street, being found quite insufficient to accommodate more than the present Congregation, whilst applications are continually received from parties, who wish to become members of it, it has become imperatively necessary to adopt measures for meeting the want thus created. For this purpose, various members of the Congregation, with other well-disposed individuals, have resolved to attempt the erection of another and more commodious place of worship, sufficient not only for the present Congregation, and of those, who are seeking to become members of it, but also for the gratuitous accommodation of the poorer classes, who are virtually excluded from the present Chapel, but many of whom are

New S. John's Built.

desirous of worshipping God after the manner of their fathers. A large addition has lately been made to the population of Perth, consisting chiefly of people from England, who are connected with the different lines of railway. And no Christian can regard it as a subject of unconcern, that these should be excluded from ordinances, to which it is found on enquiry that many of them are attached, or suffered as sheep without a shepherd to unite themselves to other bodies as fancy dictates, or, as is too probable, to fall into a state of practical heathenism. The Committee therefore urge upon all to do their best in support of the proposed scheme."

On the motion of Mr. Grant of Kilgraston, Sir Thomas Moncreiffe was appointed Chairman, and Colonel Belshes, Deputy-Chairman, of the Building Committee. By autumn the sum of £1523 had been subscribed, and thereupon the plans of Mr. Hay of Liverpool were accepted. The total cost seemed likely to be about £2000.

The Congregation made themselves responsible for the required £500, and *Sunday, September 15th*, was the last date, on which service was conducted in the old chapel of 1805. The Session of the East Kirk very kindly offered the Congregation the use of an old Chapel belonging to them in Kinnoull Street, and there they worshipped during the erection of their own new Church. The first stone of this was laid on the site of the now demolished building on *September 28th*. It occupies a position in the foundation of the east wall of the chancel close to the Greyfriars Burying-Ground. By *June, 1851*, the edifice was completed. Votes of thanks were passed to Messrs. Wood, Falshaw, and Ross, the Sub-Committee, and especially to Colonel

Belshes, the Deputy-Chairman, of the Building Committee. The next step to be taken was to secure the Consecration of the Church. Sir Thomas Moncreiffe, Mr. Grant, Colonel Belshes, and Major Jelph Sharpe were appointed to see after this.

On *October 22nd*, at eleven o'clock, the Bishop of Edinburgh (Terrot), acting for the Bishop of the Diocese, was received at the west door of the Church by the above-named gentlemen, with whom were associated Messrs. W. Ross, R. Ancell, P. D. Brown, and Mr. Henderson, constituting a majority and quorum of the Vestry. At *11.30 a.m.* the service began. The Bishop and Clergy (*i.e.*, Very Rev. Dean Torry, and Revs. G. Wood of S. John's, Milne of Cupar-Fife; C. Lyon of S. Andrews; W. Blatch of Pittenweem; W. Bruce of Dunfermline; H. Malcolm of Dunblane; J. Douglas of Kirriemuir; J. Dodgson, Perth; J. C. Chambers of S. Ninian's, Perth; J. M'Millan of Dunkeld; J. Burton of Blairgowrie; W. Warburton, Scone Palace; and C. Wordsworth, Warden of Trinity College), having proceeded from the Vestry to the Chancel, the petition for Consecration, along with a deed for holding the new Church in communion with the Episcopal Church of Scotland, was presented to the Bishop. His Lordship having formally granted the prayer, the service appropriate to the occasion was proceeded with. When the *Consecration* was finished, a deed recording the fact was read by the Bishop's Chaplain, the Rev. Henry Malcolm, and signed by the Bishop. *Morning Prayer* was then said by the Incumbent, and a celebration of the *Holy Communion*, with a *Sermon* by the Bishop, followed, the communicants numbering about 80. After the completion of these three Offices in the new Church, luncheon was given by the Vestry in the George Hotel. After a short interval, those of the company, who could, returned for *Evening Prayer* at 4 p.m., which was conducted by the Dean. At the close of this, *Confirmation* was administered to upwards of 30 persons by the Bishop. The general sentiment with regard to the day's proceedings was thus summed up by a contemporary writer :—" Every one," he said, " was pleased and delighted at the manner in which the service was conducted, and with everything connected with this day's proceedings."

There was, however, at least one "who cast a longing, lingering look behind," and that was the widow of the late Incumbent. A new Church and a Bishop might be all very well for the rising generation, but " Mrs. Skete having signified her wish to have the pulpit cushion of the old Chapel, as it was used by her husband, the Vestry agreed to the same, and requested their Secretary to transmit it to her" (*October 25th, 1851*).

This will be the best place to notice certain additions to the Church property that were subsequently made from time to time. On *March 17th, 1851*, a new Pulpit of Caen Stone was ordered. This was afterwards enriched by bas-reliefs in white marble by Miss Grant (*October, 1872*). In 1857 a new organ was erected at the cost of £350, which lasted till it was superseded by a still better instrument in 1890. In 1857 a Parsonage was obtained for the sum of £900, which sum was cleared off in 1863. In the latter year Colonel Belshes bequeathed £200 for a set of Communion plate. In 1865 Mr. Stewart left £1000 for the Clergy Endowment Fund, which was paid over in due time. Another £500 seems to have come in by the end of 1868. In 1871 a member of the Congregation, Mr. Stuart, left £500 for the endowment of the Bishoprick.

In 1855, Rev. G. Wood resigned the Incumbency and went to England. He was succeeded by the Rev. W. Blatch, who had formerly been an English Wesleyan Minister, but had joined the Church and been ordained by the Bishop of Edinburgh. He held the Incumbency of Pittenweem at the time of his appointment to Perth. Under his supervision the latter Congregation prospered and increased.

On Easter Day, 1867, there were 30 more communicants than there ever had been before, and by 1871 the Congregation numbered altogether 650. The guaranteed stipend was £250; and in Mr. Blatch's day, for the first time, the Clergyman obtained a seat on the Vestry.

A few words on ecclesiastical customs and suchlike will be appropriate here. In 1864 it was resolved to adopt the new financial schemes of the Scottish Episcopal Church, and Mr. Grant was elected Lay Representative. The subscriptions forwarded to headquarters have long been amongst the very best in the Diocese. It is evident that the Union of 1849 was sincerely entered into. In 1871 the black gown was still used in the Pulpit. In the same year "*Hymns, Ancient and Modern,*" the *Offertory* during Service, the *New Lectionary*, and Evening in place of Afternoon Service were all adopted.

From 1860 for about ten years the Bishop and his family occupied a seat in the Church.

The history of S. John's has now been given with as much completeness as possible, from its foundation in 1740 to the building of the present Church, exactly 110 years later. If we do not trace the fortunes of this Congregation, subsequent to the date we have reached, with the same fullness as before, the reader is requested to note the reason why this course has been taken. It is clearly recognised that the omission means the loss of half (often much more than half) of our Church life in Perth. But, on the other hand, for a Clergyman of one Congregation in the town to approach the office-bearers of the other with the proposal that their private *Minute Books* and *Records* of the present day should be submitted to his inspection, with a view to the publication of the results, was felt to be too delicate a task to be undertaken. Sincere friendships and brotherly relations are possessions so valuable that it was considered wiser not even to try experiments with them. Nevertheless, a few statements of facts, which are public property, will be found in some of the following chapters.

CHAPTER XXX.

HOW THE CATHEDRAL WAS PARTLY BUILT, CONSTITUTED, AND CONSECRATED, 1849-50.

But, in order to give a consecutive account of S. John's, we have gone far ahead of the point, at which we left Mr. Chambers and his Mission in Athole Street. We left it at the time when the proposal to erect a Cathedral, or at least a portion of one, was beginning to take practical shape. Let us, therefore, return to this point.

(I).—As long as the scheme was merely floating as an ideal before the minds of its promoters, we hear of no opposition. But, as Dr. Walker has pointed out,* this first period of revived life in the Scottish Church was marked also by no little controversy, which arose from the very same region whence the fresh strength was being derived, *i.e.*, from England. Not a few of the Clergy from the south went to work in this country exactly as they would have done in their own, making no allowance for the Scottish character. A more serious drawback also on progress was the entanglement of the small Northern Church in the disputes, which were agitating its great sister in the south.

And Perth was destined to have a fuller and far longer share of these controversies than almost any other place in the country. At the present crisis, accordingly, when the proposed Cathedral was beginning to become a reality, and the subscription lists already showed £5800 collected from upwards of 200 subscribers,

* *Last Hundred Years*, p. 12.

we begin to hear of "every possible phase of discouragement" springing up.

First came that arising from the contact of the common sentiment of the country with this new outcome of southern Tractarian zeal. Without the least intentional irreverence—far from it!—the people had for generations been accustomed to regard religion in the most matter-of-fact way. The serenity of mind, with which they held their services in sordidly-furnished, barn-like structures, was never troubled by the slightest misgivings. Indeed, the very idea of worship, as distinct from preaching, had been starved out of their thoughts. Calvinism had accustomed them to believe that the whole scheme of salvation had not only been worked out for us long ago, but also irrevocably applied (or not applied, as the case might be) to every individual soul from all eternity, and the sole object of repairing to Church was simply to contemplate this fact intellectually from time to time. Nothing that the individual could do, either by way of conduct or prayer, had power to make the very slightest difference to what had been fixed by God's Sovereign decree from everlasting. Language, therefore, almost breaks down, when an attempt is made to express how meaningless, nay, how repulsive, to the ordinary Scotch mind the spectacle of worship appeared. Men knelt, stood, chanted, bowed, and uttered the short supplicating cries of the responsive Liturgy before Him, who was the immutable embodiment of unchangeable predestination! Only one conclusion was possible; people, who did such a preposterously useless thing, must be either weak in the intellect or else playing the part of hypocrites! There was some colour lent to the former hypothesis, in that those, who so behaved themselves, did not speak in the broad, deliberate, rough tones, to which Perth was accustomed, but in an unfamiliar, soft, and apparently womanish dialect from the south. But whether it were the outcome of brainlessness or hypocrisy, the inhabitants of the Fair City were not prepared to welcome the proposed institution in their midst.

Public opinion, then, was hostile to the Cathedral scheme. But it was not only those outside who opposed it. There were some Churchmen, who were such not by principle but by accident. Having long lived on terms of friendliness with Presbyterians, they had to all intents and purposes embraced their principles. And Churchmen there were also, who were such by conviction, but who, like the Warden of Glenalmond, sympathized with the old-fashioned party, which in England was opposing the Oxford leaders, and who, therefore, distrusted the Cathedral scheme owing to its ultimate parentage. And there were also Churchmen who, though they upon the whole sympathized with the Catholic movement in general, yet objected to the Cathedral project in particular, inasmuch as it was being carried through, not with the concurrence of the Diocese, but solely on the authority of the Bishop, who, moreover, was too old and frail to visit his jurisdiction in person.

Objections and expostulations made themselves heard from all these different quarters. But the Bishop withstood them. As regards the utter dislike, with which the scheme was regarded by Presbyterian, or Presbyterianized, opinion, he probably consoled himself with the thought that this was a case where he could justly take that saying to himself:—" Blessed are ye when all men shall speak evil of you falsely for My sake." With regard to the opposition of *bona fide*

Churchmen, however, there was more difficulty. Still, was it merely objected that he was plunging into a scheme too large and comprehensive for his small Diocese to carry out? Well, but he actually had £6500 in hand, which was enough, or nearly so, wherewith to erect that part of the Cathedral which was intended. And he had also the promise of future help in the matter from Lord Forbes and Mr. Boyle (the Earl of Glasgow). Was it objected that he was carrying the whole thing through on his own authority, and that the Diocesan Synod had not been consulted? He could reply that theoretically a Bishop is not bound to be governed by his Clergy, and that practically this principle had been universally recognised throughout the Scottish Church. Was it objected that, granting he had the *right* to constitute a Cathedral, still it was *inexpedient* to ignore his Synod? He could reply that, as a general rule, the proposition might be admitted, but that in the present instance a great opportunity would probably be thrown away, if, by putting it to the vote in times of such excitement and difference of opinion, he hesitated to close with the generous offer. Lastly, if it was objected to as simply a move of the "Puseyite" party, he could answer that "Puseyite" was a nickname, and that, without altogether identifying himself with that party, he found substantial agreement between the theology of the Catholic Revival in England and that, which he had inherited from his predecessors.

And so the Bishop determined to ignore the opposition, and proceed with the scheme.* On *January 8th, 1848*, we find him discussing with Lord Forbes, no longer whether the Cathedral is to be built, but which part

* For the rest of this section see Neale's *Torry*, pp. 343 348 349.

of it is to be built first. The "engineer," it seems, had dissented from the idea that the east end should be fixed upon as the part to be proceeded with. But the Bishop adheres to his proposal, and gives his reasons for it :—"Whatever portion of the Church," he says, "in the meantime be erected, it is in my judgment highly desirable that the genuine symbols of the Christian Faith and Worship should be plainly indicated by the very form of its structure, and *that* from the very day it is made available for Divine Service. Now, no part of the Church does that sufficiently without a Sanctuary. Its purpose, mark, or distinction, its separation from the body of the Church, although still a part, is to make every humble and faithful worshipper, casting his eyes upon it, to *feel* and *say* in his heart, ' *That place is holy to the Lord.*' There the riches of Divine Bounty are most plentifully bestowed on Christian worshippers; there they are spiritually fed and sustained during their earthly pilgrimage, in order to their endless enjoyment of celestial peace and rest!" On *June 6th* he writes to Bishop Forbes, "The hope of the ultimate accomplishment of the Cathedral at Perth is still cherished by the estimable Lord Forbes."

The next letter shews us another step in advance. Mr. Butterfield has been selected as Architect, and on *December 23rd, 1848*, we find the Bishop writing:— "The plans of the proposed Cathedral in Perth reached me two days ago, the designs of which I think extremely beautiful, and admirably adapted for its high and holy purpose. . . . . The portion of that structure intended for erection in the meantime will, I hope, be sufficient for all the worshippers that may reasonably be expected to attend the daily services of God for some time to come. . . . The finishing of the Choir, in conformity with the beautiful plan given, may, I hope, be accomplished in my own lifetime, if it be not presumptuous for a man in his 86th year to entertain such an expectation. The Choir will form in itself a very beautiful small Church, with all appropriate symbols adapted for the solemn service of God; and the very sight of it will give new vigour to the Mission."

On *December 9th, 1849*, Mr. Boyle writes:—"A plan engages the attention of the Committee for taking a large house, and giving each Prebendary a room, rent free, as part of his stipend, and fitting up the remainder as a Collegiate School. . . . This plan, if it can be carried into effect, will save the necessity of commencing Collegiate buildings, and enable all our means to be concentrated on the Cathedral. It will help to support the Clergy; it will furnish an efficient Choir for the Cathedral without any annual expense to its funds; it will bring many of the middle class, who cannot afford Trinity College, under the influence of the Church, and would not in any way interfere with that institution. Lord Forbes and I and some others are going to become answerable for the rent should the annual offerings prove insufficient."

Soon after this, Mr. Boyle was empowered to sign the contracts, and what had so long existed in idea only, began also to exist in fact. *" On *September 15th*, being the Eve of S. Ninian's Day (1849) to whose memory the Church is to be dedicated, the first stone was laid. . . . The Clergy present were the Lord Bishop of Brechin, who acted for the venerable Diocesan, and [21 other Clergy]. The Services began at 8 a.m. with *Morning Prayer*. At 9 a.m. the Bishop held a

* *Scottish Magazine*, 1849, p. 513.

Confirmation, when eight adult candidates were admitted. This is the second Confirmation held within three months. The *Holy Communion* was celebrated at 10 a.m., and about 11.30 a.m. the procession was formed, and moved towards the ground. The choristers, 12 in number, vested in white surplices, advanced first; next, the Deacons, Priests, and Bishop, followed by the whole Congregation, walking two and two. On being arranged at the ground, the Bishop, Clergy, and choristers began the appointed Service, in which the people joined. There was also present a large concourse of spectators, who behaved with the greatest decorum,—the most part of those within hearing being uncovered when the Service began. The morning was rather gloomy; but, as the day advanced, it brightened, and, while the stone was being laid, the sun shone forth in all his splendour—an omen, we trust, that the Divine blessing rested on the work of the day!" A symbol, certainly, of that epoch of Church history, not least in Perth: "*Progress amid the clouds of Controversy.*"

Thereafter, building operations, of which "Mr. Chambers was a daily witness," proceeded regularly. It was, of course, hoped that the portion of the edifice taken in hand would be completed by S. Ninian's Day, 1850, but this was not possible: it was not finished till about three months later. As it then stood, the Cathedral consisted of Choir, Dwarf-Transepts, and one bay of the Nave, and there was room for about 350 of a Congregation. The style of architecture adopted was early middle pointed, plain and severe, but the great height of the building (70 feet), compared with its width and the elevation of the Chancel, gave it a dignity and proportions, which stamped it at once as a Cathedral, and not as an ordinary Church.

(II).—So the material building was completed, and we must now pay attention to the Statutes, which were drawn up for the administration of the Institution.

On *December 9th, 1849*, Mr. Boyle wrote to the Bishop:—" I delayed writing to you until I had seen Lord Forbes, whom I am now visiting. The meeting of Committee passed off well. A large portion of the Statutes were considered, but a good deal more remains to be done. The meeting was adjourned, but will, I trust, meet again in the course of next month, having completed the draft, and be enabled to submit it to you for your ratification."

*The Statutes were 27 in number, and, especially in view of future events, it will be necessary to indicate their leading features. All the real power was lodged in the lesser *Chapter*,—that is, in the Dean and Canons residentiary. The entire patronage was in their hands; that is, they elected the Dean, Canons, Prebendaries, and appointed all other officials. They could increase or decrease the number of these. They had the right of altering the Constitution ; and thus they took the initiative in everything. The position of the *Bishop* was of a more passive kind : ordinarily, the work of the Institution would go on without him. He had no more authority over the Cathedral than over any other Incumbency. He was to adjudge all disputes, *when referred to him*; he had a veto upon all appointments, and everything that was done was ineffectual without his ratification. *The Scottish Communion Office*, with the ancient usages thereof, was to be exclusively used in the Cathedral. The *Clergy of*

* Canon Humble's *Letter to the Bishop*, p. 71.

the Diocese were hardly connected with the foundation; since, when installing the Prebendaries, the Chapter were not free to select from the whole body, but must only choose those, who held Incumbencies founded by the Cathedral, or the patronage of which was somehow vested in the hands of its officials.

As yet the Dean was not nominated, but the following Priests were appointed Canons by the Bishop's authority, and therefore constituted the Chapter, *i.e.*, the Revs. J. C. Chambers, H. Humble, and J. Haskoll.* Although, however, the Deanery was for the present left vacant, it is interesting to remember that it was first offered to Mr. Kenrick, but declined by him. The celebrated Dr. Neale was then invited to accept the post.† And herein, it may be remarked, our authorities did themselves honour. For, notwithstanding Dr. Neale's untiring zeal, remarkable attainments, and his sounding title of "Warden of Sackville College," it is to be remembered that (since that College was only an Almshouse) no post worthy of his eminence had ever been made his in the South. We may, therefore, be proud that our Chapter did what it could to reward worth, and to secure the services of such a distinguished divine for the service of the Diocese. But, unfortunately, private considerations obliged him to decline the office. Mr. Wordsworth was to the last very anxious to have the Statute, which required the exclusive use of the *Scotch Office*, changed into a stipulation that both offices should be adopted; but the Bishop remained firm, as was to have

* The Rev. Joseph Haskoll was Incumbent of Laurencekirk. —Fraser's *Laurencekirk*, p. 260.

† Neale's *Torry*, p. 363.

been expected on that point, and signed the Constitution as sketched above on *January 16th, 1851.*

(III).—And now, there being a Cathedral in existence, we must proceed to give some account of the Consecration ceremonies.

On *December 7th, 1850*, Lord Forbes wrote to the Bishop saying that, "with a view to the Consecration of Perth Cathedral Church, which is being erected on two pieces of ground acquired for that purpose and vested in his name, he engaged to convey and make over the said ground" to the Cathedral authorities; but with this proviso, "that the same shall be held inalienably and solely for the use and behoof of a Cathedral Church . . in strict connection with the Episcopal Church of Scotland, etc."

The way was clear, and therefore our aged Diocesan wrote as follows, on *August 12th, 1850*, to Bishop Forbes, who acted in a most cordial way throughout:—"I beg to ask whether you will have the goodness to discharge in my place the duty of consecrating the Cathedral in Perth, when it shall be so far finished as to admit of that solemnity. The 16th day of September (S. Ninian's Day) is designed for the day of Consecration, but much will depend on the progress made towards completing the structure, so far as presently intended. Mr. Chambers will be able to give the necessary information, and I shall not fail to draw it from him nor lose time in making the communication to you, in the hope that sympathy with an aged brother will induce you to comply with the request."

As we have already seen, the Cathedral was not finished by S. Ninian's Day, and so the Bishop had again to write to Bishop Forbes on *November 7th.* In this letter he repeats the request that his brother of Brechin will perform the Consecration, and also that he will ordain Mr. John Comper about the same time, and read the deeds of institution of the three Canons. "On the whole," he concludes, "I grieve to be so burdensome to you, but it is all for the Glory of God."

"I may now," says Dr. Neale,* "relate the Consecration of S. Ninian's, the first British Cathedral, be it remembered (with the single exception of S. Paul's), that has been consecrated since the Reformation, as I had the privilege to be present and assist at it. It was just about sunset on a fine December day that I arrived in Perth. There had been a slight fall of snow on the grampians, and the stillness of the Fair City and the setting in of the frost seemed to bring out in greater relief the bustle within the walls of the Cathedral: and the glare of its lights, as the workmen were hurrying to the conclusion of their task, was in strange contrast with the darkness and quietness of the adjacent street. That night I shall ever remember as one of the strangest in my life. Many of the most necessary arrangements had been driven off to the very last: the carpenter's hammer and the mason's chisel were still to be heard; a crowd of workmen were yet engaged in putting the finishing touches to their respective departments; the frescoes were still incomplete, and in the later hours of the evening the Choir was practising the Chants and Hymns for the next day. An English reader can hardly form any idea of the interest and curiosity, with which our proceedings were regarded by Presbyterian spectators, to whom the whole ritual of the Church was then so

* P. 367.

The Consecration. 303

utterly unknown, that, as I remember, the leading Perth newspaper of the following week gave an elaborate description to its readers of what was meant by chanting. Perfect silence settled down over the City; but still, as we visited the Cathedral at twelve, at two, at four, and at six, the workmen were still engaged in their various occupations; nor was it till the late morning of a Scottish December day had fairly broken that everything was prepared for the approaching solemnity. . . . The doors of the Cathedral were thrown open at 10.30 a.m., and by a simple arrangement the members of the Scotch Church were separated from others, whom curiosity or a better feeling drew to the ceremonial. In the meantime the Choir, which is exceedingly elevated, was gradually filled by the Canons, Clergy, Lay-Vicars, and Choristers to the number of about 50 in all. The Bishop of Brechin, who officiated for the Bishop of S. Andrews, arrived at 11.30 a.m., and was met at the western door by the whole body of the Clergy, by whom he was conducted to the Altar. The usual formularies having been gone through, the procession was formed. . . Proceeding down the Nave and round the north and south Aisles, they returned up the Nave again, and such was the length of the procession that the foremost chorister had already passed the Chancel doors on his way to the north Aisle before the Bishop had reached the west door. At that moment the Precentor intoned ' *The earth is the Lord's and all that therein is*,' and the Choir thundered out, ' *The compass of the world and they that dwell therein*,' with the rest of the Psalm. . . The Bishop having again taken his place at the Altar, pronounced the usual Prayers of Consecration; that for the Font being followed by the Anthem, '*If ye love Me;*' that for the Pulpit, '*The Lord gave the Word;*' and that for the Altar by the '*Hallelujah Chorus.*' The Clergy then returned into the Sacristy, while the doors of the Church being thrown open, it was soon crammed. The Bishop having taken his seat on his Throne, prayers were sung by the Rev. H. F. Humble, Chanter; the lessons were read by the Rev. J. Haskoll, Sacrist, and the Rev. J. C. Chambers, Chancellor, and the Litany by the Rev. T. Helmore, and the Rev. W. Wilson. For the anthem '*Angularis Fundamentum.*' The Holy Communion was celebrated, of course, according to the Scotch use by the Bishop, assisted by three Canons as Epistler, Gospeller, and Assistant Priest. After the Nicene Creed, letters missive were read from the Bishop of S. Andrews, by which he erected the Collegiate Church into the Cathedral of the united Diocese. The Rev. J. M. Neale, Warden of Sackville College, preached from *S. Matthew vi., 5.* The Nave was crowded with hearers, a great portion of them standing. . . . In the evening the Rev. T. Chamberlain delivered the sermon.

"On Thursday, during the Communion, J. Comper was ordained Deacon, the address being given by the Rev. E. B. K. Fortescue. In the evening several adults received Baptism, and some, who had done so in other religious bodies, were admitted into the Church, as they knelt at the west door, with the words, '*We receive this person,*' etc. After prayer, these, with certain of those who had just been baptized, were confirmed by the Bishop according to the Scottish form, '*I sign thee,*' etc. On account of the extreme length of the Service, which was not over till 10 p.m., there was no Sermon. On Friday morning, after Prayers, the Bishop was enthroned (by proxy) and the Canons were installed. The Rev. C. T. Erskine, representing the Bishop, was received at the west door by the Canons and conducted to the Altar, where prayers were said over him, and thence to the Throne, after which *Te Deum* was sung. The Sermon at the early Communion was preached by the Rev. C. T. Erskine; that at the second Celebration by the Rev. P. Cheyne; and that in the evening by the Rev. A. Lendrum."

*After the Consecration the Clergy, Choir, and a number of lay friends partook of luncheon in the dining hall of S. Ninian's College, the Chancellor of the Cathedral presiding. When it was over, the guests were requested to remain and Mr. Chambers to withdraw. A statement was then made pointing out some of the difficulties, with which the latter had to struggle in establishing the Mission, and the laborious, self-denying, and unwearied exertions he had made to bring it to what it now was. The fact was also stated that he had almost kept open house since he came to Perth, extending his hospitality alike to English and Scotch, who had occasion to be there, and that on very limited means, which he could not have done without great personal self-denial. A proposal was then made to raise and present him with a purse, if possible, of not less than £100, as a testimonial of the way, in which his labours and conduct were appreciated by the friends of the Church, and a very slight acknowledgment and return for his hospitality. The statement was corroborated in every particular by the Bishop of Brechin, and the suggestion warmly taken up by all present. £56 was immediately subscribed in the room, and several contributions were subsequently received.

* *Scottish Magazine*, 1851, p. 31.

T

Our account of the completion of the Cathedral will be fitly closed by the following letter, dated from Peterhead, *December 13th, 1850*, by Bishop Torry to Bishop Forbes:—"My dear Right Rev. Brother: I acknowledge with grateful heart the receipt of your letter of yesterday's date, and I beg further to say that I can never adequately recompense you for the services done on my behalf on the day of the Consecration of the Cathedral at Perth, and subsequent days. But as your Divine Master, Whom you faithfully serve, is not only kind but generous, it is comfortable to think that a day is approaching, when you will meet with an ample reward, not only for the work alluded to, but, I trust, for long-continued services in this Church, which greatly needs such a friend. If I may judge from present appearances, it is to me clear that, but for you, the good work must have remained undone until my removal hence. May God stir up many such as yourself to co-operate with you, and then the object, for which Christ shed His Blood, will be accomplished more successfully than heretofore. It is with difficulty that I have been able to write thus far; and must conclude with a reiteration of my thanks and an aged Bishop's blessing to yourself and all friends of the Institution at Perth, both clerical and lay; being ever yours most affectionately, Patrick Torry, Bishop of St. Andrews,"

CHAPTER XXXI.

HOW THE CATHEDRAL FARED FROM ITS CONSECRATION TILL BISHOP TORRY'S DEATH, 1850-2.

HAVING now traced the revival of our affairs in Perth after the long desolation of 1810-1846, first by the opening of the Athole Street Mission; secondly by the reconciliation of the (so-called) "English" Chapel, and then by the erection and consecration both of S. John's Church and S. Ninian's Cathedral, we must enter upon a new phase of our narrative and relate the history of (at least) the latter after its establishment.

(I).—And first let us deal with the relation of the Bishop towards it.

This, it is gratifying to relate, continued to the end to be characterised by the utmost friendship and cordiality.

He defended it stoutly against all opposition. At the present day, indeed, after the founding of so many Cathedrals, it may be difficult to understand why the idea that something revolutionary was being done did not soon die away. To us it appears natural that a Bishop should have a central Church wherein to fix his official seat (or *cathedra*). But it was not so then. As there was resistance of various kinds to the scheme before it was more than a project, so also was there hostility now that it was fairly started. The Presbyterians continued to despise and dislike it, and traditions still (1894) survive to the effect that the

Clergy used to be stoned in the street. The Protestant party of our own communion continued their antagonism, and the Rev. C. J. Lyon of S. Andrews agreed with the Rev. W. Blatch of Pittenweem that "the Bishop was doing an act utterly incompetent for any Bishop to propose or even for a Diocesan Synod to accept." Even staunch Churchmen, such as the Warden of Glenalmond and the Rev. W. Farquhar of Pitscandly, failed to have their doubts as to the expediency of our Prelate's policy—*i.e.*, doing all on his own responsibility—removed; they were afraid that in reality he was, unknown to himself, being used by a party. The Synod also threw difficulties in the way, and disputed the right of the Cathedral Clergy to vote in its Debates*; and the Church Society raised objections to paying Mr. Chambers's salary. The Episcopal College itself (with the exception of Bishop Forbes) frowned upon the new institution, and wrote on *March 12th, 1851*, to enquire,† "as they could not have the advantage of the Bishop's presence, and as the question is one, in which the Church at large is interested, what was the Bishop's own view of the position of the Clergy in connection with the new Church at Perth?" And the Bishop of Moray (Eden) expressed an opinion to his aged colleague that the scholastic work commenced in connection with the Cathedral might end in rivalry to Trinity College.

But the Bishop continued stoutly to defend the Cathedral from all these attacks. And, whatever may be thought of each of the steps which he took, yet, since the matter related essentially to the constitution of his own Diocese, was nowhere forbidden by

* *Scottish Magazine*, 1852, p. 353.   † Neale's *Torry*, p. 376.

our Canons, and was in harmony with ancient custom, there can be no doubt but that, strictly speaking, he was within his rights; that his action was valid; and that he was labouring for the good of his Diocese. Accordingly he replied to the Clerk of the Episcopal College that, as a Diocesan Bishop, he claimed the right to act as he was doing, and added :—" The usage of the Universal Church has been that where there is a Christian Bishop there ought, if possible, to be a Cathedral," and, of course, a staff of Clergy to keep up suitable services. To the Bishop of Moray he wrote :—" The Schools . . may be productive of good to each other by the Middle School at Perth becoming a feeder to that at Glenalmond. I have never looked upon it in any other view." And all other attacks he warded off in a similar manner.

Indeed, he was the enthusiastic patron of the scheme. The following letter to Dr. Neale shews this :—" My heart is in the prosperity of S. Ninian's Cathedral. For every testimony, therefore, in its favour I feel grateful, because I heartily wish it God-speed. I shall, however, never see it, because of my extreme old age, being now in my 88th year, and my locomotive powers being almost entirely gone. But I will not cease to pray for its welfare while I live and retain my senses; because, if well served, its obvious tendency is to promote the glory of God and the endless benefit of many precious and immortal souls."

(II.)—Meantime, while it was being thus defended by its Bishop, how were matters proceeding at the Cathedral itself?

On the very day after the Statutes had received the Episcopal signature (*January 7th, 1851*) the newly-installed Canons met for the election of a Dean, that being their privilege by the Constitution. Their unanimous choice fell upon the Rev. E. B. K. Fortescue, M.A., Incumbent of Wilmcote, near Stratford-on-Avon, who accepted the appointment. We, indeed, who know the subsequent history, and are in a position to be wise after the event, may be permitted to doubt whether a refined and emotional Englishman, very little versed in Scotch affairs, and whose leading interest was Ritual, was the most suitable appointment that could have been made at that particular time. In these early days of renewed English sympathy with the Scottish Church, it might have been useful to have had at least one Scotchman on the Chapter. Even Bishop Torry, from his distant residence at Peterhead, seems to have had an inkling of this a month or two before he died. For when Dean Fortescue, in the zeal of his soul, resolved that the Cathedral should become a supporter of some English Church Societies, our Prelate wrote thus to him in reply (*June, 1852*):—"I am not at all inclined to accept the burden of collections for societies, who are basking under the sun of a rich and powerful establishment. There is non-congruity between their condition and that of a poor disestablished Church like our own, which greatly needs to receive such pecuniary aid as generous dispositions are inclined to give, and has little to bestow beyond a scanty allowance to their own pastors." But it is easy to criticise, and it is much pleasanter to bring forward the following testimony to the energy with which the new Dean threw himself into the discharge of his duties. "I mention these gentlemen," says Mr. Wordsworth, alluding to the Dean and Canon Chambers, "as the only two members of the Chapter who have been constantly resident. They have done much, very much, I believe, to attach earnest minds to the scheme."*

The ambition of the Chapter and the Founders was that the Cathedral Services should be a model of Catholic Worship. Starting on a new foundation, they thought that they could go back to more orthodox forms than, owing to Puritan corruptions, many even of the great English Churches were now able to adopt. On this head Canon Humble says :—†" Our whole Ritual was settled with the assistance and by the advice of the first Ritual Scholar of our Communion. We could not and did not regard this as a mere question of prettiness or hollow show; we were minded to render it as fitting an expression as we could of the holy Services, which it was to embody. We did not go exclusively to the existing Cathedrals of England for our model, because, however good the Ritual might have been at the period of the Restoration (1661), time had very seriously impaired it, and a cry had gone forth, joined in even by Churchmen, to pull down and destroy those venerable institutions as utterly effete and dead. Neither did we regard the latter end of the 17th century [*i.e.*, the time of the Revolution, when the High Church party were being chased out of the establishment both in England and Scotland] as favourable to correct Ritualism. Like its Architecture, its Ritual and Music were a composite mixture of religious and secular. As, therefore, we carefully abandoned the one, so too we went back to an earlier period for the other. . . . Upon this point of Ritual we felt strongly, for we could not see why the Christian Church should treat with disregard that, which formed so considerable a feature

* *Charge* of 1853, p. 28. † *Letter to the Bishop of S. Andrews*, p. 6.

in the Divine commandments respecting the Jewish Worship. We knew, too, what pains some of our holiest Bishops had bestowed on these things—Andrews, Cosin, Butler, and many more. Using, therefore, all available means to fix a Ritual at once worthy of a new Cathedral and of the Service to be therein rendered, we had the satisfaction of knowing that we were not engaged on unmeaning mummeries when worshipping Almighty God. We could not see any reason why ignorance and mere prejudice should dictate our Worship, so nothing was done contrary to the rubrical directions of the *Prayer Book*—more than our architectural forms."

The customs in connection with the Celebration of the Eucharist, which they chiefly valued at this time, were the use of the Scotch Office; the Eastward position; unleavened bread; the Mixture of Water with the Wine; the Lights; Incense; Vestments; and the use of Gregorian music. It is, however, curious to notice in this connection that the Black Gown was worn in the Pulpit for afternoon Sermon.

And here it may be interesting to record the impression which Services conducted on such principles by our English friends had on one, who had been brought up in the old-fashioned Scotch traditions of the Aberdeen school. It is evident indeed that, while the symbolic Ritual was quite strange to the Rev. W. Farquhar of Forfar, the general drift of the doctrines symbolized was congenial to his mind. *"I confess," he said, "for myself, speaking as a Scotchman, that the first two or three times I was present at the Cathedral Service, I felt a strong opposition and dislike to it; but I have also no hesitation in saying that

* *Report of Special Synod of 1853*, p. 55.

this soon wore off in a great degree. I believe, if the Scotch people were properly trained, they would be as capable of relishing the Cathedral Service as the English are."

(III).—And now we may turn from the Cathedral to the Pastoral or Congregational aspect of the institution.

At that time in Scotland the outward paraphernalia of a funeral were of the most gloomy and hope-destroying description. It is indeed possible to go too far in the opposite direction, and ignore alike the natural feelings of the human heart and the awfulness of God's severity, by adopting the untimely symbols of gladness at a burial. But certainly in those days the element of hope needed to be strongly accentuated in order to make our funerals Christian, and evidently the Cathedral Clergy set themselves to effect this reform. For, when an infant child of Canon Chambers' died, the obsequies were of the following character:—
*" The funeral procession started from the house at 8 a.m. It was led by a very young boy bearing a cross with an interwoven crown of everlasting flowers. This is, in fact, the mere revival of the mute's staff, which (originally a dressed cross) has become changed into a nondescript dressed stick. Behind the little cross-bearer followed six young girls in white, with hoods and scarfs, carrying baskets of flowers, which they scattered as the body was borne from the Church gate up to the Chancel and back to the grave, into which, after it was lowered, they emptied their baskets and threw their wreaths. Behind them came the bier, covered with a blue cloth with a white cross upon it, borne by eight young females also dressed in white."

* *Scottish Magazine*, 1852, p. 249.

There was a Celebration of the Holy Communion, and "*Since by man came death*," from the "Messiah," was sung as an Anthem in the Funeral Service.

*The number of Baptisms recorded respectively in 1850, 1851, and 1852 were 50, 28, and 21; of Marriages—1, 0, 1; of Funerals—4, 0, 9; and, altogether, 74 persons had been confirmed since the opening of the Mission. This was encouraging, and shewed what might be done, when the Church's missionary character was fairly brought to bear on the people.

†On *March 6th, 1852*, "the Rev. John Comper, Curate of Crieff, was admitted to the holy order of Priests, and Charles M'Ghee Keith to that of Deacons —the candidates being presented by the Rev. J. C. Chambers. . . The Bishop (of Brechin) and Clergy afterwards partook of a Lenten refreshment in the hall of the College."

‡The latter was "a middle school, wherein the sons of commercial men should be fitted for active employment; and those of them who are intended for the professions, should be educated up to the point where specific instruction in the faculty they are afterwards to cultivate commences. . . The desire is to impress a religious character on each individual." The maximum number of boarders at any one time was 30, of whom 16 were choristers. There was, besides, a school for the poor, the largest attendance at which was 80.

(IV).—We may conclude this chapter with a rapid glance round the Diocese, of which S. Ninian's was now the Cathedral. It was still the day of small things. Excluding the Bishop and the clerical masters at

* Cathedral MS. *Register*. † *Scottish Magazine*, 1852, p. 193.
‡ *Scottish Magazine*, 1852, p. 293.

Glenalmond, there were only 15 Clergy in the united Diocese in 1849, and 21 in 1852. Small, however, as these numbers were, an important change had come over the scene. The Church, which had too long been but the battered wreck of a stormy past, was at last confident that it had a future before it.

CHAPTER XXXII.

HOW BISHOP TORRY AUTHORIZED A SCOTTISH PRAYER BOOK, 1847-1852.

IT has at once to be confessed that the differences of opinion, which attended the birth of the Cathedral, became rather intensified than mitigated as time went on. We have seen that, during the period, with which we are dealing, the state of the Church at large has been characterized as one of "*Progress* amid *Controversy.*" Substantial *progress* has already appeared in Perth. It is now our duty to describe a *controversy*, the effects of which in our midst were by no means slight.

Why not pass it over in silence? Because it is far better to know the Truth. "*Magna est Veritas et prævalebit.*" It has unlooked-for ways of rewarding its disciples. Secondly, because it seems hard that, on the mere ground that they had to deal with difficulties, we should forget not merely those, who were to blame, but also those, who struggled hard to do their duty in perplexing times. Thirdly, because the discussion is now a thing of the long past, and an exhibition of its subject-matter may serve, while not rekindling old fires, as suggestive food for thought. And lastly, because the episode, both in the Church at large and even in Perth, where it was most severe and prolonged, did less injury to progress than might have been expected.

(I).—What, therefore, was the occasion of the present controversy?

It is to be remembered that, at the epoch, with

which we are dealing, the Law of the Scottish Church was the *Code of Canons* of 1838. Now, it was *impossible* for this, or any other Scotch Code whatever, to accept the English "*Book of Common Prayer*" *simpliciter*. For example, in a Church where Archdeacons were to all intents and purposes unknown, the English Rubric directing that functionary to present the Ordination candidates to the Bishop, simply could not be officially adopted. It was equally impossible that, in a Church, where there were no Archbishops, the Rubrics, which assume the existence of such a personage, should be authoritatively received. The very attempt to do so would have produced serious complications. It was also an impossibility that that branch of the Catholic Church, which was in *Scotland*, should adopt a *Prayer Book*, the title-page of which described it as that of "*The United Church of England and Ireland.*" And again the title, "*Articles agreed upon by the Archbishops and Bishops of both Provinces,*" and "*His Majesty's Declaration,*" could not possibly find formal place in a book, which, if it was to be adopted in Scotland, could not be adopted on the authority either of the Bishops, etc., of the Provinces of Canterbury and York, nor yet on that of His Majesty's Declaration. The only authority, on which the Book could be adopted, was that of the Bishops (and Synods) of the Province of the Church, which consisted of Scotland. Considerations such as these are absolute demonstration of the fact that the English Prayer Book *cannot*, as it stands, be adopted *simpliciter* as that of the Scottish Church.

This being the state of affairs, what is done? That branch of the Church, which is in America, and that in Ireland have (the former always, and the latter since its Disestablishment) proceeded as follows: they have both re-edited the *Prayer Book* from beginning to end; have introduced important changes everywhere; and have authorized the results as the *American* and *Irish Prayer Books* respectively. The Scottish branch of the Church has never gone so far as its sisters across the seas. Its policy was, at the time, with which we are dealing, as follows (and it has continued substantially the same ever since): by the *Code of 1838*, certain portions, and certain portions only, of the *English Book* were made of entire obligation, *i.e.*, *Holy Communion; Morning and Evening Prayer; the Litany; the Baptismal Service; the Catechism;* and the *Offices of Ordination and Consecration*,—and these, of course, subject to such changes as have before been shown to be absolutely necessary. The English *Marriage, Visitation,* and *Burial Services* were less strictly enjoined, and the English *Confirmation Office* nowhere so. Thus, not the English *Book, simpliciter*, but only those portions of it now mentioned, were the authorized Services of the Scottish Church; and to these a most important addition was made by the *Code* then in force, *i.e.*, the *Scotch Communion Office*. But, even of this (as now), no particular edition was specified in the *Canons*, and there were several differing from one another in existence.

Altogether, while the English, American, and Irish Churches can put a particular volume into an enquirer's hands, and say, "This is my Prayer Book," the Scottish (in common with the Indian, Canadian, South African, and other branches of the Church) cannot do so, and could not do so in Bishop Torry's time. She could only say, "Such and such portions of the *English Book*, with certain unavoidable changes, together with the *Scottish Office*, according to the traditional text, constitute my Service Book." Whether this is the most satisfactory arrangement or not, is a different question. So the case canonically stood, however, for Bishop Torry.

Under these circumstances, the idea was suggested to him of compiling a volume, which should practically represent the Scottish variation of the *Book of Common Prayer*. "In the month of *September, 1847*," he says,* "when I went to Perth, Muthill, and Crieff, for purposes peculiarly restricted to my official position, an address was presented to me in the vestry-room of the Church of Muthill, signed by seven of the Clergy of my Diocese . . . stating that they were deeply sensible of the importance of having the Liturgy and Usages of the Church in Scotland for the last century attested by a Prelate of my age and experience, and begging to express their desire that such a book might be edited under my sanction, as shall serve for a document of reference and authority in regard to the practice of our Church."

Accordingly, the work so recommended was edited by certain Presbyters of the Diocese, every proof being forwarded to and revised by the Bishop. In *April, 1850*, it was published.

So far all was in order and calculated to be for the benefit of the Church. The venerable editor had been born so long ago as 1763, and there was probably no one whose testimony to the usages of the Scottish Church was more original, comprehensive, and accurate.

But, as a matter of fact, the appearance of the book was the occasion of a perfect tempest, and it is because this tempest had such lasting consequences to

* Neale's *Torry*, p. 273.

the Church in Perth that it has been necessary to go into the matter.

What was it which caused the storm? If, indeed, the Bishop had merely fulfilled the intention of the original petition of editing "such a book as should serve for a document of reference and authority in regard to the practice of the Church," all would have been well. But, as a matter of fact, there appeared on the title-page these words :—" The Book of Common Prayer, etc., *according to the use of the Church of Scotland,*" with nothing to shew that it was not official, and the following certificate was actually prefixed by the Bishop :—" I hereby certify that I have carefully examined this edition of the Book of Common Prayer, and that it is in strict accordance with the usage of the Church of Scotland, and *I accordingly recommend it to the use of the Clergy of my own Diocese.*"

Thus the volume was distinctly something more than the mere "document of reference," for which the seven Clergy at Muthill had petitioned. And on account of the Episcopal recommendation it was actually brought into use as the *Office Book* of a few Churches, the Cathedral at Perth being one of the number.

Mr. Wordsworth wrote seven letters to the English *Guardian* against the book.

His arguments may be gathered under three heads. (1) He objected to the *manner* in which it had been produced. The Diocesan Synod was the lawful Council of the Bishop; but, without consulting them, he had allowed himself to be guided in the matter by a party. (2) But granted that the book did have the Bishop's authority fully enough, yet that authority was inadequate for the matter in hand. Even allowing that in the troublous times of the preceding

century, when there was no *Code of Canons*, individual
Bishops had greater liberty in liturgical matters, yet,
now that he had signed the *Code* of 1838, every
Bishop had, for the good of the Church at large,
recognised certain limitations on his own power and
certain powers to be possessed by the College of
Bishops for the sake of unity. And what the
limitations were in liturgical matters was made very
clear by *Canon xxviii.*, the preamble of which stated
that "In all ordinary parts of Divine Service it is
necessary to fix by authority (*i.e.*, not Episcopal, but
Canonical, authority) the precise form, from which no
Bishop, Presbyter, or Deacon shall depart by his own
alterations or insertions lest such liberty should
produce consequences destructive of decency and order."
And, in fact, "the very theory itself of General
Synods meeting to determine such points is at
variance with the claim of a single Bishop to legislate
in such matters for himself alone," as Bishop Torry
was taking upon himself to do. (3) And Mr. Wordsworth objected not only to the manner in which, and
the authority by which, the book was set forward
as "*The Book of Common Prayer according to the Use
of the Church of Scotland*," but he also maintained that
the *matter* contained in it was an unfair representation of
the Church's use. (*a*) First, a book professing to be
the *Prayer Book* according to the Use of any Church
ought to have no omissions of any of that Church's
Offices. This Book, however, did not contain the
English *Communion Service*, which was an official form
in the Scottish Church, and used by 5 out of the 7
Scottish Bishops and 78 out of the 118 Clergy in the
country. By its omissions, therefore, it was not the
Prayer Book of the Scottish Church. (*b*) And secondly,

he also disputed whether what actually appeared in the book could rightly claim to be according to the Use of the Scottish Church. After mentioning some other points, he directed attention to the Rubrics requiring *Absolution* (*i.e.*, private) on penitents before re-admission to the Altar, the *mixture* of water with the wine, liberty to celebrate with only one communicant present, and *Reservation* for the sick. He disputed the Canonical or Rubrical authority of these requirements in Bishop Torry's book.

*As a matter of fact, the vast majority of the Church decided that the weight of argument lay on the Warden's side, and the *Prayer Book* was condemned in strong terms by the Episcopal and Diocesan Synods. As a specimen of the resolutions arrived at, that passed by a majority of more than two to one in our own Diocese may be given. Its terms were as follows:—

†(1) "That this Synod, having received and heard the resolution of the Episcopal Synod ordering the suppression of 'the Book,' desires to express its entire concurrence in the said resolution, and to convey to the Bishops its hearty thanks for the same."

(2) "That this Synod feels bound in duty to record its strong disapproval of the use of the Book, which has been so condemned, and also its determination, should the Book be adopted or recommended by any Clergyman of the Diocese, to institute Canonical proceedings against the offender."

Reviewing the whole controversy, we may observe (1) that Bishop Torry had considerable reason for

* Neale's *Torry*, p. 283; Wordsworth's *Annals*, ii., p. 85.
† Wordsworth's *Seven Letters*, p. 9.

acting in the matter as he did. It was an excellent practical idea to collect into one handy volume all the canonically authorized Offices of the Scottish Church, and that this was the Bishop's real intention to the last is evidenced by these words, which he used in his own defence:—*"What I did was merely to recommend the *Prayer Book* to the use of the Clergy of my Diocese, certifying that it was in strict conformity with the Usages of the Church of Scotland."

But (2) we can only say that there seemed even more considerable reasons on the side of his opponents. Mr. Wordsworth's arguments were surely conclusive when he maintained that, as to its subject-matter, the Book did not by any means perfectly represent the Canonical Services of the Church. And as to the authority, by which the work was issued, it is plain that there was a wide distinction to be drawn between the cases of the Prayer Book and the Cathedral. Both, indeed, were alike, so far as they rested solely on the Bishop's authority. But they were unlike in this, *i.e.*, that a Bishop had a right to fix his seat formally at one Church within his jurisdiction, and to gather round him an official "lesser Council" (or Chapter); in a word, to constitute a Cathedral for his own Diocese, but he had not a right to publish a Service Book that purported on its title page to represent the use of the whole Church officially. The Bishop of S. Andrews, Dunkeld, and Dunblane could constitute a Cathedral of *S. Andrews, Dunkeld, and Dunblane*, but he could not issue an official "Prayer Book according to the use of the Church of *Scotland.*"

* *Scottish Magazine*, 1851, p. 337.

CHAPTER XXXIII.

HOW BISHOP TORRY DIED AND WAS BURIED, AND HOW HIS SUCCESSOR WAS ELECTED.

BUT now the aged Prelate, who had ruled the Diocese so faithfully since his Consecration to Dunkeld in 1808 (for Dunblane and S. Andrews see chapter xxv., p. 254) was about to pass away. On *August 14th, 1852*, Bishop Torry wrote on the back of an envelope:— " Unable to take any concern in the future matters of the Church." Towards the end of September he took ill, and "at length, in his 89th year, on the morning of *Sunday, October 3rd*, attended by the Rev. Dr. Rorison, and surrounded by all the living members of his family, without a groan or a sigh, his spirit returned to God, who gave it."

*"At the earnest solicitation of the Provost 'and Canons of Perth, and, indeed, in accordance with the Bishop's request, it was agreed by the family that his remains should be interred in his own Cathedral. They were removed from Peterhead to Aberdeen on *October 12th*; were received in that City by the Primus and some of the Clergy, and by them escorted to the Southern Railway. At Perth Station the Canons and others of the Cathedral body were in waiting; the Choristers and Vergers preceded the hearse to S. Ninian's, and the Coffin was deposited in the Nave under a Canopy of black cloth, emblazoned with the arms of the three Sees, and surrounded by six lighted

* Neale's *Torry*, pp. 381-8.

candles. The Dean of the Cathedral, having laid on it the Pastoral Staff and the Mitre,* took his place at the head, and every three hours the various watchers, all of them connected with the Cathedral, were relieved. That," continues Dr. Neale, "was a second night at S. Ninian's which I shall not easily forget. The inhabitants of the Town were admitted about 9 o'clock, passed round the coffin, and went out by the same door, at which they had entered, and never, in any foreign church, did I see so large a crowd conduct themselves with greater decorum. It was very late before all that wished had visited the scene; the doors were then closed, and the rest of the watch was kept by the Cathedral Clergy alone. On the following day, after an early Celebration, the funeral took place. The pall was borne by the Warden of Trinity College and seven other Clergy of the Diocese; the Bishops of Brechin and Moray were in attendance, and by the former the service itself was performed. The Psalms and Anthems were chanted by the Choir, by whom also, at the conclusion of the solemnity, the *Dies Iræ*, from the *Hymnal Noted*, was sung. The Bishop was buried on the north side of the Altar, and, as the ancient custom was, facing the west."

"Bishop Torry," Dr. Neale goes on to remark, "presents an example of the service, which may be wrought for God by the steady, undeviating support of one acknowledged principle. . . Possessed of no extraordinary talents, he set himself to uphold the Eucharistic treasure, of which he seemed to be the providentially-constituted guardian, and, in connection

* As had been done at the funeral of Bishop Torry's predecessor, Archbishop Sharpe, in 1679 (Gordon's *Scotichronicon*, iv., 94). In his old age, Bishop Torry wore the Rochet and Chimere.

with its defence, to maintain the independence of that Church, in which he ruled, as well from external danger as from Collegiate usurpation. For the *Scottish Office* he may almost be said to have lived during the last twenty years of his life, . . even Perth Cathedral was chiefly interesting to him as connected more or less with the National Liturgy."

The Rev. Gilbert Rorison, LL.D., Incumbent of Peterhead, who, as we saw, attended the Bishop during his last illness, spoke thus of him in a sermon delivered in S. Peter's Church there :—" Though he was mild and conciliating where no principle was touched, on questions which he apprehended to involve principle, he was rooted as a rock. '*Firm to the last*' was his answer to me, when he mistakingly supposed for a moment that he was solicited, in a letter from a brother Bishop, to modify a certain course he had deemed it his duty to pursue. Pattern of pristine faith and godly simplicity, of apostolic manners and unvarnished truth, he has been taken by the Master, and we are left to lament his loss, or rather our own."

In one respect Bishop Torry was unique, and that is that he was probably the only Prelate in the United Kingdom, who, in the sad year 1845, was prepared heartily to welcome the representatives of the Oxford Movement into his Diocese. Now, as it was the all but universal reprobation of his views by the Episcopal bench that made Newman feel an alien in the English Church and look elsewhere for sympathy, we may perhaps hazard the suggestion that the old-fashioned, non-juring Theology of the Scottish Church, which Bishop Torry represented, although differing in certain respects from that of the

Tractarians,* might, if it had been more largely disseminated, have availed to keep the future Cardinal amongst us.

But, however that may be, "under the shadow of his own Cathedral the Bishop awaits the reward of his labours at the Second Coming of the Lord."

(2) But, whenever one general fails in the Church militant here on earth, another must step forward to take his place. Accordingly, on *October 14th, 1852*, the Primus issued a Mandate for an election to fill up the vacant See, and the Dean of the Diocese summoned the Clergy to meet in S. Anne's Church, Coupar-Angus, for the purpose of choosing a successor to his deceased Father.

As we have already seen, public opinion was in a very excited state, and the Clergy of the Diocese were divided into two opposite and, numerically speaking, equal camps. This controversial position of affairs, however, we must by no means altogether attribute to local animosities. The fact is that, although the late Bishop had welcomed the Tractarians from England into his Diocese and protected them there as restorers of the ancient ways, his death now made an opening for those, who were opposing the Oxonians in the south, to appear actively in our Diocese also. This is what was happening. But, though the contest was thus the widespread one of Tractarianism *versus* the world, it, of course, assumed a special form in these parts, which was as follows:—" Puseyism," led by the Rev. G. Forbes, A. Lendrum, C. J. Chambers, H. Humble, and Dean Fortescue, entrenched itself in two positions, *i.e.*, in Perth Cathedral and Bishop

* The statement on p. 269 that the two views of Theology were *identical* perhaps puts the matter rather too strongly.

Torry's Prayer Book. The attack was led by the Warden of Trinity College, who rallied half of the Clergy of the Diocese, including Dean Torry, to his standard. Only here it must be understood that our Anti-Tractarianism did not assume a violently Protestant hue. If Mr. Wordsworth could by no means be described as a "Puseyite," yet he was not to be classed either as a "Low" or a "Broad" Churchman. His mind not being of a metaphysical or rationalistic character, he had no sympathy with the latter; and, being an accomplished student acquainted with history, the narrow individualistic views of the former could never wholly satisfy him. His was an essentially English mind—scholarly, objective, conservative. He was perfectly satisfied with the English Church as it was before the days of "Puseyism." He would simply engraft some of the energy of the new Movement upon things as they were in his native land. And so it came to pass that the opposition to our local Tractarianism was made from the prevailing "Church and State" point of view, and not chiefly by a narrow Protestantism.

Such were the two parties, which found themselves confronting one another, when Bishop Torry died. With which was the victory to lie? Was the leader, who conscientiously believed it to be his mission to prevent Tractarianism absorbing the Scottish Church; or was Puseyism, as embodied in the Cathedral and Bishop Torry's Prayer Book, to carry the day? When the hour of election[*] came round, the candidates proposed were Bishop Eden of Moray, who was the excellent and judicious nominee of the Tractarians, and the Rev. Charles Wordsworth, M.A., Warden of

[*] For a full report of which, see *Scottish Magazine*, 1852, pp. 585-601.

Glenalmond, the brilliant champion of the other side. The speeches made on the occasion reflected the excitement of the time, and, when the matter came to the point, there were eight for the Bishop of Moray and eight for the Warden. There was still one elector who had not recorded his vote, and that was Mr. Wordsworth. Evidently all depended on his action. What was he to do under these excessively difficult circumstances? There was no difficulty at all, said his opponents. Personal considerations clearly shewed that he ought to vote for the Bishop of Moray. In view of subsequent events we may say that that might possibly have been the best course to take. But in the thick of the contest matters did not present themselves to the Warden at all in this light. Let us do him justice. On the one hand he was conscious to himself of no personal ambition for the vacant Office. A man of his calibre and influence must have known that, so far as ambition went, he might do much better for himself.* "Friends," he says, "in England shared my indifference. They disliked the thought of my becoming a Scottish Bishop, which they feared would entail banishment from England permanently." On the other hand, merely because it was a personally disagreeable thing to vote for himself, was he to allow an extreme faction to capture the Diocese and inflict a deadly blow on the Scottish Church? And, even if he were himself inclined to allow this to happen, his friends in the Diocese would not hear of it. They plied him with every argument in their power to support the cause, which they deemed sacred, whatever his personal aversion to doing so in the circumstances might be.

* Wordsworth's *Annals*, vol. ii., pp. 125, 128, 137.

They carried the day. To vote for himself appeared in the light of a duty to the Warden, and he did so. Thus he was elected. But, because the Dean only, and not the majority of the electors, signed the return, the Primus ruled that the latter was informal. A second Mandate was, therefore, issued. But the result was precisely the same. Of course it was appealed against, but the College of Bishops decided that the Warden's conduct was both canonically and morally justifiable, and so the election was confirmed, and the Consecration took place at Aberdeen on *January 25th, 1853 (Conversion of S. Paul)*.

On *March 7th* a deputation of the Laity of the United Diocese waited on the new Bishop at Trinity College, and presented to him a congratulatory address, which had received the signatures of the great body of the influential lay members (heads of families) of the Diocese, to the number of 237. Certainly not since the death of Bishop Rattray, one hundred and ten years previously, had so strong a personality presided over the See. *The new Bishop was the son of Dr. Wordsworth, Master of Trinity College, Cambridge; nephew of William Wordsworth, the celebrated Lake Poet; brother of Christopher Wordsworth, the great Bishop of Lincoln; and uncle of John Wordsworth, the present learned Bishop of Salisbury. Both he and his two brothers, John and Christopher, were distinguished for the remarkable number of University prizes, which they carried off between them at Oxford and Cambridge. Our Prelate had himself been the winner of the University Latin Verse Prize on *Mexico*,† the Christ Church Latin Verse Prize on *Athenæ*, and a Fell Exhibition, all in 1827. For these

* See *Annals*, vol. i., *passim*.   † Quoted on p. 166.

distinctions he was named for a Senior Studentship by the Dean of Christ Church at the end of the same year, being the first in whose favour the system of patronage nomination was laid aside. When he took his B.A. degree in 1830, his name appeared in the first class in *Litteræ humaniores*. After completing his own course at the University, he acted as private tutor to a very distinguished roll of pupils, including Hope Scott of Abbotsford, W. E. Gladstone (the future Prime Minister), H. E. Manning (the future Cardinal), Francis Doyle (the future Professor of Poetry), W. K. Hamilton (the future Bishop of Salisbury), Lord Lincoln, and others. It may not be amiss also to record that he had been as distinguished for Athletics as for Scholarship, having rowed in the first inter-University boat race, and played in the first inter-University cricket match. After leaving Oxford he became Second Master and Fellow of Winchester, in which capacity he had laboured zealously as well for the religious as for the educational good of the boys—a thing, which had been by no means so common as it is now in the great English Schools. As we have seen, he was Warden of Trinity College at the time of his election to the Bishopric, a post which he continued still to hold for a few years.

The present Episcopate brings us into a fresh era. Alone of all his Right Reverend brethren, Bishop Torry had survived to represent the Eighteenth in the middle of the Nineteenth Century. He was the bond of connection between the old and the new. With his death the past was quite gone. With the advent of his successor the Diocese assumed an Anglican, as distinguished from a merely Scottish, complexion. The directing mind was itself now part of that wave of life, which came north from England; and, in that mind, the Church to be directed was conceived of, not merely as the descendant of the old Non-jurors, but as the united body, which resulted from the amalgamation of that school of divines with the "Qualified" Chapels. And, *as* the leading passion of Bishop Torry had been the preservation of the "*Scottish Office*," so the dominating enthusiasm of Bishop Wordsworth was a scheme to effect union between the Establishment and the Communion, in which he himself now held so distinguished a position.

CHAPTER XXXIV.

HOW THE CATHEDRAL WAS ACCEPTED BY THE DIOCESAN SYNOD OF 1853.

THE Anti-Ritualists were thus established in power. The question was therefore agitated amongst them :— What to do with the two principal schemes of their opponents : namely, the Cathedral, and Bishop Torry's *Prayer Book?*

As for the latter we hear of it no more. The new Bishop had publicly maintained that it was an utterly unauthorized publication, and no attempt was made to obtain his sanction for it. And, as all the sanction it ever had was that of the Diocesan, it of course disappeared, now that that was no longer forthcoming. Bishop Wordsworth had destroyed one of the engines whereby our Tractarians had hoped to disseminate their principles.

But what about the Cathedral ? Was it to be wrested from them also ? Great must have been their relief when a friend wrote as follows :—" We are happy to hear that the Bishop of the Diocese has exhibited the utmost anxiety to promote and further the efficiency of this valuable institution." And shortly afterwards his Lordship himself said :—*" No true Churchman can fail earnestly to desire and to long for the restoration of Cathedrals . . . It is only a question of *time* and *place* and *means*. In respect to time and place as they concern S. Ninian's—considering

* The *Report of Special Synod of 1853* is the basis of what follows.

what has been already done, I trust that you will all agree with me that it is the part alike of Christian prudence and Christian charity to look upon the decision as already made."

These being his ascertained sentiments, the Bishop "was given to understand that, as his Predecessor had been enthroned (by proxy) in the Church in question, it was expected that the same ceremony of solemn inauguration into his office should be performed for him also."

But the Cathedral authorities were going on too fast. It did not follow that because the Bishop was willing to recognize S. Ninian's as his Cathedral, he would do so, and that in such a public manner as consenting to be enthroned there, until considerable alterations had been made in its constitution. The changes upon which he insisted were of three kinds :—

First, financial. The Institution was already nearly £3,000 in debt, chiefly in connection with the Middle School. Some remedy for this must be found, and a satisfactory minimum income secured for the future. This reasonable requirement was at once munificently met by two individuals. The Hon. G. F. Boyle cleared off the entire deficit and also bound himself to make over a capital sum of £3,000 at some time, and, in the meanwhile, to guarantee an income of £200 a year from himself ; and, on his part, Lord Forbes promised £100 *per annum*.

So the first difficulty disappeared. The *second* requirement was that the concurrence of the Diocesan Synod should be secured. This the Bishop proposed to obtain, as it were, by instalments. He would hold two meetings of the body referred to : the one he would ask to *affirm the general principle* that, supposing it were satisfactorily reformed, it would be well to recognize S. Ninian's as the Cathedral; and the other he would ask *actually to accept* the Institution as reconstituted.

Accordingly a special Synod assembled at Trinity College, where the Bishop still resided, on *April 6th, 1853.* At this his Lordship proposed:—" That the act, by which our late holy and revered Diocesan constituted S. Ninian's, Perth, to be the Cathedral of this united Diocese, be *ad interim* accepted by this Synod, *provided*—*(a)* that such arrangements be made as may settle the Chapter upon the basis settled below (*i.e.*, a Dean with at least £200 a year secure; two Canons with £100 a year each, resident; and the Dean of the Diocese as *ex officio* a Canon non-resident); (*b*) that such other modifications be made in the existing Constitution as the Bishop may think necessary, according to the method, which the Constitution provides for its own revision." This was the important part of the Bishop's proposals. He now invited free discussion on the general principle.

The *Rev. C. Lyon* of S. Andrews moved an amendment, to the effect "that, as there is no recognition of Cathedral Churches with Deans and Chapters by the Canons of this Church, it is incompetent for this Diocesan Synod—or, if competent, inexpedient—to acknowledge S. Ninian's, Perth, as anything more than an ordinary Chapel of the Diocese; and, therefore, the question of recognising it as a Cathedral, even *ad interim*, be postponed, until the subject be taken up by a General Synod."

The *Rev. W. Blatch* of Pittenweem seconded the amendment in a long speech. His *first* argument was that, as they had all along been opposed to the

Cathedral, they would be stultifying themselves by accepting it now. His *second*, that, as Cathedrals were not in the Canons, it was incompetent even for a Bishop to propose to create one. His *third*, that, as the Church was so poor, it was inexpedient to spend so much money as would be requisite on one undertaking. His *fourth*, that in no case could they offer to the Cathedral dignitaries "that learned leisure, which was one great object, he believed, of kindred institutions in England." His *fifth*, that there were no Cathedrals in America. His *sixth*, that the scheme would excite the hostility of the Presbyterians. And his *seventh*, that the Ritualism of Rome was not to be tolerated.

The *Rev. A. Lendrum* followed, and replied to each of these arguments at some length. (1) The Synod, having never been consulted on the Cathedral question, could not be stultifying itself, if it now expressed approval of the scheme. (2) Cathedrals had only disappeared from the Church's system against her will at the Revolution: the Canons only professed to regulate what was practically in existence in the year 1838, when they were drawn up: the fact, therefore, that Cathedrals were not mentioned in them could not be held to forbid them. (3) To create enthusiasm for one large scheme would, so far from paralyzing effort in other directions, stimulate Church life in a variety of ways. (4) "Learned leisure," in Mr. Blatch's sense, so far from being the use, was the abuse of Cathedrals. (5) Although there were no Cathedrals in America, a movement in favour of erecting them was in progress there. (6) As for the Presbyterians, he held that they would speak well of the Church only so long as it did nothing. (7) As for Ritualism being a stumbling-block, the fact that four or five years ago there were only 20 or 30 members belonging to S. Ninian's, whereas now there were 200, proved the contrary.

When all the members of the Synod, and some of the Laity (whom the Bishop, for the first time, had invited to be present), had spoken, and spoken with great fulness, the curious result appeared that all, who had been hostile to his election, supported his present proposal, and all, who had supported his election, were hostile to his present proposal. Under these circumstances his Lordship evidently felt that he could count on the concurrence of the Synod in his policy. His late opponents were conciliated, and the present dissent of his electors would not be carried so far as active opposition to his plan, should he persevere with it. Accordingly he summed up as follows:—"So then I am prepared to defend the act of my revered predecessor to a certain extent. I am prepared to maintain its legality; but I am not prepared to uphold either the wisdom or the charity of all the steps, by which it has been brought to its present condition." And he concluded thus:—"I shall give my best consideration to everything that has been stated here to-day. I had no intention of putting anything to the vote on the present occasion. I shall do the best I can against the time of our next Synod."

Altogether the meeting had passed successfully off. The *Scottish Magazine*, which was the organ of the Cathedral party, remarked:—"Although this Synod was assembled to consider a most knotty point, we are happy to say that throughout the whole proceedings the utmost fairness prevailed." It also congratulated the Bishop on the happy idea of inviting the presence of the Laity.

So now two of the Bishop's requirements had been met, the financial question was settled, and the preliminary concurrence of the Synod obtained. His Lordship therefore addressed himself to his *third* demand, *viz.*:—That a new Constitution should be adopted. *Accordingly, with the help of the Rev. John Jebb, Prebendary of Hereford, he set to work to prepare a new draft of Statutes. His leading idea in doing this was that the Chapter should no longer be an *imperium in imperio*; a close corporation, independent of the Bishop and the Diocese. This seemed to strike at the root of the primitive functions of a Cathedral. He desired, on the contrary, "to maintain the unity and singleness of Diocesan Episcopacy: not according to the mediæval plan of checks and counterpoises of Government (which arose in part out of the aggrandizing spirit of the Church of Rome)." Accordingly his new Code depressed the power of the *Chapter*. They were no longer to have the appointment of the Dean, Canons, and other officials exclusively in their own hands; they were no longer to be the sole originators of all business at the meetings; they were no longer to have power to increase and decrease the number of stalls at their pleasure; in fact, the initiative in the government of the Institution was to be no longer theirs. They were to act strictly under the *Bishop*, whose powers were therefore largely increased; he was to be no longer passive, and merely sanctioning or vetoing what came up to him from the Chapter. He was to be the ordinary president of the Chapter; he was to initiate all business there; he was to have the power of proceeding against the members of the Chapter for

---

* Bishop's *Address* to Special Synod of 1873; *Annals*, vol. ii., 152-6; Humble's *Letter*, pp. 63-73.

Statutes of 1853. 339

insubordination, etc., and of making new laws or altering the Statutes, provided he obtained a two-thirds majority. As regards the *Clergy of the Diocese* they were to be so connected with the Cathedral that, the Patronage of the Chapter having been done away, the five oldest Presbyters in the Diocese were always to be invited to become Prebendaries. Thus every school of thought would have an opening. As for the *Scottish Communion Office*, though he would not interfere with its actual exclusive use, yet, it must not stand on the formal Statutes of the Cathedral, that any Canonical Service, such as the *English Office*, was to be constitutionally excluded.

When this Code had taken shape, copies were sent to all the Bishops, to the Clergy, and to the leading Laity of the Diocese, and suggestions invited. The answers received were altogether extremely favourable.

Thus armed, the Bishop summoned another meeting of the Synod at Glenalmond for *July 6th.** It assembled accordingly. *Morning Prayer* was said in the College Chapel at 9 a.m., and the *Litany* sung at noon, the Service concluding with the *Holy Communion*, according to the *Scotch Office*. Immediately after Service the Bishop and his Clergy took their appointed places in the Ante-chapel, where the Synod was formed and solemnly constituted with Prayer.

After some preliminary business, the subject of "The Position of S. Ninian's, Perth," came up. During the course of a long address the Bishop remarked that he had thoroughly considered the transactions of the last Synod, and that he now submitted to them his new Draft of *Statutes*. He begged also to state that "he would have made no progress whatever had it not

* *Report of Ordinary Synod of 1853.*

been for the forbearing, considerate, and truly charitable spirit, in which he was met by the Clergy and other friends of S. Ninian's, and especially by Mr. Boyle:" he pleaded for an exhibition of the same spirit on the other side.

Proceeding to give answers to all the objections against the Cathedral that had been made at the last Synod, he first developed Mr. Lendrum's argument in favour of the *legality* of reviving Cathedrals: "it was sufficient in this connection to say that what once existed in our Church, and what she never of herself repudiated or condemned, it cannot be against her authority to restore." He next proposed to change the title of the head of the Cathedral from "Dean" to "Provost," in order that there might be no confusion between the Dean of the Diocese and the Dean of the Cathedral. Eventually he hoped that both offices might be united in one person; meantime "Provost" was an ancient ecclesiastical designation. The alteration with regard to the *Scottish Liturgy* was then explained. Thus he put the thing in legal shape before them. But now for an answer to the alleged *inexpediency* of the project. It would work, he said, far more damage to destroy an institution that has reached the present dimensions of S. Ninian's, than to accept it on reasonable terms; by accepting the Cathedral "they would encourage their best friends, give a new impulse to other schemes, and take one of the most effectual steps to secure peace amongst themselves." As for the danger of *Ritualism*, the Cathedral Clergy were now *on the same footing as all the other Clergy of the Diocese*, and the Bishop would keep a vigilant watch over them. His Lordship ended with an exhortation to remember the importance and sacredness of the question before them.

Synod accepts Cathedral.

The *Dean of the Diocese* then moved :—" That the Draft of *Statutes* for S. Ninian's, Perth, which the Bishop has submitted to our deliberate counsel, be unanimously approved and accepted by this Synod. That the foregoing resolution be passed subject to the approval of the next general Synod."

A full discussion having ensued, the resolution was carried unanimously.

Thereupon the Bishop requested the Provost of S. Ninian's to take the place which had been accorded to him by the Synod, *i.e.*, on his left hand, as second in rank in the Diocese. The meeting then closed with expressions of good will on the part of his Lordship towards the Cathedral, and of thankfulness that such a conciliatory spirit had been shewn on all sides in discussing this burning question.

Certainly each party made real sacrifices in order to meet the other half way. The Chapter had accepted a Constitution, which was understood by the Synod greatly to curtail their power, and, on the other side, the Bishop and Diocese had accepted a Foundation, which was originally the creation of their opponents. So far the Church might be congratulated on the course, which events had taken in the Diocese.

The Bishop, therefore, at last closed with the invitation formerly mentioned, and was enthroned in the Cathedral on *S. Matthew's Day (September 21st), 1853*. He preached an eloquent sermon upon the occasion, his subject being " *S. Matthew an example for Scotland.*" It was afterwards published with the following dedication :—" To the Very Rev. John Torry, M.A., Dean of the United Diocese, &c., and to the Very Rev. E. B. K. Fortescue, M.A., Provost, and the other members of the Chapter of the Cathedral Church in Perth, the following discourse, being the first, that has been preached at the enthroning of a Scottish Bishop for nearly two centuries, is affectionately inscribed."

CHAPTER XXXV.

HOW MATTERS WENT IN PERTH DURING BISHOP WORDSWORTH'S FIRST THREE YEARS, 1853-6.

HAVING now narrated the reconstruction of the Cathedral and its acceptance by the new Bishop and the Diocesan Synod, let us leave these constitutional questions and watch the establishment at work, confining our view to the period, when the Bishop resided elsewhere than Perth.

Fortunately, it is characterized by an admirable spirit of conciliation and consequent harmony. It almost seemed as if the Fair City, having endured the advent of the Tractarians and the onset of their opponents, had already got over the epoch of controversy, which marked the history of the Scottish Church in the third quarter of the Nineteenth Century.

That this time of peace, however, was not gained without some sacrifice soon appeared; for Canon Chambers found the new *régime* so uncongenial that he sent in his resignation, which was accepted by the Bishop. He certainly was a great loss. It was he, who had originally gathered the Congregation together, and we saw at the time of the Consecration what his brethren of the Clergy and the leading Laity thought of that work. To this day—that is, forty years after the date, with which we are dealing—he is remembered with respect and affection by the oldest members of of the flock. It is related that, some years after he resigned, one of our Perth people called on him in London, and found him with his coat off in the garden, and that, when he looked up and suddenly recognized his friend from S. Ninian's, he could scarcely restrain his tears. Canon Haskoll also ceased to reside, not approving of the recent changes. The two vacant stalls were filled by the Revs. J. Sellar and R. Campbell, who were to oversee the educational part of the work.

The other Cathedral Clergy were also called upon to put a considerable strain upon their loyalty to the Bishop, but they yielded, if not gladly, yet at least quietly. They had, as we have seen, taken the utmost pains to study the subject of Ritual and to make theirs as correct as possible. But at the demand of their Ordinary they now made the following changes in their use, "painful" as they confessed they were to their feelings:*—(a) During the Introit the Celebrant was to kneel at the North side, instead of in the midst of the Altar. (b) The Celebrant was to receive kneeling. (c) Not to Communicate with less than one. (d) No lighted candles. (e) Choir not to go to the Nave to hear the Sermon. (f) Offertory Sentences not to be sung. (g) No singing during the Communion of the people. (h) The sacred vessels to be covered with fair linen cloth instead of the silk veil before the second Celebration. As for the Eastward Position, it was the Bishop's own practice at this time in the College Chapel, and therefore no objection was made to its continuance in the Cathedral.

These preliminaries having been amicably arranged, our Prelate paid his first visit to the Cathedral during the Glenalmond summer holidays of 1853. It was upon a week day, and his Lordship sat amongst the Congregation. On *August 29th*, after returning home,

* Humble's *Letter*, pp. 7, 73.

he wrote as follows to Provost Fortescue :—*"I must not omit to say how extremely pleased I was with all I have seen of your Church Services (including the early Service), both morning and evening, when I was in Perth. I certainly never was present at any Celebration of Divine Service which I liked—to speak with all reverence—so well." And to Mr. Boyle he wrote in the same strain. He thought the Cathedral Services were simpler than many, and therefore better : "*simpler*, he meant, from the use of Gregorian chants, and that not only for the Psalms, but also for the Canticles, in place of the elaborate and too often undevotional (so-called) Services found in English Cathedrals, and from the use of a plain hymn in place of the Anthem: *better*, because the Choir was composed, for the most part, of a better class of boys, carefully trained under the Provost's own eye in his own house, while the Organist was known to possess superior qualifications for his office." And as for the low celebration of the Eucharist in the early morning, the Bishop liked it, " because it was not of a character highly ritualistic. Nothing but the plain Service plainly read, or rather rehearsed from memory by the Provost; not in the Choir, but in the North Transept, with no singing or ritual of any kind, and with a congregation of say half-a-dozen of all ages—such as in those days I commonly joined in, when I was staying in the Cloister at Westminster."

Their Diocesan having thus shown himself amongst the Congregation, the latter felt that the way was now open to address him on a certain point.† They claimed the right of nominating their own Pastor, now that

* *Address* to Synod of 1873, p. 25.
† *Some Considerations respecting S. Ninian's*, 1873, pp. 40-2, 34.

Mr. Chambers had retired. In a letter to Dr. White the Bishop replied, pointing out that this claim was inconsistent with the new Constitution, which placed the Patronage in the hands of the Bishop. A letter from the Provost to his Lordship both closed the discussion and shewed that not only the Cathedral Chapter but also the Congregation were prepared to yield to their Father in Christ. The Provost said:— "It will, I am sure, afford you as much pleasure to learn, as it does me to communicate, that those present (forming a very distinct majority of the whole body) unanimously agreed heartily to accept your decision on the matter of the Patronage of the pastoral care of the Congregation assembling in the Cathedral." A slight counterbalancing concession on the part of the Bishop was also acquiesced in. His Lordship had suggested "the addition of one or more members to the present number of lay Trustees, to be elected by the Congregation," and the Provost reported that the latter had agreed to the suggestion.

*In 1854 the Bishop (who had received the degree of D.C.L. from Oxford University *honoris causâ*) made a short stay in Perth. "We returned," he says, "early in September to our lodging in Rose Terrace—a pleasant situation facing the North Inch, with the glorious Tay flowing full in view, and the woods of Scone Palace spreading to the north-east."

On S. Matthew's day, the first anniversary of his enthronement, he held the annual Synod in the Cathedral. Besides this assembly there was also a Visitation, by which was meant a combined meeting of Clergy and Laity. It had occurred to the Bishop that the latter ought to have a more prominent place

* For what follows, see *Annals*, vol. ii.

in the Councils of the Church than was then accorded to them. The addition of a Visitation therefore to the purely clerical Synod seemed to him to be the best way of meeting the difficulty under the circumstances. At the latter there was a Sermon delivered by the Provost. The Bishop reserved his charge for the larger assembly. It was the first of that long series of remarkable utterances on the subject of Union between the Episcopal and Presbyterian Communions, which were destined to make his name a household word in Scotland. "At the close of the two days," he says, "which were spent in the business of our Synod and Visitation, it was remarked, publicly, and I believe with perfect truth, that greater harmony of sentiment, or more perfect evidence of cordial and brotherly affection, could scarcely be conceived than had been shewn amongst us." The Bishop also delivered a striking series of Lectures on his favourite topic in the City Hall.

Before the autumn was over he left for Bournemouth, and in November the Provost's Father wrote thus to him:—"Your residence in Perth has been a great blessing to the Church and neighbourhood. My son's letters have been filled with accounts of the advantages resulting to the Cathedral and population from your presence and preaching." And, even now (forty years afterwards), there are those who can recal the crowds that used to resort to the Cathedral to hear him at this time. We may be sure that it was with conscientiously elaborated and intellectual discourses that he edified them. He was a truly eloquent man.

After having settled his family at Bournemouth for the winter, the Bishop returned in a few weeks to Muthill, and then, about Whitsunday, 1855, having been rejoined by his household, took up his residence at Birnam Cottage, Dunkeld. "While here," he says, "I frequently went into Perth for the Sunday, to preach either at S. Ninian's or at S. John's—especially at the latter, the Incumbency of which was then vacant, through the resignation of Mr. Wood."

"On one such occasion," he continues, "I was met with a curious illustration of the effect which our worship, as then conducted at the Cathedral, was likely to have upon the minds even of the more respectable portion of the humbler orders in Perth. I was travelling outside the Inverness Mail from Dunkeld, before the days of Highland Railways, late one Saturday evening, in order to preach at S. Ninian's on the day following, and I had as a companion an elderly and intelligent woman, whom I took to be the wife of a small farmer, who had interested me by the sensible and religious tone of her conversation. She had no suspicion who I was, for the night was dark and stormy, and I was wrapped up closely in travelling costume; and, as we came to our journey's end, the coach had stopped to allow a passenger to dismount at the corner of the street opposite the Cathedral (which had a light in the sacristy, probably for choral practice). Pointing to the building, she said to me—'Were you ever in that place?' and, without waiting for an answer, continued—'I was once there, but never intend to go again. When I came out, I said to myself, *I wonder now whether they know what they have been about, for I'm sure I don't!*' There was no ill-nature in the remark; it was merely the simple record of her own experience."

The Synod of this year (1855) was again held in the Cathedral, and it will be interesting to quote the following passage from the Bishop's Charge, in order to show of what kind of a Diocese S. Ninian's was then the centre:—

"In January, 1853," he said, "the number of Incumbencies in the Diocese was 16, now it is 20. The number of souls in our several Congregations was then returned as 2552; it is now 3239, making an increase of nearly 700—mostly, I should imagine, arising from the children who have been added to our schools. This will account for the smaller increase (though still not inconsiderable), which appears in the number of our Communicants. In 1853, they were 1132; in 1855, they are 1366. The increase in the number of confirmed is not so large as might be expected, being only the difference between 122 and 114; but this I attribute to the fact that during last year (1853-4), being the first year of my Episcopate, Confirmation had been administered to more than the usual numbers. The return of the number of baptized for 1853 was 91; for 1855, it is 213. The number of schools (which, though not returned in 1853, is known to have been 9 in that year) is now 15, and the number of children who attend them is 1193. I have also added a column to the present schedule, which exhibits the sum-total, both of the contributions made by the Diocese to the Church Society, and of the grants of all kinds made to the Diocese by the Church Society. The former amounts to £371 3s. 7d.; the latter to £294 16s. 4d.: which leaves a balance in favour of the Society of £77 7s. 7d.,—a sum certainly not greater than might reasonably have been expected, considering the wealth and extent of this united Diocese." The entire income of the latter for the year was about £2500, and there were also four parsonages.

Turning now to the statistics of the Cathedral,* we find that the number of souls was 519; of Communicants, 121; that since 1853 there had been 137 Baptisms; 25 Burials; 40 Confirmed; and only 1 Marriage is recorded, but possibly this return is incomplete. "Reckoning by the number of Communicants," the Bishop said, "the Cathedral was thus the third largest Congregation in the Diocese." Considering that there was already the largest Congregation in the Diocese (*i.e.*, S. John's) in the Fair City, and taking into account the prevailing prejudice against the Church, it is evident that much earnest pastoral work must have been done by the Cathedral Clergy in the period under review.

At Whitsuntide, 1856, the Bishop left Dunkeld and took up his abode at Pitcullen Bank, a commodious house just out of Perth, on the east side, with grounds pleasantly laid out. Here a new chapter of our history opens.

* MS. *Register.*

CHAPTER XXXVI.

HOW THE THIRTY YEARS' WAR WAS WAGED, 1856-1886.

IT has been so ordered by Providence, since the Revolution of 1688, that whatever trials beset the Disestablished Church of Scotland at large, they should appear in their acutest form in Perth. In no district, as we already observed, could the Presbytery have been more severe towards the ousted Clergy than was ours against those in this neighbourhood between 1689-1712. When the first Jacobite rising took place in 1715, the Fair City had the doubtful privilege of being made Prince James's headquarters. In 1716 our two Clergy had to fly the town, and the subsequent penal laws pressed heavily on our people. When Bishop Rose's death, in 1720, compelled the Church at last to face the question of adopting a new and permanent organization, nowhere could the resulting controversy have been keener or more prolonged than it was here—from the dispute over the "College" Bishop Norrie, to the schism of his party in the Fair City in 1740. When the second Jacobite rising took place in 1745, we had again the doubtful privilege of providing headquarters for the Stuart Prince, and Mr. Lyon, our Priest was hanged and disembowelled. The subsequent repressive legislation further weakened our cause by turning the anti-usage congregation into an "English Qualified" charge, and had the further effect of rendering the orthodox flock liable "to be frighted at a shadow." The latter half of the Eighteenth Century saw us afflicted with the continuance of the split, and the first half of the Nineteenth Century, which in other places was marked by the reconciliation of the separated bodies, produced in Perth the disappearance of the orthodox and the thirty-six years' triumph of the schismatics. The period 1846-1856 brought in, to be sure, a very substantial change of fortune by the submission of the alienated Vestry and the not unsuccessful launching of the Cathedral scheme. But we have now reached a period, when differences were again acute in the Church at large, and we must be once more prepared to find that they gathered more thickly round Perth, and stayed longer there, than in other parts of the country.

To speak shortly, the controversies, upon which we are now entering, were simply the exaggeration of those, which we have already described as the results of the coming of the Oxford Movement to our midst. The Bishop, who looked upon it as his mission to prevent the extravagances of Puseyism (as he conceived them to be) from taking root in his adopted country, had hitherto been too much occupied with his duties as Warden and with the initiatory labours of his Episcopate to devote his whole attention to S. Ninian's, or even to take up his residence near it. And on their side, the members of the Chapter, as every true Churchman must, had been ready to make even great sacrifices in order to meet the requirements of their Diocesan. But now, by the latter's settlement in Perth, the two parties were brought into close proximity, and the result was that on his side the Bishop felt that there was still something to be done before his Cathedral was got into thorough working order, and, owing to the progress of Ritualism in the Church at large, this meant the abandonment of certain practices, such as the Eastward Position, which he himself had formerly considered lawful. On the other side, the Cathedral Clergy reflected that they had already made large concessions in their method of conducting service, and the new Episcopal demands appeared to them in the light of violations of the *Concordate* of 1853. We need not go into all the ceremonial details, which the Bishop wished to have changed, but the controversy lasted from 1856 to 1858.

To the question, how could the Residentaries, who had recognized the Bishop as actual head of the Cathedral by the new Statutes of 1853, find a colourable pretext for now resisting his requirements, the answer is this—No doubt his Lordship's intention in formulating the new Constitution, and the Synod's purpose in agreeing to it, had been to make the Diocesan supreme even in details. But the very clause, which was intended to assert the Episcopal supremacy, really placed definite limits to it.* "*The Clergy of the Cathedral*" (said the Statute) *shall be subject to the Bishop and amenable to canonical jurisdiction—provincial and diocesan—in all respects as the other Clergy of the Diocese.*" Now, whatever the Bishop may be able to effect in each of the Congregations of his Diocese by a judicious use of his paternal authority and personal influence, it will not be disputed that he cannot issue and

*In fairness it must be remembered that the task of determining the relative positions of Bishop, Provost, Residentaries, Non-residentaries, Chapter, Trustees, Synod, and Congregation in this, the first Cathedral founded since the Reformation, was by no means so easy a matter as outsiders may be disposed to imagine. The circumstances of the great English Cathedrals were so different that they could give little help. Experience was to be the great teacher, and, as everyone knows, its methods of instruction are not always pleasant at the time.

enforce a formal Episcopal *order* against practices, which are not contrary to the Rubrics and Canons. It followed, therefore, that, in the present instance, those, who commanded the majority of votes on the Chapter, were within their formal rights, if, while submitting to the Bishop's canonical jurisdiction, they began to demur to his personal requests. This, at least, was the defence of themselves, which they made. And, as we may be sure that the Bishop was thoroughly persuaded that he was acting in accordance with the spirit of the Statutes and of the Church's ritual, so we may believe that the Chapter was conscientiously convinced that it was acting lawfully for the good of Religion. Neither party saw fit to bring the matter to a test before the final Court of Appeal.

In the year 1858 the five Prebendaries, *i.e.*, the Revs. J. Torry (Dean), G. Milne, J. M'Millan, N. Johnstone, and W. Farquhar, declared their disagreement with the residentaries and their sympathy with the Bishop by resigning their stalls.*

The controversy then took a wider scope, and the fact was evidenced that the troubles at Perth were only part of the larger movement going on all over the country. In the same year, in which our Prebendaries resigned, the Rev. P. Cheyne, Incumbent of S. John's, Aberdeen, was at least temporarily suspended from the exercise of his Priestly (though not Diaconal) functions, on account of the expression he had given to high sacramental views. An agitation was also in progress against the Bishop of Brechin for his *Charge* on the Holy Eucharist, which culminated in a somewhat mild sentence against him in *March, 1860*. With a view to testifying their sympathy with the

* Humble's *Letter*, pp. 15, 97.

Bishop leaves Cathedral. 355

beliefs of the accused Bishop and Priest, the Cathedral Clergy drew up a declaration of their Faith* (although without alluding to the legal proceedings), and it was signed by 105 communicant members of the Congregation. Hereupon the Bishop, whose views, it was well known, were adverse to those of Bishop Forbes on the disputed points, ceased to attend the Cathedral, and began, thenceforth, to officiate at S. John's.

This unfortunate climax had been preceded by the resignation of Canons Campbell and Sellar and the consequent closing of the Grammar School. Nevertheless the communicants had increased during the four years from 121 to 135; no less than 190 persons had been baptized; there had been 3 marriages performed, and 39 funerals taken.†

(2) 1860-1871.—With the termination of the Forbes case in 1860, or at least with the General Synod of 1863, at which the *English* was accorded precedence over the *Scottish Office*, as being of primary authority, the period of the Eucharistic controversy may be said to have come to an end in the Church at large. It is a mistake to think of the incident as pure loss. It directed men's minds to a question, which they had not been in the habit of sufficiently considering, and left them upon the whole with higher views. No one would dream now of trying to procure a Synodical condemnation of the views held by Bishop Forbes or Mr. Cheyne.

But, whereas, before the great Controversy, the revival had been due to a few; now, after it was over, fresh life seemed to stir everywhere. And, doctrine being out of the way, the form, which this revival took, was a business one.

* Humble's *Letter*, pp. 15, 97.   † MS. *Register*.

With the exception of the *Friendly Society* for the widows and orphans of the Clergy and the Gaelic Society of 1830, our Communion had been devoid of any general financial organization until the foundation of the *Church Society* in 1838. This, indeed, had been a vast improvement upon everything that had gone before; but by the year 1853 it was in a retrograding condition, and in 1862 the annual income, which it had to distribute, was only £2888. The year 1864, however, marked a wonderful renewal of vitality.* New regulations were adopted by the Society, and something like £16,000 were collected in the twelvemonth. This, to be sure, was a special effort, which could not be kept up, for in 1867 the receipts had fallen to £8366. But, when this tendency to decline became apparent, good was brought out of evil, for thoughtful men began to enquire into its cause, and they perceived that they had been running on lines too entirely financial and business. The idea, therefore, took shape that the Church would prosper more, if she were to provide, not only for her own existing wants, but also to gird up her loins for spiritual work of an aggressive kind. It was hoped that, if her funds were treated as the widow of Zarephath treated her oil and her flour (*i.e.*, given to others), a greater blessing would rest upon herself. Hence sprang our Home and Foreign Mission Movements, which ultimately brought such strength to our ecclesiastical life. The year 1864 was also marked by the repeal of the humiliating restriction of the Relief Act of 1792. Henceforth Clergy in Scotch Orders became eligible for livings in England.

Active controversy, indeed, ceased in Perth with the Bishop's withdrawal from the Cathedral in 1859, but,

* *Scottish Guardian*, 1864, p. 233.

alas! it was impossible for the new blood, which was now coursing through the veins of the Church, to make its way hither. So long as the relations between the Diocesan and the Cathedral authorities were so strained, the Institution, however strong its case might really be, could not look for public confidence in itself. And though the zeal of Provost Fortescue and Canon Humble, who could go on year after year with their hands at the plough, despite the heavy burden of their Bishop's displeasure (unjust as, from their point of view, it appeared to be), is worthy of admiration, yet it is not to be wondered at, if they made little headway. Still, there was an annual average of 33 baptisms in the Congregation; 26 candidates were confirmed in 1864; a new school was acquired in 1865; and the Bishop occasionally preached* in the Cathedral pulpit.

As for S. John's, it was a large and influential Incumbency, quietly pursuing the even tenor of its way; but after the Bishop had been there about six years, he was convinced that the exclusive spirit of Congregationalism pervaded its members.† There was plenty of wealth amongst them; and, as they found it so easy a thing to keep the Services going for themselves in a successful manner, they failed to realize how necessary it was that they should help to support the struggling mission congregations of poor people, which were now springing into existence. The Bishop, therefore, severed his particular connection with them, and endeavoured to stimulate the Mission movement in Perth by building the Chapel of S. Andrew* near the Station, where, with the help of the Rev. James

* *Some Considerations*, p. 25.
† *Claims of the Poorer Brethren*—a sermon, 1866.

Christie, he began to officiate in 1868 in an always crowded Church. He also delivered a course of lectures in the City Hall in *April, 1865*.

In 1869 the Earl of Glasgow, who, along with Lord Forbes, had already done so much for the Cathedral, began to pay £400 per annum as a voluntary augmentation, over and above the £200 for which he had become responsible in 1853.

In 1871 Provost Fortescue resigned his post, and shortly afterwards seceded to the Church of Rome. In announcing the fact to the Synod at S. Andrew's Mission, the Bishop said :*—" Of Mr. Fortescue's uniform courtesy and kindness to myself personally—and I am sure I may say, as far as private intercourse extended, to us all—and of his devoted fidelity to his own convictions upon all matters of public and official duty, it would be impossible for me to speak too highly. That his convictions led him, as statutable governor and superintendent of our Cathedral, into a line, in which few of you I believe were able to concur with him, and from which, as his Diocesan and Ordinary of S. Ninian's, I felt obliged, no less conscientiously, to withdraw my countenance—this was a source of no little distress, I am sure, to us both ; and it must be added, I fear, of weakness to the Church throughout the Diocese, and especially in Perth."

(3) 1871-1876.—The vacancy of the Provostship, and the fact that only one member of the Chapter, *i.e.*, Canon Humble, now remained, seemed to open the way for a fresh start.

The arrangement, which first commended itself to the Bishop, was that " he should take upon himself the duties of the Provostship for two years without

* *Charge*, 1871, pp. 5-6.

remuneration; that the Precentor should retain the senior stall with the title of Vice-Provost."* This proposal, however, which had some obvious advantages, came to nothing. After some correspondence, therefore, with the Earl of Glasgow, the Bishop, as sole Patron, offered the vacant post to Mr. Shute, who was acceptable to that nobleman. After a fortnight's consideration, Mr. Shute declined the offer. What followed is best told in the Bishop's own words. "The fact," he said, "that Mr. Burton had already laboured for upwards of 20 years in the Diocese (at Blairgowrie, Alyth, and Meigle), and consequently could not fail to know more or less concerning the difficulties of the post, and how those difficulties had arisen—this fact, combined with the confidence, which I had reason to feel in his ability, his learning, his conciliatory disposition, and, above all, in his faithfulness, appeared to me to give him a superior claim; and I am glad to say that, after due consideration, he was induced to undertake the office." "The Dean also, and Mr. Johnstone, who withdrew from S. Ninian's fourteen years ago, have, at my urgent request, consented to act again as Prebendaries; and, under the difficulty of determining the true term 'Presbyter of the Diocese,' as used in the Constitution, six other seniors have been added to the list of Prebendaries, *pro hac vice*, instead of four, *viz.*:—the Revs. H. Malcolm, J. Douglas, G. Forbes, L. Tuttiett, W. Bruce, and W. Minniken." Also the vacant Lay Trusteeships were filled by John Grant, Esq. of Kilgraston; Sir Patrick Keith Murray of Ochtertyre; and John Stirling, Esq. of Kippendavie.

†By Canon Humble's advice the Congregation now reasserted their right to appoint their own Pastor;

* *Synodical Address*, 1872, p. 4.   † *Some Considerations*, p. 40.

but this claim was met by a reference to Provost Fortescue's letter, by which, at the settlement of 1853, the Congregation had recognized the Bishop as Patron. The matter, therefore, went no further.

His Lordship now attended a morning Service at the Cathedral, and began to preach there at night regularly.*

Thus there seemed to be prospect of a new and more prosperous state of affairs. But unfortunately the events of 1856-1859 were precisely re-enacted. †The new Provost began in a way, which was calculated to please the Bishop. He abandoned a good many points of ritual, which, it seems, Provost Fortescue had lately been introducing after visits paid to England and the Continent. And then he decided to make the settlement, reached at the re-founding of the Cathedral on the Bishop's accession in 1853, the rule of his Services. That is, he went back to the state of affairs, which prevailed before the Bishop settled in Perth in 1856.

But as the latter objected in 1856 to what he had (as he maintained, provisionally,) sanctioned in 1853, so now again he found fault with that comparatively reduced Ritual. Amongst other points he wrote to the Provost saying, "(1) Your use of the *chasuble* in the Altar Service, and (2) your *eastward posture* in the earlier part of that service and down to the Consecration Prayer, I consider objectionable."

The result was therefore exactly the same as it had been under similar circumstances thirteen years previously. Provost Burton and Canon Humble were able to gain a majority of votes in Chapter for the interpretation of the Statutes, which had been formerly asserted, and

* *Some Considerations*, pp. 15, 42.   † *Ib.*, pp. 14, 16.

Death of Canon Humble.

on his side the Bishop prolonged his previous attitude. Accordingly, he discontinued his resumed attendances at the Cathedral (1876), and went to reside in S. Andrews, leaving the Chapel, which he had built near the Station, under the charge of the Incumbent of S. John's.

This latter Congregation, indeed, as coming before the public with the confidence of the Bishop, was *"no longer (1873) able to accommodate all the applications that were made for sittings, and the few pews that were reckoned free, even if not forestalled by the military, as mostly happened, were utterly insufficient to meet the ordinary demand." But S. Ninian's just held its own. The late Provost's secession to Rome had been a severe blow to the Congregation, and, to make matters worse, although Canon Humble's zeal continued unabated (as testified by his exclamation, that "he would live and die for the Cathedral"), yet it was becoming apparent that his health was in a far from satisfactory condition. In the year after the catastrophe (1872), there are only 8 Baptisms recorded; but, by 1875, they had gradually risen again to 22, and this gives a fair indication of how matters were going.

On *February 7th, 1876*, Canon Humble, who had been ordered to a warmer climate for the sake of his health, died in San Remo, at the age of 57. Dr. Freeman, who attended him, relates that, when he was sitting up for the fourth night with his patient, the latter remonstrated with him and urged him to take some rest. The physician at last yielded, and went to his own house. At a certain hour of the night, however, he woke up suddenly, and, looking at his

* *Address to Chapter*, 1873.

watch, said to himself: "Canon Humble died just now; if I had been awake I should have seen him." On dressing and going out, he found that his suspicion as to the fact was exactly true. The funeral took place at San Remo. At home, the east window of the Cathedral was filled with stained glass in his memory.

From all accounts, Canon Humble appears to have been a strong man. Local tradition considers that it was his powerful will that enabled the two successive Provosts to continue administering the Cathedral, through evil report and good report, during twenty years, on lines opposed to those demanded by the Bishop. He had considerable knowledge of Ritual and of Canon Law, and was the author of several pamphlets, including *A Letter to the Bishop of S. Andrews* (1859); *Convocation and the Scotch Liturgy* (1862); *The Rights of the Faithful Laity* (1870); *The Administration of Canon Law* (1873).

(4) *1876-1885.*—We have now reached the last, and, indeed, a mild phase of the "thirty years' war." From Canon Humble's death till 1878, Provost Burton was single-handed. In that year, however, the vacant stall was at last filled. The new Canon and Precentor was the Rev. Donald J. Mackey, B.A., Cantab., who, notwithstanding his name, was an Englishman. His previous clerical history consisted of Ordination in the Diocese of London in 1868, and service as Chaplain in India from 1870 to 1878. His ecclesiastical views were similar to those of his predecessor, and he continued that Priest's attitude towards the Bishop. By arrangement with the Provost he confined his attention at the Cathedral to the duties of the Precentorship, the pastoral work of the Congregation being otherwise provided for. Canon Mackey was thus able to devote

some of his energies to literature. He contributed articles to several ecclesiastical Magazines; published Diocesan maps of England, Ireland, Scotland, and India; composed a *Communion Service in A*; compiled the Scottish Report for the "*Official Year Book of the Church of England*;" and last, but not least, wrote a "*Life of Bishop Forbes.*" This last has scarcely had justice done to it. According to the terms of that Prelate's will, the time had not yet come, when his MSS. could be put at the disposal of the public, and our Author has therefore been blamed for the imperfection of his Biography. But this is hardly fair. What he proposed to do was to compile a "*Life*" of the Bishop out of such material as had already been printed, and this (if we except some remarks on Bishop Wordsworth introduced into the Appendix) he accomplished very successfully. Until we can have a story based on private and original sources, it is satisfactory to have the materials already existing collected and put into order. In 1883 Canon Mackey organized a Diocesan Choral Festival at the Cathedral, and the Bishop accepted the invitation to preach on the occasion.

The same year (1878) that brought our second Precentor to Perth saw another addition to the clerical staff there.

But to understand the exact nature of the appointment, a slight retrospect is necessary. The following letter, therefore, from the Rev. Canon Bruce, Dunimarle, is quoted to explain the situation :—

"In reply," he says, "to your query regarding the provision for supernumerary work in the Diocese before 1878, I think I may say that there was none at all. When I came to the Diocese nearly 47 years ago it was not so customary as it is now for the Clergy to take holidays. There were hardly any railways; travelling by coach was costly; and clerical work was taken more quietly and easily than now, so that the Clergy did not greatly suffer from the tear and wear of over-exertion. Sometimes two brethren would exchange for a fortnight or so—the rural parson and his family going to some seaside place, while the seaboard neighbour migrated with his belongings for the same period to the landward Parsonage. But this was not very common. Sometimes a Clergyman from England would come on a visit to some country family, and would kindly take the duty for a Sunday or two, so letting the Incumbent away for a fortnight or three weeks. This was the way, by which I got most of my holidays while I was at Dunfermline. Then latterly there were two or three retired Clergymen in the Diocese. These would occasionally take a Sunday's duty; and there were also one or two stray parsons in Edinburgh, who might be had on an emergency. But, before the date you mention, I do not think there was any regular provision for the taking of occasional duty."

It was now determined, however, to make such provision. A Presbyter was to be attached to the Cathedral, who, while working there during the week, should be at the Bishop's disposal for duty in any part of the Diocese upon Sundays. Accordingly, the Rev. S. B. Hodson, an Englishman, who had passed through the Theological course at Glenalmond, and was at present Curate of S. Mary Magdalene's, Dundee, accepted the offer of the post. He was shortly afterwards installed as a Canon. To him the pastoral oversight of the Congregation was delegated by

Canon Hodson. 365

Provost Burton, and in this sphere he did an excellent work. Owing to the illness and death of Canon Humble and the two years, during which the Provost had been left single-handed, the number of Communicants in 1878 was not more than 60. In a few years Canon Hodson's zeal in connection with parochial visitation, the School, the Men's Club, and other organizations raised the number to fully double what he found it on his arrival. Another satisfactory result also flowed from this Priest's labours. His duties as Supernumerary took him not infrequently to S. Andrews, and there he was so happy as, not only to secure the Bishop's confidence in himself, but also in some degree to restore his interest in the Cathedral, from which he had been so long absent. The consequence was that the Diocesan Synods began once more to be held here in their natural home. In the spring of 1883 Canon Hodson, at the Bishop's request, undertook the opening of a Mission at Newport-on-Tay, and, therefore, resigned the position which he held in Perth.

In September of the same year his place was filled, on the joint appointment of the Bishop and Provost, by the Rev. George T. S. Farquhar, M.A., at that time Curate of S. Mary Magdalene's, Dundee. The new Assistant-Presbyter and Supernumerary made it his endeavour to follow in the steps of his predecessor, and to hope that the partial agreement, which had been practically come to between the Bishop and the Cathedral would ere long be thoroughly completed. At Easter, 1885, the number of those, who communicated in the Cathedral, was 116.

The reason why Provost Burton almost entirely delegated the Pastoral work of the Congregation in these later years to his subordinates was to be found in the state of his health. This was causing much anxiety to those about him, and by the year 1883 he was obliged, under medical advice, to spend the winters in the south of England. At last, on *July 8th, 1885*, the end came rather suddenly. On the Sunday previous he had taken his usual part in the Cathedral Services, celebrating the Holy Communion and preaching, but on Wednesday he became ill, and died on Thursday at his residence of Newfargic, in Glenfarg. On the following Monday the body was brought to the Cathedral and received by the remaining Clergy and a number of Communicants. Watch was kept, chiefly by relatives, all night, and on the following morning Canon Mackey celebrated the Holy Eucharist. At 1 P.M. the Burial Office was begun in the Cathedral by the Dean of the Diocese (Johnstone), and ended at the grave in Wellshill Cemetery by the Bishop. There was a considerable number of mourners present, and the Choir sang their portion of the Service. Provost Burton's memory is recalled with affection by all, who knew him. Although, on coming to Perth in 1871, he had been drawn into the contest between the Bishop, on the one side, and Canon Humble and Lord Glasgow on the other, and (contrary to his previous sentiments) had been led to take part with the latter, he was personally a man of peace, and possessed of a kindly and amiable nature. As, under his auspices, monuments, in the shape of a Reredos and the stained glass of the east window, were erected to the memories respectively of Bishop and Dean Torry and of Canon Humble, so also ought something to be done to perpetuate his name in the Cathedral, over which he presided.

S. John's.

While dealing with this subject, it will be appropriate to anticipate the course of events by a few months, and to record the fact that Canon Mackey resigned in October of the same year. His health also had given way, and, after holding one or two brief appointments in England, he was taken to his rest in the spring of 1888.

The chief event, which occurred at S. John's during this period, was the resignation of the Rev. W. Blatch in 1879, on receiving preferment in England. Under him the Congregation had been in a quiet but flourishing condition, the only weak point being (in the Bishop's words) that *"the sittings were mostly let at a rate above the means of those who were in humbler life, and about 200 of them practically excluded from public worship." Mr. Blatch was succeeded by his Curate, the Rev. Carl Weiss, who had at one time been a German Evangelical Pastor.

* *Claims of the Poorer Brethren*, p. 10.

CHAPTER XXXVII.

HOW A NEW START WAS MADE, 1885-1889.

THE opportunity of making an entirely new start at the Cathedral, which had once already come to Bishop Wordsworth in 1871 and proved fruitless, had again presented itself to him, when his age was now almost exactly fourscore. This time he had no thoughts of himself assuming the Provostship. On *August 30th, 1885*, therefore, he offered the vacant post to the Rev. V. L. Rorison, M.A., Incumbent of Forfar, who accepted the nomination.

The new Provost (a Scotchman) was the son of the Rev. Gilbert Rorison, LL.D., Incumbent of Peterhead, (who, as we saw, had attended Bishop Torry on his deathbed, and who was the author of the well-known hymn "*Three in One*," and of the Essay on "*The Creative Week*," in "*Replies to Essays and Reviews*.") Mr. Rorison was born in 1851; educated at Trinity College, Glenalmond, and at Aberdeen University, where he graduated. He was ordained in 1874 by the Bishop of Aberdeen (Suther), and elected early in 1875, while still a Deacon, to the important charge of Forfar. During his tenure of that post a new Church was built free of debt, costing £10,000, and more than 500 persons were confirmed. At Christmas, 1875, the communicants there numbered 89; when he left at Christmas, 1885, they numbered 435.

A fortnight after his appointment, however, what appeared to be a fatal blow fell upon the Cathedral.

A Catastrophe. 369

Although the Earl of Glasgow heartily concurred in the appointment, the days of that generous Nobleman's influence had come to an end. For, owing to some crisis in his private affairs, it was found that the whole of the endowment, to the amount of £8750, which, it was universally believed, he had made over to the Cathedral, was no more available. Combined with the effects of the "thirty years' war," as related in the last chapter, this sudden loss of nearly all the external support, on which the Cathedral leaned, rendered it possible that it might have to be closed, like Cumbrae College, which was involved in the same disaster. Mr. Rorison, who had not yet resigned Forfar, could honourably enough have now retired from all connection with the Provostship.

But, having said that he would undertake the post when the weather seemed fair, he would not withdraw, simply because the sky had become suddenly overcast. Indeed the Bishop had many years before expressed an opinion, which seemed strange at the time, that *"he wished to see Lord Glasgow released from some portion of his yearly contribution, which ought no longer to be required in full." He had always been of opinion that there would be a termination of the Cathedral difficulties, if the institution were no longer almost entirely dependent on one man's munificence, but if the necessary income were to be provided by the Diocese at large. The catastrophe, therefore, he thought, might ultimately prove to be a blessing in disguise. These sentiments were so far shared by the Provost designate that, while deploring the misfortune of the generous Earl and regretting the loss of his support, he trusted that, despite all that had

* *Synodal Address*, 1873, p. 31.

occurred, the Diocese would rally to the aid of their Cathedral in the day of its distress.

It was while matters were in this doubtful state that the Precentor, Canon Mackey, resigned, as related in last chapter. Inasmuch as the endowment of his stall had happily been secured to the Cathedral by Lord Forbes, about £200 a year was now set free, and would suffice to keep the work going until the Diocese had obtained time to fill the gap caused by Lord Glasgow's failure.

Accordingly, on *November 26th*, the Rev. G. T. S. Farquhar, M.A., who, as we have seen, was already attached to the Cathedral in the capacity of Diocesan Supernumerary, was appointed to the vacant Canonry, it being understood that he should also retain his Supernumeraryship. The new Precentor was the son of the Rev. W. Farquhar, M.A., of Pitscandly, Forfar (one of the Prebendaries who resigned in 1859, and author of a learned work, "*Prelacy not Presbytery*"). Mr. Farquhar was thus a Scotchman, like the new Provost, and also a former pupil of Trinity College, Glenalmond. He had graduated at Keble College, Oxford, in 1882.

Despite the misfortune, therefore, Service was kept up without a break, and the Congregation cared for during the necessary months of anxious waiting. At Christmastide there were about 100 persons, who communicated. Such was the flock which had survived the thirty years' war.

Before the festival that long period shewed unmistakable signs of being at a full end. By this time it had been ascertained that the Diocese, or at least many of its prominent members, were truly anxious to do all that was possible to set the finances of the

Turn of the Tide. 371

Cathedral on a satisfactory basis. As a result of this favourable disposition on their part, the Bishop came to Perth on *December 16th*, and formally installed the Provost, who subsequently, at the same Service, installed the Precentor. The whole Chapter was also once more re-constituted, the list of Prebendaries being as follows :—Revs. H. Malcolm, B.A., Dunblane ; J. J. Douglas, B.D., Kirriemuir; L. Tuttiett, S. Andrews; W. Bruce, B.D., Culross ; Hon. John Baillie, M.A., Cupar Fife, Senior Canon of York. On the death of the last of these, his place was taken by the Rev. R. Cole, M.A., Doune, Synod Clerk.

At the beginning of 1886 the leading Laity, amongst whom the Earl of Strathmore was prominent, were forwarding the cause of the Cathedral so successfully in the Diocesan Council, that the Provost was at last justified in formally resigning his Forfar Incumbency, and coming to reside in Perth. This was towards the end of February, by which time an income of £300, and £100 to help with the Services, had been guaranteed by the Diocese.

The tide had at length turned, and it was soon observed with joy that it bore promise of being a full one. Shortly after the Provost had come into residence, the *Scottish Guardian* published the following paragraph :—" All friends of the Diocese will be glad to hear that affairs at the Cathedral are looking bright. The Provost has only been in Perth for a week or two, but on Sunday the Cathedral was filled with large congregations, both forenoon and evening. Altogether, although he is quite clear that one, who is buckling on his armour, ought not to boast as one that taketh it off, he declares that things are looking very hopeful, and all the more so, as the Bishop is soon coming to encourage us and ordain an assistant Deacon."

Both in 1856 and in 1871 his Lordship's arrival had been followed by outbreaks of the ritual controversy; but on the present occasion he assured the Clergy that, although he did not wish to be quoted as responsible for every custom observed at the Cathedral, yet it was far from his desire to find fault with anything. The Services were carried on by Provost Rorison just as they had been at his predecessor's death. At the early Celebrations the Eastward Position, Scotch Office, Linen Vestments, Lights, Mixture, and Ablutions were continued, and at midday all these usages, with the exception of the Vestments and Lights, were likewise retained. In no quarter was any disposition shewn to rekindle a dispute on such points. Henceforth there was a thoroughly good understanding between the Bishop and Chapter.

And so there was nothing, as in former instances, to prevent the early promise of the Provost's incumbency bringing forth fruit. A new phenomenon persistently appeared. The Cathedral was constantly crowded to a surprising extent. The following description of the Christmas of 1886 may be taken as typical of the state of affairs between that and Christmas 1889, that is, as long as the Congregation worshipped in the Building as erected in 1849. "The Cathedral," said the *Scottish Guardian*, " is always well filled on Sunday mornings, and regularly every Sunday evening it is simply crowded. But on the Sunday after Christmas '*crowded*' is not the word to express the state of affairs, because, though it quite expresses it inside the building, it does not suggest to the reader the knowledge of the fact that the crowding began more than an hour before the commencement of the Service, and that, all through that hour, numbers of people were continually arriving, a great proportion of whom, including many faithful members of the congregation, had simply to turn and go home again. And it was not only the Nave and Transepts, including all the passages, that were crowded, and not only the Chancel, including the very Altar steps, but, bitterly cold though the weather was, the temporary entrance porch as well."

And this phenomenon shewed itself not only within the walls of the Cathedral, but elsewhere also. For the Provost, having been invited by the Ancient Order of Foresters to preach a Sermon to them one Sunday evening, found that it would have been hopeless to accommodate the assembly in the Cathedral. About 2000 people were therefore gathered together in the City Hall, and took part in the devotions of the *Book of Common Prayer*, the Provost officiating in his Surplice. At the same hour the usual Evensong was conducted in the Cathedral and S. John's in the presence of what, not so long before, would have been considered good congregations. No doubt this very uncommon state of affairs partook to some extent of the nature of a temporary wave of excitement. The Church having been hitherto vexed by controversy, the public had been able to ignore it, and now it had all the novelty of a new discovery. But, even if it had only been a temporary wave of excitement, yet, even so, it would have been a remarkable occurrence. Readers of this *History* will know only too well that a fit of popular enthusiasm in favour of the Scottish Episcopal Church in Perth had been an impossibility for nearly 200 years. Evidently there had been a great change in the northern ecclesiastical atmosphere.

But it would be altogether a mistake to imagine that the movement was merely a passing craze and no more. In the first place, the Cathedral continued to be overcrowded for, at least, the four years, with which this chapter deals. In the second place, the candidates, who presented themselves for Confirmation, were numerous beyond precedent. In 1886 the Bishop administered the Apostolic Ordinance to 34 persons; in 1887 to 62; in 1888 to 40; in 1889 to 37: that is, in all, to 173 people. And this number is, of course, exclusive of members of other congregations, who received the laying-on of hands here. In the third place, that this addition to the communicants was not merely formal is evident from the fact that whereas, as we have seen at Christmas, 1885, the number of those, who knelt at the Altar, was about 100, it was pretty nearly 250 in 1889. Nor can any one rightly say that these Confirmations and Communions were merely formal, because it is God only, who sees the heart, and there was every sign of spiritual earnestness about the worshippers. And lastly, we may point to the solid and lasting results, which sprang from the new state of affairs, and which will be recounted in the next Chapter.

During this period two candidates were ordained to the Diaconate and Priesthood, and afterwards licensed to serve as Chaplains at the Cathedral. These were the Rev. W. Arbuthnot, now Chaplain at Taymouth, and the Rev. F. Smith, now Rector of S. Luke's, Glasgow, and both did good work while they were here, the latter being the successor of the former. Such help was all the more needed, as the Provost

The Cathedral School. 375

was prostrated by an illness in 1889, which obliged him to be absent for six months.

As an appendix to this Chapter, we may conclude with a short sketch of the fortunes of the Primary School attached to the Cathedral. Previous to the *Education Act* of 1872, the headmaster for 25 years had been Mr. Joshua Stott, who was known as a strict disciplinarian and a good teacher. He was succeeded by one of his pupils, Mr. Leslie Macdonald, who brought the School into a high state of efficiency. But, as if misfortunes never come single, just at the very time that Lord Glasgow's support failed, the Education Department sent notice that our Buildings were condemned. Amid the general crash, there appeared to be no other course but to make preparations for reluctantly closing the establishment. The teachers were therefore informed that their services would no longer be required after the next Inspection. Thereupon Mr. Leslie Macdonald accepted the headmastership of Jedburgh Church School. Mrs. Campbell, however, struggled on at the request of the Managers, although by this time merely a handful of children remained. But, just when the end seemed certain and near, the Earl of Strathmore intervened with his influence and his purse, and the School was saved. A substantial stone building, in accordance with government requirements, was erected. Mr. Robert Macdonald, another of Mr. Stott's former pupils, was engaged as headmaster, with Miss Helen J. Dorward (succeeded in 1893 by Miss E. Sim) as Mistress of the Infant Department. Thenceforth, under their efficient control, the School, with an average attendance of over 200 (213 in 1893), has been enabled to pay its own way without recourse to subscriptions, except at first. It is certainly not the least valuable work done in connection with the Cathedral. In the Board Schools Religion may or may not be a part of the education given. The play of Hamlet, in fact, may be represented without the Prince of Denmark. But by means of the Cathedral School, and that in connection with S. John's at S. Andrew's Mission Chapel, witness is borne in Perth to the sadly forgotten principle that no education is complete, which, even while providing to perfection for the intellectual and physical development of those submitted to its training, ignores and neglects the need of doing something (and doing it under Christ) for the spiritual element in their nature. Nor have the working classes hitherto failed to respond in an encouraging manner to the uprightness of the Church's intentions towards them in this matter.

CHAPTER XXXVIII.

HOW THE NAVE OF THE CATHEDRAL WAS BUILT, 1886-1890.

CONSIDERING the financial disaster, which had occurred, and also the fact that, so far, the only remedy forthcoming was an income of no great magnitude temporarily guaranteed by the Diocese, the friends of the Cathedral now desired to provide something permanent. A certain amount of progress was accordingly made towards the creation of an endowment and the building of a Provost's residence.

But this movement was for the time brought to a standstill. The unexpectedly large additions to the Congregation, which have been described in the last chapter, pointed to the imperative necessity of at once securing further accommodation in the Cathedral. The Provost, therefore, determined that the matter should be brought before the Diocesan Council. After communicating with the Bishop, he accordingly laid the subject before the meeting in *October, 1886*, at which there was a considerable attendance of Clergy and Laity. In the absence of his Lordship and the Dean, the Earl of Strathmore was appointed Chairman. After the transaction of other business, the following letter from the Bishop was read:—

*" I am sorry that I shall not be able to be with you in Perth to-morrow, but it must not be supposed that my absence is due to indifference to the cause, for which

For the quotations in this Chapter, see the *Scottish Guardian*.

your meeting is to be held. I am very anxious that everything should be done that can be done to help S. Ninian's out of its difficulties, and to place it upon a firm and satisfactory basis; and I am glad and thankful that such a harmonious spirit has been shewn, both by the Clergy and Laity of the Diocese, to endeavour to accomplish that result. It is greatly to be wished that the Congregation should be in a position to do more for itself; and, with that view, *I begin to look forward to the time, when the building shall be completed*, as a condition almost indispensible towards permanent and effectual improvement in that respect."

A long and interesting discussion followed, in which the necessity and advantages of enlarging the edifice (which, it will be remembered, consisted at that time only of the Chancel, quasi-Transepts, and one Bay of the Nave) were dwelt upon by several speakers. The Provost urged the meeting to consider the endowment fund, and the project of a residence for himself as of secondary importance in the meantime. An estimate for the completion of the Nave, without the two western towers, was submitted. From this it appeared that the cost would be about £3000. It was eventually agreed unanimously :—

" That the Council resolves to turn its attention specially to the enlargement of the Cathedral by the completion of the Nave in accordance with the original designs, the present accommodation being altogether inadequate."

It was further resolved :—

" That the Council authorizes the transfer from the endowment fund of any donations, which the donors prefer to give to the building fund."

Before the meeting closed one subscription of £250,

Appeal for Funds.

two of £100, and one of £50 (soon afterwards doubled), were intimated. This gave a start and spirit to the movement.

A small sub-committee, which was appointed, drew up the following appeal :—

"The accompanying report of the meeting of the Diocesan Council, held in Perth on *October 29th*, fully explains the grounds, on which we appeal for funds to aid in the completion of S. Ninian's Cathedral, so as to make it more worthy of the name, and also more efficient as the Cathedral of the Diocese. The practical necessity for the enlargement of the building, so as to accommodate the members desirous of attending the Services, has now become a matter for serious and immediate consideration; and it is believed that the expenditure of comparatively so small a sum as £3000, which is the estimated cost of the proposed extension of the Nave, will make the Cathedral not only more useful and seemly, but, as indicated in the last paragraph of the letter written by the Bishop of S. Andrews, and quoted in the report above referred to, will enable it, to a much larger extent than is at present possible, to contribute to its own support.— Strathmore, *Lay Representative (i.e., Elector)*; A. Hay Drummond, *Cromlix*; V. L. Rorison. *Provost of the Cathedral*; T. T. Oliphant, *Hon. Treasurer*; P. Stirling, *Kippenross*; F. Buchanan White, *Lay Representative*; C. L. Wood, *Freeland.*"

Along with this appeal a letter from the Bishop was circulated, in which his Lordship emphasised the resolutions of the Council and the statements of the Committee, and added :—

"Under these circumstances, it appears to me to be a very plain duty to endeavour to carry out the scheme now proposed, and, with this view, I earnestly and heartily recommend the foregoing appeal."

All those, who have read our *History* from the beginning, will see that this meeting of the Diocesan Council in *October, 1886*, was a very memorable one. It afforded proof, on the one hand, that the controversies of the middle of the century, which came to an end in the Church at large about the year 1863, had at last terminated, even in Perth; and, on the other, that the attitude of the general Presbyterian public had undergone a very great change for the better towards the disestablished Church.

It was one thing, however, to resolve to build the Nave, and another to do it. There was the strongest objection expressed from the first against having any resort to bazaars, and such-like means of raising money. It was felt that all, which should be subscribed for a Cathedral, ought to be given directly and simply as a gift to the House of God. There was nothing, therefore, for it but to circulate appeals as widely as might be; and so, armed with the Committee's letter, as endorsed by the Bishop, more than one person began to ask for contributions, and that not altogether unsuccessfully. But it is merely the barest justice to say that all the other labourers in this good work were completely out-distanced by the Provost. The energy, with which he undertook the toil, and the success, which crowned his efforts, not only delighted, but astonished, the friends of the scheme.

The result was that, when the Diocesan Council re-assembled in *September, 1887*, Mr. Oliphant, as Hon. Treasurer, was enabled to submit a report, from which the following is a summarized extract:—

"The result has been satisfactory beyond expectation.

Building Committee. 381

Up to the present date (only ten months from the date of the resolution), £2500 has been subscribed, mainly owing to the untiring energy and personal influence of the Provost; and the Diocesan Standing Committee, at a recent meeting, have come to the conclusion that this Council would now be justified in obtaining plans and specifications from the architect, in accordance with the original designs, with a view to commencing the work next spring, and carrying it on, as far as the funds then in hand permitted."

After full discussion, the following resolution, moved by Colonel Stirling of Kippendavie, and seconded by Captain the Hon. A. Hay Drummond of Cromlix, was unanimously agreed to:—

"That this meeting, having heard Mr. Oliphant's report, are of opinion that the funds promised, and in hand, are sufficient to warrant the building of the Cathedral being proceeded with in spring, and that a Building Committee be appointed, etc., etc."

The Committee was accordingly appointed, as follows:— The Earl of Strathmore, *Chairman*; the Very Rev. the Provost; T. T. Oliphant, Esq., *Secretary*; Patrick Stirling, Esq. of Kippendavie; C. L. Wood, Esq. of Freeland; Canon the Hon. J. Baillie; E. Baxter, Esq. of Teasses; J. B. Don, Esq.; Sir Robert Moncreiffe of Moncreiffe; Henry Mercer, Esq. of Gorthy; Rev. Canon Malcolm; C. T. C. Grant, Esq. of Kilgraston; Lord Forbes; and to these were afterwards added the Earl of Kinnoull and the Precentor.

In October, for the first time for fourteen years, there was a meeting of the Chapter presided over by the Bishop. The building, being vested in their name, it was necessary that their consent should be obtained before the scheme was actually put into execution.

It was, of course, given unanimously,—a recommendation being added that the matter should be so gone about as that no debt should be incurred.

Mr. Butterfield now got his plans into working order, and made the following announcement with regard to an important change, which commended itself to his judgment:—

"The west end of the Cathedral will abut so closely on the wall of the Queen's Barracks, as to make a western entrance impossible. One high western tower takes the place, in the present design, of the two very much smaller towers in the first plan. In the absence of a central tower at the intersection of the Choir and Nave with the transepts, it is felt by the architect that a single tower is more suitable than two would be. Two towers in that position demand a third, which, in this case, does not exist. Neither of the two towers in the first design would have been imposing features, and in one only of them would there have been bells to justify its existence. The single tower, with its spire, as now proposed, is of imposing proportions: it will be a commanding feature in any distant view of the Fair City, and will serve for a full peal of bells."

To carry out this design in its entirety, it was estimated that about £10,000 would be required. Such a sum, indeed, was considered more than it was prudent to aim at in the meantime. But, seeing that the £3000 needed for the completion of the Nave, without the western Tower (which was the extent of their original ambition), had now been nearly all promised, the Building Committee resolved to endeavour to collect another £2000, and carry the Tower, without its Transepts, as high as the apex of the Nave roof.

Building Begun.

As therefore the appeals on behalf of the Nave had been entirely successful, another effort must now be made on behalf of the Tower, its Transepts, and some necessary internal fittings. The Provost renewed his exertions ; the Building Committee personally contributed £1125 in addition to their previous donations, and a Committee of the Congregation made themselves responsible for £200 to be raised by any legitimate means in their power. The consequence was that, when the Diocesan Council met in *August, 1888*, Mr. Oliphant was able to announce both that building operations had been begun in Spring, and also that the sum subscribed now stood at £4649. It was thereupon resolved that not only should the Tower to the height of the Nave roof be added to the original working scheme, but also its Transepts and the internal fittings, which were necessary.

So then from the Spring of 1888 there were not only interesting discussions on the subject being held in the Diocesan Council and appeals being vigorously issued, but the contractors, Messrs. Fraser & Morton of Perth, were busily engaged in practical operations at the Cathedral. It may possibly be considered interesting hereafter by members of the Congregation to know how the present site of the Nave and Tower used to be occupied. That of the North Aisle was filled by a temporary room, which was at first used as the School and afterwards as the Library, and in which Bishop Wordsworth delivered many of his celebrated " Charges." He used to read them sitting where there is now an archway leading from the west door into the North Aisle. In the centre of the present Nave used to stand buildings utilized for Vestry and lesser Schoolroom, and the site of the

South Aisle and Western Porch were parts of the girls' playground and Schoolmaster's garden respectively.

At the beginning of 1889, while the Provost was absent on account of his illness, and when the walls had now risen to a considerable height, some anxiety and delay were caused by the sinking of the Tower. The cause of this was the excessively soft and unsubstantial nature of the soil beneath the foundations. The settlement, however, soon reached its limits, and no more damage was done than could be remedied. Mr Butterfield therefore ordered the Contractors to resume operations, and by October the Nave was so far advanced that the old temporary west wall was pulled down. The new and the old parts therefore formed, at last, one large Church, as it is now.

At the usual Autumn meeting of the Diocesan Council this year (1889), the Earl of Strathmore, who had all along actively performed the duties of Chairman of the Building Committee, made the following observations, which will shew how the finances stood at this time :—

"They must," he said, "express their thanks to Mr. Oliphant for the very hearty way, in which he had entered upon the report he had just given them, and to the Very Rev. the Provost for the great number of applications, which he had made, and the money he had obtained by them. It had been rather a hard work for the Building Committee to get on with the funds up to the present time, since the matter was first set on foot three years ago. There was then a rough estimate that £3000 would be needed, and everybody wondered how that would be raised. Not only, however, was this now accomplished,

The Nave Completed.

but they had raised the sum to about £5500, and now all except the Spire would be completed."

The long-wished-for goal was thus nearly within reach: at Christmas, 1889, the Cathedral was "approaching completion." It may here therefore be recorded that, just as S. Giles', Edinburgh, was restored after the completion of S. Mary's Cathedral in that City, so now that S. Ninian's, Perth, was in the same condition, the public began to hear of a design to restore their old Church of S. John.* Our Communion may be small in numbers, but there can be no doubt that its presence in the midst of Scotland has been the means of perserving the knowledge of more than one article of the Faith, which would have been forgotten without her. These present instances of the renovation of true principles of ecclesiastical building are matters of congratulation. For not Eloquence, nor Music, alone have the power of setting forth the Truth, but Architecture also can help in its own degree to preach Catholicism, even to a rationalistic generation.

But to return. Immediately before Easter the Nave was completed, and Service was held in it for the first time on that great Festival. The Building consists of the original Choir, dwarf Transepts, and one bay of the Nave, together with the three new bays of the Nave, and the space under the Tower and its Transepts at the west end. The new portion is, of course, in harmony with the old as to style. The whole is 200 feet in length; the Nave 70 feet in height and 50 feet in breadth. Although the funds at the Architect's disposal were but small for the erection of a Cathedral, yet it cannot be denied that, by throwing all his

* The Choir, or East Church, has actually been restored.

strength into the general outline rather than on elaborateness of detail, Mr. Butterfield has been successful in producing a very stately edifice, decidedly of a Cathedral, and not merely of a parochial, character.

And not only was S. Ninian's now completed, but completed clear of debt. For at the meeting of the Diocesan Council in *September, 1890*, Mr. Oliphant was able to make the following satisfactory report on the finances:—

BUILDING FUND.—The total cost of completing the Cathedral, which, as all present know, had been consecrated a few weeks ago, was £6842 9 9
1. The subscriptions prior to the
 date of Consecration were, £5909 15 0
2. Grant from Walker Trustees, 500 0 0
3. Collection on day of Consecration, 258 6 3
4. Sums since received, ... 39 18 3
 ——— £6707 18 3
 Deficit, ... £134 11 6

And as this deficit of £134 was at once cleared off by the Lay Members of the Building Committee, there was not a penny of debt left at the completion of the arduous undertaking.

This will be the proper place to add that before long more than £1000 additional was spent on the Cathedral. On the death of Mr. Carnegy of Stronvar, who had been a generous contributor to the various schemes, his son, the present Laird, filled in the great west window with stained glass, by Burlisson and Grills, to his Father's memory. The present Lord Forbes also presented one of the Nave windows as a memorial to the original Founders, Walter, Lord Forbes, and the Earl of Glasgow. The collections, too, at the

Children's Services, supplemented by offerings made at Baptisms, sufficed to fill a second Nave window. Somewhat later, the Earl of Kinnoull presented a third, in memory of various members of his family. And on the deaths of C. T. C. Grant, Esq. of Kilgraston, Lay Representative, and of Henry Mercer, Esq. of Gorthy, two of the Clerestory windows were filled in, as was also a third by T. T. Oliphant, Esq., the Treasurer of the Building fund. A tablet was also erected to Mr. Grant's memory, and the Countess of Glasgow subsequently presented a handsome Altar Frontal and a Cope. Various other offerings from working people, as well as from their richer brethren, were also made for the Service of the Sanctuary.

APPENDIX TO CHAPTER XXXVIII.

THE matter-of-fact narrative, contained in the Chapter, gives a true account of the building of the Nave. And yet it is not altogether true, inasmuch as it is not full. There was something else at work all the time besides Committees on business and finance. There was a religious enthusiasm animating the various workers in the scheme. The story is not complete without some attempt to chronicle this ; and, therefore, here follows a series of Sonnets written at the time by the Precentor to express it—preceded by a set of verses on the same subject by the Bishop :—

Ad G. T. S. F.

Aedis S. Niniani apud Pertham Praecentorem et Poetam.

> *Salvere jubeo te, Poeta jam noster.*
> *O si quod olim in Conditore Thebano,*
> *Lapides canendo qui movere callebat,*
> *Accidere posset, te canente tam belle !*
> *Tum quam repente surgeret Cathedralis*
> *Perfecta moles ; tumque cordibus gratis*
> *Quot vota caelo solverentur exsultim !*
> *Et qui Poeta es, Conditor fores noster.*
>
> —*Episcop. Sanct. Andr.*

Translation.

All hail to thee, who art become our bard!
O! that Amphion's wonder-working lyre,
Which built the walls of Thebes, might be transferred
 To thee, who sing'st so sweetly! All entire
How swiftly then would our Cathedral pile
 Rise up! How full would the exulting strain
Of thanks to Heaven be raised! And thou, meanwhile,
 "Building the lofty rhyme," would'st build our Fane!
    —BISHOP OF S. ANDREWS.

THE SONNETS.

1.—*On the prospect of seeing the Cathedral completed*, 1886.

Through many tribulations must we go
 Before to Heav'n's high kingdom we attain ;
 Nor must our feet reluctantly disdain
To tread the footsteps of our Master's woe.
By this the patient Church was taught to grow ;
 Through many griefs her upward path hath lain ;
 Nor least in Scotia hath she suffered pain—
Deprest and to a shadow's shade brought low.
But see! God breaks her Scottish gloom at last :
 At His command the long black night departs,
 And the blue day returns. Awhile remain
To us, dear life! for here approacheth fast
 The gladness longed for by our prayerful hearts—
 The hope to see S. Ninian's full-grown fane!

2.—*Prayer for the Cathedral in* 1887.

Prevent us, Lord, with Thy continual aid,
 In whatso'er we do ; but chiefly now
 Advance the work, for which full many a vow
Ascends to Thee. May offerings still be made
For Thy dear sake, until, securely laid,
 We see the last stone on the topmost row
 Of these Cathedral walls, that all may know
A debt of love has here to Thee been paid.
And let not sin make void our future hours
 With empty rites ; but kindle brightly here
 In many souls the Faith's authentic flame.

Add here one more to Zion's own true towers;
    O'er this new Fane shed grace, so rich and clear,
    That it may spread the glory of Thy Name !

        3.—*Building begun*, 1888.

If 'tis enquired, wherefore I tune my lyre
    To these Cathedral songs, I proudly say
    That, while I'm weaving thus my humble lay,
I see an end to which I would aspire ;
For though 'tis much that other men should tire
    Body and mind throughout the livelong day ;
    And though 'tis much that they should give away
Their wealth to gain the end of our desire,
Yet is there left me one thing to fulfil—
    One thing which, if it be beyond my skill,
    Is yet a wise delight to have essayed :
I fain would leave a message to proclaim,
    When I shall only be a bye-gone name,
    With what deep joy were these foundations laid !

    4.—*A reply to Sanballat, Geshem, and Tobiah*, 1888.

There are who view our dear Emprise with scorn,
    And, never guessing at our inward glow
    Of love, demand sagaciously to know
How we shall fill this Church each holy morn,
When 'tis complete. But I have still forborne
    To answer questions, which are seen to grow
    From hearts whose stream of sympathy runs low,
And would not rise though we were left forlorn.
    Since, when this growing Pile stands forth at length
        A perfect whole, I hope perhaps that less
            Shall we *fill it*, than it shall wondrously
Fill us with sense of soul-subduing strength ;
    Fill us with sense of sacred lovliness ;
        Fill us with sense of God's own Majesty !

        5.—*On seeing the Masons at work*, 1888.

Beside the Minsters of the South, 'tis true,
    As fits the Northern Church of our small isle—
    A Church all strange to this world's friendly smile—
Thou wilt seem slight, when strangers come to view.
Nor will thy walls be rich with age's hue,

Nor kings bedeck thee in their gorgeous style,
Nor ancient memories hang round each aisle,
But thou will be unhistoried and new.
Yet, though in many a way thou'lt be surpassed,
Let all the coming generations know
   Thou art the birth of fervent Christian prayer :
Thy goodly columns, tall as some ship's mast,
   Are traced by Christian hands, and as they grow,
     Our hearts rise with them through the upper air !

6.—*Suggested by the Very Rev. the Provost's Illness.*
Delightful task, indeed, to watch the hand
Of sturdy craftsman ply the skilful steel,
Compelling so the shapeless stones to feel
The pressure of his powerful blows, and stand
New-formed and comely as his purpose planned !
   Delightful, too, as ever upwards steal
   The rising walls, to note the builders seal
Each well-hewn block in its appointed band !
But ah ! the pain when we ourselves are stones,
   And the great Builder of the Eternal Fane
   Hews us and moulds us for its walls on high !
His loving strokes are answered by our groans,
   Until, at last, the soul's new form made plain,
   We joy to own our heavenly destiny !

7.—*While watching the Masons at work*, 1889.
A strong desire still moves me to behold
   The slowly-growing fabric day by day :
I love to haunt the spot, and dreamingly
Descry the finished vision all unrolled
Before my wistful eyes. Then uncontrolled
   My sanguine fancy ranges on its way,
   And sees the Church successfully essay
To don the glory, which was hers of old.
And yet do I desire this thing aright ?
   Is there no mingling wish that I may then
     Win reflex glory from the triumph gained ?
Put this thought from me, Lord, and by Thy might
   Make love of Church one with the love of men
     And of Thine Image in their souls contained !

Cathedral Sonnet.

8.—*Our point of view explained to Posterity*, 1890.

Rejoiced to see these holy walls arise,
  In simple strains. I sang my gratitude,
  Proclaiming that, where once a sheep-fold stood,
This noble Pile now points us to the skies.
Whereon methought, "Such words will breed surprise,
  Perchance, in future minds to learn what food
  For rapture lay in this Cathedral—good.
Yet oft surpassed, where happier England lies."
But, if the next age choose to marvel so,
I judge they have no bitter cause to know
  How deep the Church can fall through adverse fate!
For, if they felt what crushed our father's heart
They would not ask why, playing Jeshua's† part,
  Our souls with humbler mercies grow elate!

† See Ezra, iii, 2

CHAPTER XXXIX.

HOW THE NAVE WAS CONSECRATED, 1890.

NOTHING now remained but to consecrate the newly-raised edifice to God. Thursday, *August 7th, 1890*, was selected as the memorable day for the performance of this duty. The weather was fortunately all that could be wished. It may have been fanciful, but there were those to whom it occurred at the time, that the bright summer sun, which smiled upon the completion of the labour, was a good omen, when contrasted with the cold winter's day, on which the older part of the building had been consecrated in 1850.

The religious services of the day were begun by an administration of the Holy Eucharist according to the Scottish rite, which had been the sole Use of the Cathedral since its foundation. The Celebrant was assisted by the Rev. V. Fortescue, a son of the first Provost. At 11 o'clock the worshippers were admitted. Of these there were about 1000, and the Nave was completely filled by a congregation drawn from all ranks of Society. A very large number of people had come from a distance, but places were also reserved for members of the Congregation. It was generally remarked that the arrangements for receiving and seating the worshippers were carried out so smoothly that there were none of the small worries, which sometimes, on such occasions, disturb the devotional atmosphere of Churches.

The Procession.

The Bishops, Clergy, and Choristers robed in the Schoolroom, and entered by the North-West door. So long was the surpliced procession that a Priest, who was coming down from Glenalmond to take part in it, had only reached the Jubilee Building in the Dunkeld Road, when he saw the leaders beginning to quit the Schoolroom and enter the Cathedral, and yet he was able to walk rapidly down, put on his robes, and fall into his place amongst the rest. The order of the Procession was as follows:—

                Cross Bearer.
        The Choir (about 60 in number).
       Stranger Clergy (28 in number).
Diocesan Clergy (17 in number: others of them followed later).
        The Warden of Glenalmond.
          Three English Canons.
           Two Scotch Canons.
       Five Canons of the Cathedral.
Deans of Moray, Edinburgh, and S. Andrews.
        The Very Rev. the Provost.
           Bishop Mitchinson.
    Bishop of Glasgow, and Chaplain.
    Bishop of Edinburgh, and Chaplain.
     Bishop of Argyll, and Chaplain.
    Bishop of Aberdeen, and Chaplain.
     Bishop of Moray, and Chaplain.
    Bishop of Lichfield, and Chaplain.
   Archbishop of Dublin, and Chaplain.
Bishop of Brechin, Primus, and Chaplain.
   Bishop of S. Andrews, and Chaplain.
   Rev. J. W. Hunter, Ceremoniarius.

It was a happy circumstance that not only were English, Irish, and Scottish Clergy here mingled together, but also that every one of the Scottish Bishops was present. The opening voluntary, played by the Organist, Mr. J. E. Pirrie, was the *Overture* to the *Messiah,* after which, as the Clergy proceeded up the Nave, "*The Church's One Foundation*" was sung. Prayers were intoned by the Precentor, the Responses being *Tallis' Festal in G.* The Proper *Psalms* were the 24th, 34th, and 87th. The first lesson (*Isaiah lviii., 8 to end*) was read by the Rev. Prebendary Stephenson, Treasurer of Wells Cathedral, and the Second *(I. S. Peter ii., 1-10)* by the Very Rev. the Dean of Edinburgh. The *Te Deum* was *Dykes in F,* and the Anthem *(" I was glad ")* by Dr. E. Bennett. Instead of the *Collect* for the day, the Bishop of the Diocese said special prayers, in which he besought God "to accept the work of His servants' hands, whom He had moved to erect and enlarge this House." At the conclusion of *Matins,* the formal presentation of the deed of Consecration was made by the Earl of Strathmore, as Chairman of the Building Committee, accompanied by Colonel Stirling and Mr. T. T. Oliphant, as Diocesan Trustees for the Cathedral, and Mr. C. T. C. Grant, as Lay Representative of the Congregation. The document having been read, it was signed by the Bishop upon the Altar. Thereafter, prefaced by the Hymn "*O Word of God above*," the *Communion Service* was proceeded with. The Office used was that in the English "*Book of Common Prayer,*" the Bishop considering that this was required by Canon upon such an occasion as the present. To many it seemed a great pity that the distinguished ecclesiastics from England and Ireland should have been deprived of this opportunity of joining in the grand and primitive Liturgy of the Scottish Church. The Provost was the Celebrant, the Bishop of Moray, Epistoler, and the Primus, Gospeler. The Sermon was preached by the Right Rev. Dr. Maclagan, Bishop of

Lichfield (now Archbishop of York), who wore his scarlet robes.

Taking as his text Eph. iii., 10, and, after some preliminary remarks, his Lordship said:—

"Look at the story of your own Church, the Church of your forefathers—yours and mine. What a lineage, what a heritage is yours! Think of your own S. Ninian, and of the place, which he occupies in the religious life of Scotland. Himself one of the few survivors of an ancient Christianity well nigh extinguished by a savage heathenism; yet, destined to be one. of the spiritual forefathers, not only of the Church of Scotland, but of Northern England also, and not the least in my own midland Diocese. It was through the Church of S. Ninian; through S. Columba and S. Aidan; from *Candida Casa*, through Iona and Lindisfarne that my good predecessor, S. Chad, was sent forth to restore the life of the Church in heathen Mercia. Not through Augustine and his companions, but through Scotland and her Saints, did the light of the Gospel shine forth out of the darkness in that ancient See, now committed to my unworthy hands. Its earliest Bishop was a Scot, who was succeeded by another. I need not tell you, for you know better than I, through what troubles and adversities your Church has fought its way from the days of S. Ninian to the present hour; you know the cruel sorrows and the sad mistakes, and the many failures, which have marked its course; but you know too the heroic faith, the steadfast hope, the fervent love that from time to time have been displayed by its persecuted members. You do not forget the almost incredible restrictions imposed upon its worship till within a century ago. And, as you watch it now and mark its reviving life and power, even within one short lifetime, you may well see in its growth and progress 'the manifold wisdom of God.' You have behind you the record of a great history. There lies before you the possibility of a great future; but it is beset by exceptional difficulties. We find around us here as elsewhere great religious communities, more or less powerful, and more or less instinct with true spiritual life, who do not appreciate the advantages we enjoy, nor realize the blessing of our spiritual lineage and heritage. We long that they may be with us, that we all may be one; but, for the time, the barriers seem almost insurmountable, and the estrangement remains. In such a case we have special need of patience—I do not say the patience of Job, but what is far higher and more beautiful, the patience of God. His longing for the oneness of His people is older than ours, older and stronger and wiser; and even in the delay of our hope we must acknowledge 'the manifold wisdom of God.' In His good time and in His own way the blessing will come. Though it tarry we must wait for it, because it will surely come—it will not tarry." After this, with an exhortation to let the heavenly watchers see us growing, not only in outward strength, but also in inward devotion, the Bishop concluded his discourse, and the *Holy Communion* proceeded (with the addition of certain special and appropriate prayers, said by the Bishop of the Diocese) to its usual end.

In the afternoon a public luncheon took place in the City Hall. About 400 persons were present. The Provost presided, and was supported by the Bishops of S. Andrews, Moray, Lichfield, Edinburgh, Glasgow, Argyll, Mitchinson, the Archbishop of Dublin, the

Earls of Strathmore, Kinnoull, Stamford, and Caithness, Lord Provost Whittet, and many others.

Colonel Stirling of Kippendavie proposed the toast of the *Bishop of the Diocese.* And it was certainly not the least striking incident of the day's proceedings, when the venerable Dr. Wordsworth, then in his 85th year, rose amid great enthusiasm to reply. He said:—

"Mr. Provost, my first duty is to thank Colonel Stirling for the compliment he has paid me, and for the kind, the far too kind, expressions, which he used, when proposing my health. And next I have to thank you all, Christian friends and brethren, for the very cordial manner in which you have received it. But I have other and more solemn thanks to render upon this occasion—I have to thank our Heavenly Father for having permitted me to live to see this day. While almost everybody, whether clergyman or layman, connected with the early days of our Cathedral— though almost all, if not all, of them younger than myself—have been called away, I have been spared. There is, indeed, one other notable exception, and I am sorry he is not with us to-day. I mean our distinguished friend Mr. Butterfield, who has now the satisfaction of seeing his noble specimen of pure ecclesiastical architecture brought almost to its final completion. And now, looking back for a moment to the past, I cannot but remember that there have been anxious times—times of difficulty, times of struggle, and times, I regret to think, even of conflict; but this, perhaps, was only to be expected, when men equally earnest, but taking different views, were brought together to carry out a new undertaking without being agreed upon the principles, upon which it would be best and most expedient to conduct it. For my own part, it has been my aim and endeavour all along that our Cathedral should command the confidence, not of one party only in the Church, but of all—that it should be, as it professes to be in name, the Church of the Bishop, who, if he is wise, will know nothing of "High", or "Low," or "Broad" or "Narrow," but only what is good and what is true. I wished it should be diocesan in the fullest and widest sense—that is, as wide and comprehensive as the Diocese itself. I have further wished that it should be so administered that, not only the Clergy, but also the Laity should feel an interest in it—that they should be prepared to rally round it, and take pride and pleasure in its success. Such, I am thankful to say, is now the case; and, therefore, in looking forward to the future, I see nothing but what is hopeful, nothing but what is encouraging, and—which is better than all, and for which we are mainly indebted to the many admirable qualities of our Provost—nothing but what is harmonious. God grant that no evil influence may ever arise, no untoward accident ever occur to mar or to blight this cheerful prospect. And if it be so, I shall feel I am handing down to my successor an invaluable instrument, by which he will be enabled to administer the affairs of the Diocese far more effectually than it has been in my power to do; by which he will not only be enabled to secure its welfare, but to promote its growth and to turn its resources to better account to God's glory and the good of His people in this distracted land. I will not detain you longer, but will once more thank you most heartily for the good wishes that have been conveyed to me in the toast, which has been so kindly given and received."

The Provost's Speech.

When the applause, which loudly greeted the Bishop's speech, had subsided, *the Provost* rose, and, after dwelling gratefully at some length upon the benefactors of old time, added, concerning the work so lately finished :—
" During these four and a half or five years they had rather a stiff task before them, but from the beginning there went with him a band of men, whose hearts God had touched. Certain laymen of this diocese, who were not content to dwell in ceiled houses, while the House of God lay waste, had stood round him. They had never suffered him to be defeated or thrown back in his building, or in his work in any respect. When he proposed the benefactors and founders of the Cathedral, he would include in that description almost everyone present. The work of building S. Ninian's had been mainly performed by a few laymen of the Diocese, who were determined to make the Cathedral worthy of its name, and worthy of the Diocese of S. Andrews. Although, however, he was grateful to every one of these laymen and to the Congregational Guarantee Committee, who had stood round him, yet among these laymen there was one, whom he must mention as their main benefactor, the Chairman of the Building Committee, the *Earl of Strathmore*."

In the course of his reply the latter said :—" There were present two friends of his own, whom he would specially select as being real benefactors to the Cathedral more truly than himself, not only from having given their money, but from having worked heart and soul in the cause. He meant his friend, the Provost, and the indefatigable Secretary, Mr. T. T. Oliphant. The former had left the charge of Forfar, where, by the influence he exerted, he was able to do much good.

He had left a comfortable home and an assured income and come to Perth. And what did he find? An unfinished Cathedral, a scattered congregation, no residence, and no income; and, as if that were not sufficient, the school buildings were in such a state that the Government Inspector had said that, unless new buildings were erected, the grant would not be given in the following year. The first thing was to go to the Scottish Department and get a year's grace for the Schools. Before the year's grace was out, the Schools were built. Then £6800 had been expended on the Cathedral. He thought no one could have entered it that day without admiring that fine interior. Altogether, during the last four years, £15,000 had, in one way or another, been devoted to the work in connection with the Cathedral. Speaking for himself (and he was also sure he spoke for every gentleman on the Committee), this had been a day of extreme gratitude and thankfulness to Almighty God." The Earls of Kinnoull and Stamford, the Bishops of Lichfield, Edinburgh, and Moray, the Lord Provost of Perth, Mr. Spier, Mr. Oliphant, and Mr. Grant also addressed the meeting.

There was *Evensong* in the Cathedral at 7.30 p.m., a large congregation being present. Prayers were intoned by the Provost, the lessons were read by the Bishops of Edinburgh and Argyll, and the Sermon was preached by the *Archbishop of Dublin*. His Grace divided his remarks under three heads. (1) First, the Services of that day seemed to him to furnish a proof of *Church Life*. He might almost have said of Church resurrection. Perhaps he could not more signally emphasize what he meant than by recalling the fact, when, forty years ago, the first stone of the Cathedral

The Archbishop's Sermon. 401

was laid, there was presiding over this See of S. Andrews, a Bishop, who could himself remember the time within the compass of his own Ministry, when it was illegal for more than four persons to worship within the walls of any Church belonging to this Communion. Yes, the late Bishop Torry, of whom he was now speaking, began his Ministry in a kitchen, and for several years had no better accommodation. The Church was reduced to the "shadow of a shade;" there were only 46 clergymen left in all Scotland. A century only had passed since the repeal of the penal laws, and what see we now? The number of its clergy increased at least sixfold; new Sees have been filled and new Churches and Cathedrals have been erected to the glory of God, amongst them the noble Cathedral of Edinburgh. Yes, and what is of far more moment, a fresh outburst of spiritual vigour has been manifested. (2) But, again, the Services of to-day supply to those who may need it, a proof of *Christian Unity*. The fact that, upon the occasion of the Consecration of the Nave of this Cathedral by your own revered and beloved Diocesan, the Pulpit has been occupied in the morning by an English, and in the evening by an Irish, Bishop, will ever stand forth in the history of our proceedings as a token of that sisterly fellowship, which, thank God, exists between the three independent Churches, which represent the Anglican Communion in the British Isles." The Archbishop then proceeded naturally to speak at some length on the subject of the union of Christendom at large, and then (3) he turned to the last thought, which the Services of the day suggested, namely, that "after all, the one great aim, with which the whole work had been undertaken, was to make further and more fitting provision for them who desire to '*draw near to God.*'" His Grace dwelt with much earnestness and at considerable length upon this last thought, and concluded with these words. "May this Cathedral, in which we are assembled, prove in very truth, for generations yet unborn, a Sanctuary to all, who come hither to meet their God! No matter how troublous the days in store for your Church or mine; no matter what strife or tumult may rage in the world without; no matter what fears or temptations may disquiet your breast within,—here, at least, may there ever be found a refuge from the storm, whither many an anxious one may come to worship God in peace and safety—a tranquil haven where many may yet find, in the presence of a loving Father, a way of escape from cowardly forebodings and torturing doubts; and may thus be enabled, by their own blessed experience, to realize the full meaning of the Psalmists exulting words, "*It is good for me to draw near to God.*"

CHAPTER XL.

HOW THE CATHEDRAL FARED DURING BISHOP WORDWORTH'S LAST THREE YEARS, 1890-2.

WE must now return from the great occasional events of the last two chapters, and resume our narrative of ordinary affairs at the point where we left it off at the end of Chapter XXXVII. And it will be convenient to group the events, with which we are to deal, under three heads :—

(a) First, Congregational. In the three years 1890-2 pastoral affairs were carried on at the Cathedral under conditions quite new in its history. There were no penal laws in force against the Church, nor any controversies raging within. On the other hand, indeed, the excitement of novelty, which had produced such an effect from 1886 to 1890, had worn off. But permanent work was nevertheless on an altogether larger scale than had been possible in former times. The number of Baptisms was 141 ; of Confirmations, 154 ; of Marriages, 23 ; of Burials, 73 ; and the number of those, who communicated at Easter in 1892, was 290.

The Clergy, who served during this period as Chaplains, were the Revs. James Farquhar, B.A. (1889-91), now of Dunblane ; W. Dundas Walker, M.A. (1890-91), now Rector of Burntisland ; John Dunn, M.A. (1891-92), now English Chaplain at Paramé-les-bains ; J. F. K. Branford, M.A. (1892-93), now Curate at Nottingham ; and J. Meeser (1892-94), now Rector of Aberchirder. In this connection it is right to state that Captain the Hon. A. Hay Drummond of Cromlix has afforded invaluable help by providing for the support of one of the Chaplains.

Mention may here be made of two or three Services of a rather unusual character, which occurred in the present period. (1) At Christmas, 1889, the state of the building operations was such that only the Chancel of the Cathedral was available. No attempt was therefore made to hold the ordinary forenoon worship. But there was a series of Eucharists beginning at 5 a.m., and those, who were present at one or more of these, will not soon forget the strange sensation of making their way, at those early hours through the Nave, which, though completed externally, was nothing internally but a scene of confusion, filled with scaffolding and heaps of rubbish, lying upon the undulating surface of the unlevelled earth. (2) Another most interesting Service was held on *Sexagesima, 1890.* While they were excluded from S. Ninian's, the Congregation used to assemble in the City Hall, but on the evening of the Sunday referred to this was impossible. The Rev. W. Stevenson, M.A., Minister of the Middle Church, was therefore generous enough to put that place of worship unconditionally at the Provost's disposal. Evensong was accordingly taken there at the time mentioned. The Choir, having vested in the Session House of the East Church, entered the Transepts of old S. John's singing a processional Hymn. The Prayers were intoned by the Precentor, and the Sermon preached by the Provost. About 1500 people are estimated to have been present. This was the first Service conducted in this Church by Clergy of Episcopal Ordination since that held by Mr. Armstrong in the presence of Prince Charlie in

1745. (3) The other noteworthy Service was the first celebrated in the completed Cathedral, which took place on Easter Day, 1890. Both morning and evening the building was crowded. It was, indeed, a red-letter day to all. While we are on the subject of worship in the Cathedral, a word may be added about the Choir. Previous to 1885, of course, it was easy to make provision for having not only the Sunday but also the Daily Offices chorally rendered. From that date to 1890, under Mr. J. E. Pirrie as Organist, the choristers, both men and boys, attended altogether voluntarily. The work which they did was very creditable, but from the nature of the case (all having their week-day occupations to attend to), could only be given on Sundays and the greater Festivals. After that year, under Mr. Stephen Richardson, enough payment was given to render the attendance of the necessary voices on Sundays certain, and consequently there was an improvement in the quality of the music, which was thoroughly satisfactory, but the Daily Offices were still plainly read. The fact is, while the Congregational Services are well provided for, something still remains to be done in order to enable a sufficient body of efficient singers to be always available on strictly Cathedral and Diocesan occasions.

The reference to money matters leads us naturally on to speak of a development in the way of organisation amongst those worshipping in the Cathedral. The original idea was that the entire financial management of the Institution in all its aspects should be undertaken, at its quarterly meetings, by the Chapter, assisted by the Lay Trustees. When, however, the latter fell into abeyance, owing to Bishop Wordsworth's withdrawal, and the governing body was reduced to the Provost and Precentor, it came about that till 1876 the latter of these, and after that the former, took the management into his own hands. So long as the principal source of revenue was supplied by the Earl of Glasgow, no fault was found with this arrangement. And even after that Nobleman's failure, at the end of 1885, when the Collections made in the Cathedral and the contributions given by the Diocese had taken his place, the same system of administration was continued. But at last, when the offerings made at Service came to be practically the chief source of income (except for the stipends of the Provost and Precentor), it was thought better that the Congregation should control the funds, which they themselves provided. And so a Congregational Committee was formed, and a constitution granted to it over and above the Cathedral statutes by the Bishop. Of this the Provost is *ex officio* Chairman, and Dr. F. Buchanan White and Sir R. Moncreiffe have successively held the post of Convener; Mr. Norie Miller being Secretary. A still more satisfactory plan would be, as has indeed been suggested, to revert to the original idea, viz:—to allow the Chapter to transact all the business of the Institution with the aid of the Lay Trustees, amongst whom the congregational deputies might find a place.

The history of S. John's had meantime been of a very much quieter and more uneventful nature. In *August, 1892*, however, the Rev. C. Weiss, Ph.D., resigned the charge, and was succeeded by the present Rector, the Rev. H. Armstrong Hall, B.D., of Durham University, and formerly Vicar of S. Mary's, Spring Grove, near Isleworth, Middlesex. Under his care it began to enter upon a new period of life and vigour.

Secondly, there was substantial progress made with the *Cathedral*, as such, as well as with the Congregation. Of course, the task, which emerged for the Churchmen of the Diocese at this time, was to provide from a public source that support, which had been so munificently given by a private individual up to the end of 1885. Towards this end, a most suitable house for the Provost, called "The Deanery," was purchased in Barossa Place in *September, 1891*, at the cost of £2400 (fully paid), and the greater part of £5000 was promised as endowment for his Stall. Thus a substantial beginning was made in the work of consolidation.

Thirdly, some account must be given of *Diocesan* affairs. This will now be done for the most part according to the order of their occurrence. In the *Autumn of 1889* the Clergy made an arrangement amongst themselves, which would have proved very beneficial had it been set on foot earlier. The only opportunity, which they ever had previously of meeting together in at once a brotherly and clerical capacity, was on the day of the annual Synod and Council. But this was practically no opportunity at all, as the meetings had generally begun before all had hurried up from the Station, and were no sooner over than trains for the return home had at once to be caught. At a meeting, however, held in Perth on *October 31st* of the year in question, the Rev. A. S. Aglen, M.A., of Alyth, proposed the formation of a Clerical Society, and his motion was unanimously carried. Since then monthly meetings, during the winter half of the year, have been held at the various houses of the members. At these a combination of theological discussion and brotherly intercourse has produced the most satisfactory results.

On *April 21st, 1890*, a meeting of the Clergy was held in the Cathedral for the purpose of electing representatives to the General Synod held that year. The Revs. J. W. Hunter, S. J. Howard, and J. Leslie were chosen. In preparation for this important gathering, the Diocesan Synod of 1889, which was held in the ante-room of the City Hall, Perth, and lasted for two days, was entirely taken up with the proposed revision of the *Canons* and of the *Scotch Office*. The aged Bishop presided over all the meetings with great efficiency. The Synod of the succeeding year (1890) was memorable in at least one way, inasmuch as it was the first to be held in the completed Cathedral. In his charge the Bishop commented upon the new *Code of Canons*. The Synod of 1891 was remarkable for the Bishop's able charge on Old Testament criticism. In this he showed cause for expecting that, as Wolff's disintegrating theories on Homer had at first been welcomed by scholars, but afterwards looked upon more coldly, so the disintegrating theories of Wellhausen on the Old Testament would probably run a similar course. The Synod of 1892 was also doubly remarkable. It was the first assembly of the kind, over which Bishop Wordsworth had not presided in person for 40 years. It was also noteworthy on account of his charge, which was read by the Dean. This was the great Advocate of Union's last official appeal to the Presbyterians to consider his scheme of amalgamation. There were also contained in it some touching words of farewell to his Clergy.

There was another matter of importance dealt with at the Synod of 1890. And this was the Decanal succession. On the death of Dean Torry on *December 15th, 1879*, at the age of 79, he had been succeeded by the Rev. N. Johnstone of Kirkcaldy. The latter, after an extremely uneventful tenure of office, died at the age of 85 on *September 19th, 1890*. It fell, therefore, to the Bishop to appoint his successor at the ensuing Synod. The course, which he followed, was unexpected in one respect. That the Provost of the Cathedral should be nominated to the vacant post was not unlooked for; but what surprised the Clergy was that the Bishop should also revive the Archidiaconate, a dignity not only little known in the Scottish Church, but also deliberately considered to be unnecessary by the late General Synod. At the same time it must be admitted (especially by those, who consider that Bishop Torry was within his right in constituting a Cathedral on his own responsibility, when such institutions were not mentioned in the *Canons*) that it was also competent for Bishop Wordsworth to create an Archdeacon, if he chose. And the case of the Archdeacon was so far stronger than that of the Cathedral, previous to its recognition by the Diocesan Synod in 1853, that, although there was no discussion in the proper sense of the word, yet the Synod was formally asked and forthwith gave its consent to the revival of the Archidiaconal Office in 1890. Since, then, the thing was to be, all were satisfied that a better appointment could not have been made than that, which the Bishop did make, when he promoted the Rev. A. S. Aglen, M.A., of Alyth. The Archdeacon was subsequently installed as a Canon of the Cathedral. He is the Author of Commentaries on several of the Old Testament Books in *Bishop Ellicot's Commentary* and in *Cassell's Bible Educator*, and of the article on *Eschatology* in the new edition of the *Encyclopædia Britannica*.

CHAPTER XLI.

HOW BISHOP WORDSWORTH DIED AND BISHOP WILKINSON SUCCEEDED, 1892-3.

AFTER the Consecration of the Nave of the Cathedral in 1890, the Bishop, although he had then reached the advanced age of 85, and was failing in his bodily faculties, continued in the full possession of his great intellectual powers. Besides the *Charges* mentioned in the last chapter, as delivered to his Synod, he published in 1890 a volume containing all the Collects of the Prayer Book turned into Latin Verse; a volume of Sermons entitled "*Primary Witness to the Truth of the Gospel*" (1892); "*Annals of my Early Life*" (1891); and only a few weeks before the end he wrote several vigorous letters to the *Scotsman* and *Scottish Guardian* containing, in a few terse sentences, an *Apologia* for his Re-union Movement. But, though mentally he was strong to the very last, he was more than once confined for weeks at a time to his bed. Consequently he gradually withdrew from the discharge of such duties as involved physical exertion.

Under these circumstances he suggested the idea of the Consecration of a Coadjutor, but the Bishop of Glasgow (Dr. Harrison) was so ready to afford him all the help necessary (just as Bishop Forbes had assisted his aged predecessor) that the project was entirely dropped. Towards the end of *November, 1892*, the Bishop's condition was such as to cause anxiety to his friends. To many throughout the Diocese, indeed, it seemed difficult to realize that the end of an Episcopate, which had been begun before they were born, and which had filled a larger space in the history of the Scottish Church than it has entered within the scope of these pages to describe, was approaching its end. But so it was. The Bishop himself realized clearly but calmly what was coming. All, who had access to his sick chamber, were impressed by the earnest spirit of charity towards men and devotion towards God which prevailed there, and at length, on *December 5th*, this distinguished Prelate peacefully drew his last breath.

The interment took place on Friday, *December 9th*, at S. Andrews. The weather was bitterly cold. Both on the day preceding and on that following, snow was falling heavily; but the 9th itself was gloriously bright and frosty. The Funeral Services consisted of an early Celebration of the Holy Communion, followed by the Burial Office at 1.30 p.m. The Primus read the Lesson in Church. A procession of about 30 surpliced Clergy was then formed and preceded the hearse along South Street to the new part of the Cathedral Cemetery. Many spectators lined the route, along which, as a mark of respect, the shops were closed. The Bishops of Edinburgh and Glasgow took the Service at the grave, and not a few tears were shed ere the mourners turned away.

Many tributes of respect were paid to the late Prelate's memory, both in the press and in the pulpit. Those only, which were uttered in Perth, concern us in these pages. The new Rector of S. John's spoke a few sympathetic words, such as became one recently settled in the Diocese. The Minister of the East Parish gracefully expressed his sense of the loss, which not only Scottish Episcopalians, but the entire Christianity of the country, had sustained. The Dean preaching at the Cathedral on the forenoon of *Sunday, December 11th (3d in Advent)*, enlarged upon the Bishop's power of standing alone against the world in whatever cause he deemed just. He also called attention to the great work, which he had done in proclaiming the duty of Christian union in a schism-distracted land. In his evening Sermon at the Cathedral, the Precentor endeavoured to give something like a complete outline of the Bishop's life-work. He dwelt not only on the *scheme of re-union* with the Presbyterians, but recalled the brilliant *scholastic work* of the departed at Oxford, Winchester, and Glenalmond, and the Christian character, which he tried to impress upon it. He mentioned Dr. Wordsworth's contributions to *general literature*, such as his delightful " *Shakespeare and the Bible ;* " his *eloquence* in the Pulpit and in the chair of the Synod, and described the *internal progress of the Diocese* during the late Episcopate. "In this department," he said, "it was evident that a great development had taken place during the late Prelate's rule."

What that development had been will be best described through comparing the figures given for 1853 by the Bishop himself (in his *Charge* for 1855, for which see *Chapter xxxvi.*) with those given in the "Year Book" of 1893 for 1892 :—

	Incumbencies.	Souls.	Communicants.	Confirmed.	Baptized.	Parsonages.
1853,	16	2552	1132	122	91	2
1892,	26†	6665	3283	1528	208	20
Increase,	10	4113	2151	1406	117	18

† Add also 18 Missions, Private Chapels, etc.

Altogether, although strong men and strong theologians, such as Bishop Rattray ; contemplative Saints, like Bishop Jolly ; able administrators, like Bishop

Bishop Wordsworth. 413

John Skinner; powerful intellects, like Bishop Gleig; and hard-working theological Saints, like Bishop Alexander Forbes, have held the Episcopate in Scotland since the disestablishment in 1689, it may well be doubted whether Bishop Charles Wordsworth does not stand out pre-eminent amongst them for a certain largeness of personality, and it is certain that he surpassed them all in the manner, in which his utterances commanded the ear of the Scottish public. Whether the particular means, by which he proposed to bring about a reconciliation between Episcopacy and Presbyterianism be considered feasible or not, it must on all hands be admitted that he impressed the duty of Unity upon Scottish Christians as it never had been impressed before, and this not upon the shifting basis of Indifferentism, but, as he always maintained, upon the solid foundation of the Historic Episcopate.

(2) Only sixteen years of the nineteenth century were not covered by the united rules of the last two Prelates. Bishop Watson, as we saw, had occupied the first eight years of the century, and the question now arose, Who was to preside for the last eight, or at least a part of that time?

It was very strongly felt by many, even of those, who acknowledged with gratitude the invaluable stimulus to Church life, which had come from England at the middle of the Century, that that impetus had now been long enough in motion to justify them in looking for a Scottish Prelate as the very fruit of its success. It was keenly felt that while the Church is a Catholic body, knowing neither Jew nor Gentile, Greek nor Barbarian, Bond nor Free, and therefore glad to welcome Englishmen in Scotland, as she welcomes Scotchmen, even to the Thrones of Canterbury and

York, in England, yet that to go on having an overwhelming majority of non-native Prelates upon the Scottish bench was stretching the principle somewhat too far.

And doubtless these considerations would have triumphed on the present occasion. Only it so happened that the Right Rev. George H. Wilkinson, D.D., who had resigned the Diocese of Truro some years before on account of illness, but had now quite recovered, was still living in retirement. And it at once became apparent that the heart of the Diocese was drawn towards him with wonderful harmony. Of course, the names of others were considered, and their merits warmly discussed in private, but, when the Electors formally met, under the presidency of the Dean, in the Cathedral on *February 9th, 1893*, it was found that, while even the minority had resolved to bring forward no other name, the majority were eager to secure the oversight of so exceptionally experienced a Prelate. The result, therefore, was that no division took place, and Bishop Wilkinson was chosen with practical unanimity in both the Clerical and Lay Chambers.

Having duly considered the outcome of the vote, the Bishop-elect acquiesced in the result, which had been confirmed by the Episcopal Synod.

After receiving the Deed of Collation from the Primus, nothing remained but that his Lordship should be publicly enthroned. As no consecration was necessary, it was determined that this ceremony should be surrounded with every circumstance of solemnity. Accordingly when the appointed day (*April 27th*) arrived, about 70 Clergy and perhaps 1000 people, including the Lord Provost and Magistrates, assembled at the Cathedral. Again, as on the day of Consecration in 1890, the arrangements for seating so large a concourse were admirable. Punctually at 11 A.M. the surpliced Procession (at the rear of which came the Bishops of Moray, Aberdeen, and S. Andrews in Rochet, Chimere, Stole, and Scarf, and the Primus in Cope and Mitre) left the Schoolroom, emerged in brilliant sunshine into Methven Street, and, passing thence into Athole Street, reached the west door of the Cathedral. Here the Bishop of the Diocese was met by the Dean and Chapter, and requested to be enthroned. The procession then advanced up the Nave, singing the appointed Psalms, and took their proper places. After this the Primus placed the Pastoral Staff in the Diocesan's hand, and the Dean led his Lordship to the Throne. When this was accomplished the Primus proceeded with the Eucharist according to the Scottish form. The Bishop himself preached the Sermon, as his predecessor had done 40 years before. The text was *Revelations i. 12-13, "I saw seven golden candlesticks, and in the midst of the seven candlesticks one like unto the Son of Man."* First the vision of Christ glorified was dwelt upon; then the long waiting and the seeming failures, which the beloved Apostle had to endure before his Saviour thus revealed Himself: then the fear of S. John on beholding the sight; then the Lord's words of encouragement with respect to the Disciple's personal life, to the Church which he loved, and to the final victory of Christ. Then came the application of all this to the occasion—an exhortation to act in harmony with the words, which Christ had so uttered, —*i.e.*, to begin with personal religion; to go on to share in the larger life of the Church, especially "this (Scottish) branch to which we belong—this branch that has all the marks of God's election (poverty, small in the eye of man, martyrs, saints, confessors, holy men, godly matrons); this Church that can lift up her hands and shew the mark of the nails. Go out and help her: stand by us." And finally they were to endure as seeing the Invisible, "where now (the Preacher added) their late Bishop was at rest together with the ten thousand times ten thousand, who have washed their robes and made them white in the Blood of the Lamb."

After the Service was over there was luncheon in the City Hall. At this the *Dean*, who presided, read a telegram from the Archbishop of Canterbury— "*Gratia et pax et salus in Domino !* "—and pointed out that this was the first occasion, at least within the period subsequent to 1689, on which one, who had ruled an English, had been translated to a Scottish Diocese. *Mr. Speir* of Culdees testified to the great religious work, which the Bishop had done at S. Peter's, Eaton Square, in London. *The Bishop* himself, who was enthusiastically cheered, "scarcely knew how fitly to acknowledge the great kindness, with which he had been received from the time at which he had been called to this See by the unanimous election of Clergy and Laity. He could no longer feel as a stranger as letter after letter reached him, and hand after hand grasped his hand with an unmistakable touch, which spoke to him of a heart that was ready to respond, of a life that was ready to be given up willingly in helping him to the work that had been entrusted to him." *The Primus* " believed they had got a Bishop appointed over them that day to take up, as it were, the mantle of Bishop

Speech by the Primus. 417

Forbes, and who came very much in the same spirit. He did not believe they could have chosen throughout the length and breadth of the Anglican Communion a man so able to take up and carry on that great torch and spiritual light which Bishop Forbes lighted up, and sent from hand to hand throughout the whole of Scotland."

After several more able speeches from *K. T. Oliphant, Esq.* of Gask, *Rev. V. S. Coles, M.A.*, Vice-Principal of the Pusey House, Oxford, and others, the meeting broke up, and those present returned "to their work and to their labour."

Epilogue.

WITH the enthronement of our present Diocesan we have reached a date so recent that any attempt at a systematic history of events, subsequent to that important occurrence, would be out of the question. With a few notes, therefore, on the present position of affairs (*Ascensiontide, 1894*), and a questioning glance into the future, we shall conclude our narrative.

As for the present, we note that the Bishop has resided at Birnam since his accession to the See. Nevertheless his Lordship has taken pains to impress upon all that he looks upon the Cathedral, both theoretically and practically, as the centre of the Diocese. The Synods and Councils continue to be held there: it is to be the point, to which candidates for Ordination are to come: the Bishop frequently takes part in its Services: the Chapter is once more a reality: the Lay Trustees are to have more active duties assigned them: a beginning has been made in the revision of the Statutes, with a view to rendering the Institution more practically efficient: within its walls and immediate vicinity Conferences and Quiet days, both for men and women, have been held by the Bishop himself, from which it is hoped that an impetus to the life of the Diocese will result. £800 has also been raised towards building a Chapter House to the memory of the late Bishop. And, if we turn from the Cathedral to the Pastoral side of things, here, too, some encouraging signs can be honestly chronicled. Considering the collapse of the Church in Perth during the first half

The Present and Future. 419

of the Nineteenth Century, it is with gratitude that we record the fact that at Easter, 1893, the number of those who communicated in S. Ninian's reached 300 for the first time, and that at the same festival of 1894 the combined totals of those, who approached the Altar in the two congregations of the Fair City, was 500. Only a few years ago it would have appeared visionary to expect such a thing. Then, too, a Congregational Chaplaincy, held at present by the Rev. J. Philip, M.A., has been established. Various organizations also, such as the Day School, the Sunday School, the Mothers' Meeting, the Young Womens' Guild, and the Boys' Brigade, are in a more or less flourishing condition in connection with the Atholl Street congregation, not to mention the similar agencies attached to that in Princes Street. A legacy of £10,000 has also been made over to S. John's by the will of the late Professor Sandeman. Humanly speaking, this comparatively favourable aspect of affairs, unparalleled (as readers of this *History* will know) during the course of the last 205 years, is due to one cause, and that is the *Peace*, that has reigned since the close of the thirty years' war. The Church has seen a new thing in Perth from that time, *viz.*, a combination of Toleration from without and Harmony within. May He, who alone fighteth for us against foes, both external and internal, continue to give Peace in our time!

Surely, as regards the future, it cannot be the will of God that our bush, which has been burning for more than two centuries, and yet has not been consumed—nay! has budded and put forth leaves in the end of the days—should perish vainly after all! Rather (we would fain believe) God has some purpose for this Church to fulfil, as in the country at large, so also in Perth. How that providential design will be attained we cannot tell. It may be that the now great and powerful Communion, which took our place as the National Establishment at the beginning of this *History*, is destined to share the same fate as befel us at that time. And it is possible that, in the unsettlement, which such a catastrophe is calculated to bring about, our long-despised assertion of the need of historical continuity with the visible Church, which Christ founded when He sojourned on earth, may at last be welcomed by many as a pearl of great price. We know not; but of one thing we are convinced, and that is, that we have not been preserved through so many crushing disasters for nothing. The message of the hour to us in this City and throughout Scotland is, that we should make ourselves as profoundly efficient Christians, intellectually, morally, practically, and religiously, as we can, and be ready for the issue whenever and however it comes! But who is sufficient for these things?

List of Authorities Cited.

(a) Manuscripts† :—

Perth Presbytery Records, 1690 to 1750.
Perth Kirk Session Records, 1690 to 1750.
Perth Town Council Records, 1746.
MSS. contained in the Episcopal Chest, Edinburgh.††
MSS. belonging to Episcopal Theological College.††
Muthill MS. Register (Episcopal Church).
Minute Books of S. John's, Princes Street. Perth.
MSS. Records of the Cathedral, Perth.
MSS. belonging to J. R. Anderson, Esq.
Scott's MSS. in the Advocates' Library.
MS. Record of the Diocese of Dunkeld.
Rev. Dr. Gordon's MSS.
The Torry MSS.
MSS. Records of the Dioceses of Brechin and Aberdeen.
MSS. lent by Rev. W. W. Hawdon.
Minute Book of the Perth Congregation, 1740-45 (Kilmavœnig MS.)
The Duninarle Ring and Pincushion.

(b) Printed Authorities :—

Rev. Thomas Stephen's "History of the Church of Scotland," vols. 3 and 4.
Rev. J. P. Lawson's "Episcopal Church since the Revolution."
Professor Grub's "Ecclesiastical History of Scotland," vols. 3 and 4.
The Scottish Magazine, 1849-54 (6 vols.)
The Scottish Guardian (various volumes).
The Scottish Standard Bearer (Dr. Walker's articles).
Scott's "*Fasti Ecclesiæ Scoticanæ.*"
"The Despot's Champion" ("Life of Claverhouse.")

---

† In quoting from MSS., I have not always been at pains to preserve the old spelling. In many instances, also, I have used my authorities without referring to them in a footnote.—G. T. S. F.

†† Amongst many other Documents, these contain Letters by Bishop Rattray, Rev G. Sempill, Rev. R. Lyon, the Perth Managers, and the Rev. George Innes.

Penny's "Traditions of Perth."
Stephen's *Episcopal Magazine*, 1834-7 (4 vols.)
Marshall's "Historic Scenes of Perthshire."
Wilson's "Perth Presbytery."
Lyon's "History of S. Andrews."
Bishop Dowden's "Annotated Scotch Communion Office."
Letter from a Gentleman in Edinburgh, 1711.
Fittis's "Gleanings concerning Perthshire."
Fittis's "Sketches of the Olden Time in Perthshire."
Oliphant's "The Jacobite Lairds of Gask."
Wood's "East Neuk of Fife."
Skinner's "Ecclesiastical History of Scotland," vol. 2.
Skinner's "Annals of Scotch Episcopacy."
Scottish Episcopal Journal.
Dr. Gordon's "*Scotichronicon*," vols. 4, 5, and 6.
Poem on Bishop Rattray in Episcopal Chest.
The Gentleman's Magazine for November, 1746.
Wodrow's Correspondence (Parker Society).
Lord Rosebery's Preface to List of Rebels in 1746.
Thackeray's "Four Georges."
Chambers's "History of the '45."
Bishop Pococke's Diary.
Harrington's "Brief Notes on the Church of Scotland."
Dr. Neale's "Life of Bishop Torry."
Dr. Walker's "Life of Bishop Gleig."
Dr. Walker's "Life of Bishop Skinner."
Rev. W. Blatch's "Life of Bishop Low."
J. M. Connolly's "Life of Bishop Low."
Canon Mackey's "Life of Bishop Forbes."
Bishop Wordsworth's "Annals of My Life," vols. 1 and 2.
Canon Archibald's "Church in Keith."
Canon Archibald's "Historic Episcopate in Moray."
A Narrative of the Repeal of Disabilities Bill, 1792.
Statistical Account of Perth.
Dr. Walker's "Last Hundred Years of Scotch Episcopacy," 1889.
Bishop Wordsworth's privately-printed Pamphlets on the Cathedral.
Bishop Wordsworth's Charges.
Dr. Rorison's Sermon on Bishop Torry.
Report of the Synod held at Glenalmond in 1853.

List of Authorities.

English Guardian, August, 1885.
Canon Humble's Letter to the Bishop of S. Andrews.
Rev. J. B. Craven's "Journals of Bishop R. Forbes."
Rev. J. B. Craven's "Episcopal Church in Moray."
Rev. J. C. Chambers's Sermons.

BY THE SAME AUTHOR.

PRICE TWO SHILLINGS AND SIXPENCE.

Sonnets.

"They are admirable."—*Canon Liddon.*

"Their sentiment and language are alike elevated: their lines move with a stately march and with a rhythm that pleases by its steadiness."—*Scotsman.*

Sold by CHRISTIE, S. John Street, Perth.

www.ingramcontent.com/pod-product-compliance
Lightning Source LLC
Chambersburg PA
CBHW020526300426
44111CB00008B/557